Donald Trump Is the Worst Person in the World

A Book on Donald Trump

The case that Donald Trump is a man lacking character
and devoid of integrity, a man seemingly without a soul.
An examination up to the election of 2016.

Tedd Levy

Donald Trump Is the Worst Person in the World by Tedd Levy
Published by Tedd Levy 2020
First Edition
Printed and bound in the United States

DTrumpIsTheWorstPerson@gmail.com

ISBN-13: 978-1986621090
ISBN-10: 198662109X

Cover Image Source: World globe showing the continents of North and South America. © Abidal - Dreamstime.com (image altered).

Contents

"If someone shows you who they really are, believe them."

– Maya Angelou

It is indeed amazing how Donald Trump exploded on the political scene and then was elected president. Give him credit for that. But not much more.

Donald Trump's political approach, his public conduct, and his personal conduct are primarily an extension of his narcissistic, bullying, lying, greedy, bigoted, unprincipled, classless, braggadocious personality. He is a man of little character, a political candidate of little substance, and a danger to our country and its values.

Trump doesn't live in a world of right and wrong, fair or unfair, kind or unkind. Trump lives in a world of Trump. He doesn't care if something is right, true, or just. That simply isn't part of the equation. He has the ethics of a rock. He will consistently lie, cheat, deceive, and coerce to get what's best for Trump. And he expects others to do the same on his behalf — he calls that loyalty. He has absolutely no moral compass. He only cares about himself and is motivated solely by the constant feeding of his ego.

This is not hyperbole. You might think he's not as horrible a human being as I say because you think people just aren't like that. But he is, believe me (to borrow a phrase). You may dismiss my assertions because my words are so harsh, but you shouldn't. Donald Trump is a one-man assault on truth, reason, and decency.

Trump's conduct is on display to America and to America's children. When we assume the crucial task of building healthy children, we look to foster positive values. We teach our children to be honest—but Trump is deceitful; to be modest—but Trump is egotistical; to be kind—but Trump is cruel; to be generous—but Trump is greedy; to be respectful—but Trump is insolent; to be fair—but Trump is partial; to be compassionate—but Trump is coldhearted.

It is my opinion that Donald Trump is a liar, a bigot, a hypocrite, a bully, a thief, a braggart, a narcissist, a religious charlatan, and a philanthropic phony; moreover, he is crude, ignorant, lewd, bizarre, and terrible. Now, to some, it might seem reckless to claim Trump has all these attributes. However, my book includes a chapter on each of these claims, offering extensive evidence to support my assertions.

This book is dedicated to the millions of people who have been or will be hurt by Donald Trump's candidacy and presidency. It is devoted to those who fear losing their health insurance, to those with preexisting conditions who fear skyrocketing premiums, to those who fear unwarranted raids and expulsion from the country, to those who are insulted by Donald Trump's misogyny, to those who are revulsed by Trump's history of sexual assaults and sexual harassment, to those who suffer because of Trump's bigotry, to those who shudder at the Trump-buoyed white nationalism, to those who worry about Trump's obsession with lies and deceit, and to all those who shed tears because of Trump's assault on American values.

I love to celebrate the goodness in people. I am constantly inspired by the human spirit. To focus on the negative, as I have in this book, is contrary to my spirit. And the direct, harsh tone I employ in this book is also something I am not pleased with. My nature is to be conciliatory, not critical. My nature is to reason, not condemn. My nature is to find common ground, not to judge people starkly. My nature is to believe there is good in all of us. In this book, I have not stayed true to those ideals. I couldn't help myself. I feel so

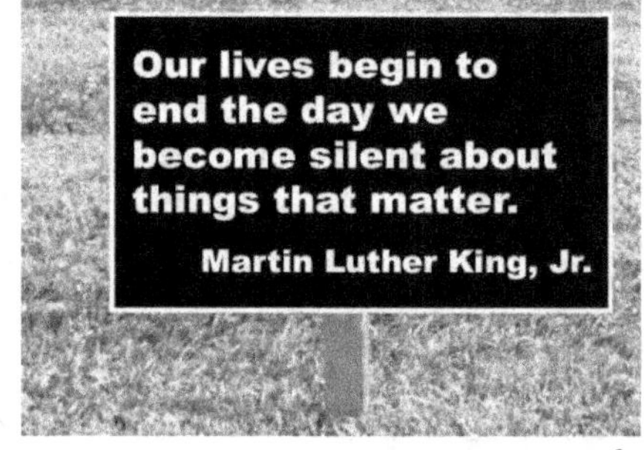

Image Source[2]

strongly about the unique evil of Donald Trump that I needed the focus and tone I've adopted to make my points honestly and to make them with impact.

My book is mostly a compilation of information that is in the public domain, with my analysis and my opinion. So now you know what you're in for: a direct, harsh, truthful examination of the evil that is Donald Trump. I warn you, it will be a bumpy ride.

One more thing. You may not believe this from my book's title or its content, but I tried very hard to be fair. I excluded or removed much that I thought could not be documented sufficiently or that overstated Donald Trump's shortcomings, the latter something that many may think is impossible. As I reviewed news stories, reports, videos, documents, and so on, I sometimes found conflicting reports on the facts of the same occurrence. When I found these different takes, I would dig deep to be fair.

I strived to be accurate. Here I present the facts and my opinions for your consideration.

This book is written with reverence for, and is dedicated to, all the patriots who helped develop and foster our remarkable American values, from before the Revolutionary War to today.

I have designed my book to be a flexible read. You need not read it continuously from beginning to end. Nothing is lost by skipping around from chapter to chapter, or even section to section. If you would like to read this book in such a way, you're invited to do so.

So here is the book on Donald Trump, up to and as of, the 2016 presidential election (with a few post-election freebies thrown in) as I see it. I hope you enjoy it.

Tedd

Chapter 1
Trump the Liar

Lie[3]

[lahy] *noun*

1. to speak untruthfully with intent to mislead or deceive.
2. to convey a false impression or practice deception.
3. an untrue or deceptive statement deliberately intended to deceive.

I think Donald Trump lies—a lot. It's what he does. He never stops lying. The frequency of his lying is overwhelming. Consider: PolitiFact.com is a website that fact-checks statements and rates the accuracy of claims by elected officials and others in American politics. They rate statements as "True," "Mostly True," "Half True," "Mostly False," "False," and "Pants on Fire." As of October 22, 2016, PolitiFact concluded that of 309 Donald Trump statements they reviewed, 70% were not true. *This means he lies more than he tells the truth.* He had 266 statements (85%) that were either not true or half true. The review is updated regularly. As I visited it throughout the campaign and Trump's early presidency, the numbers remained surprisingly constant. Trump's statements were awarded PolitiFact's 2015 Lie of the Year.

Per PolitiFact, "In considering our annual Lie of the Year, we found our only real contenders were Trump's—his various statements also led our Readers' Poll. But it was hard to single one out from the others. So we have rolled them into one big trophy."[4] Congratulations, Donald.

The Donald Trump PolitiFact Scorecard	
True	4%
Mostly True	11%
Half True	14%
Mostly False	19%
False	34%
Pants on Fire	17%

10/22/2016

The PolitiFact analysis reveals that Donald Trump lies (considering the categories of "half true" through "pants on fire") 85% of the time. That's hard to do. You would think just by accident he'd have to be truthful more than 15% of the time.

- The *Washington Post*'s fact-checker, Glenn Kessler, has said that in his six years on the job, "there's no comparison" between Trump and other politicians when it comes to falsehoods. Kessler says that when analyzing Trump's statements, he has given him his worst rating—four Pinocchios—63% of the time, compared to between 15% and 20% for politicians on average.[5]

- In September 2016, *Toronto Star* reporter Daniel Dale began counting and tracking Donald Trump's lies. In 28 days of this work, he found 560 false claims, or 20 per day, during a period from mid-September to late October. Examining the first three presidential debates, Dale found 104 false claims for Trump to 13 for Hillary Clinton.[6]

- *Politico* magazine, looking at Trump's tweets, speeches, and interviews, found 87 lies over a five-day period. That's one lie every 3.25 minutes over almost five hours of remarks.[7]

- The last time I googled "Donald Trump lies", I got more than 47 million results.

From journalist David Brooks: "Trump is perhaps the most dishonest person to run for high office in our lifetime. All politicians stretch the truth, but Trump has a steady obliviousness to accuracy."[8] A thread that runs through the entire Trump experience is his total disregard for honesty.

Alair Townsend, a former deputy mayor of New York City, said, "I wouldn't believe Donald Trump if his tongue were notarized."[9]

From Trump himself in his book *Trump: The Art of the Deal*: "That's why a little hyperbole never hurts. People want to believe that something is the biggest and the greatest and the most spectacular. I call it truthful hyperbole. It's an innocent form of exaggeration—and a very effective form of promotion."[10]

> ## Trumpspeak[11]
>
> 1. A statement of intentional lies passed off as the truth. Trumpspeak is its own language. It may, on occasion, include some verifiable facts to help bolster its overall message of lies, misdirection and puffery.
>
> 2. A statement of intentional lies or misinformation passed off as the truth.
>
> 3. Ambiguous, euphemistic, grandiloquent language used chiefly in political propaganda.

Many people lie from time to time. For Donald Trump, however, lying is so natural that he lies as easily as he talks. He can tell two lies in one sentence. He is seemingly more comfortable lying than he is telling the truth. Donald Trump has absolutely no allegiance to the truth. He doesn't accept the concept of truth. *Trump never intentionally tells the truth. If he says something that is true, it's just a coincidence.*

Donald Trump doesn't own a drop of sincerity; he is uniquely dishonest. He is the least honest person in the public eye in the past 100 years. Over time Trump tells thousands and thousands of lies. His penchant for lying is unfathomable and unmatched. He is a bottomless pit of lies. Lying is completely integrated into his personality and (lack of) character. It's tough to overstate just how routinely and how blatantly Trump lies. He is a "lie addict," a serial compulsive liar incapable of stopping himself. Each and every sentence Trump utters must be questioned as to its validity. You can't take anything he says at face value. If Trump tells you it's three o'clock, you better check your watch.

Most people speak from a foundation of truth or facts. Not Donald Trump. He speaks from a foundation of what serves his needs in the moment. Ask a normal human being how many people were at the Trump inauguration, and they will consider the facts to guide their answer. Ask Trump the same question, and he considers only what serves his needs or makes him look good to determine his response. Facts don't enter into the picture.

It is shocking to me that someone who lies so constantly, so obviously, and so blatantly, can be so effective at it. People buy his lies. Even his detractors frequently fall into the trap of thinking Trump is a normal human being and assume his utterances to be generally true, as we do of most human beings.

Those who might think that are, sadly, wrong. With Donald Trump, you must presume anything he says is likely to be untrue. Remember PolitiFact found only 4% of his statements to be true.

Donald Trump's words are often just noise. Most people are not prepared to respond to falsehoods of this frequency and scope. The world isn't prepared to respond to falsehoods of this frequency and scope. Because he lies so much, thinking about or responding to his words can simply be a waste of time. We spend hours analyzing his statements: "Well, maybe he meant…" or "I think his assertion might be based on…" Wrong. The correct explanation is one we are not quick to believe: the man lied. You must be careful because Trump can easily lead you down a path of fiction and nontruths. Politicians, elected officials, the media, and the general public frequently take the bait as they analyze, explore, and try to explain a Trump pronouncement when the real explanation is, quite simply, he's lying.

According to journalist Dara Lind, "If you try to dive into the reasons Trump lies, you've already lost. It grants his lies the dignity of a strategy. The truth is that, by all appearances, Trump seems to lie whenever it suits him."[12]

Even when caught in one of his lies, Donald Trump remains unfazed. He'll tell an outrageous lie and then later change the story, repeat the lie, or just deny he ever said it. He'll lie even if it's obvious or easy to verify that he is lying. He just doesn't care. He will tell the same lie repeatedly even if it has universally been proven false. Trump figures that if he doesn't confess that he told a lie, he really didn't, and so the lie lives. And to some extent, he's right.

Often, Trump's lies seem so pointless as to befuddle. I call these, "I lie for the heck of it" lies (or "serve no purpose lies"); lies that are unnecessary and not even useful. He will tell a bizarre lie that leaves you scratching your head. Sometimes he'll tell a pointless lie that provides him little or no advantage if believed. At times he can't tell the truth even when to do so would be to his advantage. Why? The answer is he's addicted to lying.

Donald Trump will tell you 15,000 people attended his rally when the capacity of the room is 4,200. He will tell you the lines are around the block with people wanting to get into his rally, but when a television channel shoots video outside, there is no line at all. He will tell the crowd at his rally and the television audience that the room is overflowing when video shows the rear of the room to be sparsely filled. And all these lies serve no purpose. Few would refute that Donald Trump does attract very large crowds at his rallies. There's no need to lie and overstate the crowd size. So why do so? Because Donald Trump can't help himself.

During their first debate, Hillary Clinton noted that Trump had stated climate change is a hoax perpetrated by the Chinese government. Trump aggressively interrupted and denied the assertion. But the fact is, he did say that, and it was easy to prove since he claimed it in a Twitter post. So why bother lying by denying it? He could have just ignored Clinton's claim. But lies flow so easily from Trump's mouth that he can't help himself. His gut reaction is to lie. He lies when the truth will do. It's interesting, too, that he aggressively interrupted Clinton to tell this lie. That adds some believability to it. Nice touch, Donald, but please know you're one of the few people who will even interrupt others to lie.

Dara Lind again: "Donald Trump has buried America in lies."[13] Digging out from these lies is a full-time American occupation. It's hard to have a productive discussion of the issues when one must first wade through Trump's declarations to see if they're true. Donald Trump tells so many lies, lies so effectively, and has such a massive platform to tell his lies that his lies muddle Americans' knowledge and perceptions (e.g. the birther issue). He can sell a lie like nobody else. He pounds his audience so incessantly that his lies seemingly become a new reality. The fact that they are lies disappears under the barrage. Here are some stories of lying, Trump style.

He Lies, Lies, and Lies Again

Headlines

There is much reporting on Trump's lies. Here are the headlines of just 10 articles from various sources about Trump's lying during the presidential campaign. I would estimate that thousands, of similar headlines appeared during the campaign.
- "Scope of Trump's falsehoods unprecedented for a modern presidential candidate"
- "The Lies Trump told"
- "Donald: 101 Of Trump's Greatest Lies"

- "Donald Trump is constantly lying"
- "Trump's Lies"
- "Trump's lies have already changed America: Column"
- "Donald Trump's Week of Misrepresentations, Exaggerations, and Half-Truths"
- "Donald Trump lies. All the time."
- "Donald Trump And the Summer of Lies"
- "Counting Down Trump's Litany of Lies"

The World Trade Center Lies

The World Trade Center lies come from a November 2015 Trump interview with ABC's George Stephanopoulos. "Hey, I watched when the World Trade Center came tumbling down. And I watched in Jersey City, New Jersey, where thousands and thousands of people were cheering as that building was coming down. Thousands of people were cheering. . . .It did happen. I saw it . . . . It was on television. I saw it. . . . George, it did happen."

Trump went on: "There were people that were cheering on the other side of New Jersey, where you have large Arab populations. They were cheering as the World Trade Center came down. I know it might be not politically correct for you to talk about it, but there were people cheering as that building came down—as those buildings came down. And that tells you something. It was well covered at the time, George. Now, I know they don't like to talk about it, but it was well covered at the time. There were people over in New Jersey that were watching it, a heavy Arab population, that were cheering as the buildings came down. Not good."[14] Typical Trump: tell a lie and then double and triple down on it.

Notice that Trump argued, "It was on television. I saw it," and "It was well covered at the time." If it was well covered, why is it that no government official and no television outlet has any record of this happening? Trump knows "it" wasn't well covered. He just created that lie to somehow bolster his original untruth of people cheering.

Jersey City Mayor Steven Fulop tweeted in response to Trump's claims that Trump "has memory issues or willfully distorts the truth."[15] TV and newspaper reporters, law enforcement, and elected officials have all refuted Trump's assertions. There is no such television report as claimed by

Trump. Trump simply, plainly lied. And it seems a little perverted to lie about a horrendous tragedy such as 9/11.

It should be noted that there were, however, stories of Muslim Americans repudiating the attacks. In Paterson, New Jersey, in the center of the city's Middle Eastern community, residents put up banners that read, "The Muslim Community Does Not Support Terrorism."

The Serge Kovaleski Lie

To back up his assertion that he saw thousands of people in the streets celebrating the destruction of 9/11, Donald Trump referred to a 2001 newspaper article by Serge Kovaleski. The report noted that New Jersey authorities had detained and questioned a number of people (not Muslims) who allegedly were seen celebrating the attacks on rooftops in Jersey City, but it added that these incidents had not been confirmed. The article also did not say that "thousands" were seen celebrating. Mr. Kovaleski has since said he has no recollection of any evidence that any such incidents did actually occur.

Kovaleski and his article did not confirm Trump's claims, so Trump, in his usual perverted style, took to denigrating Kovaleski himself (see: "I would never mock a person that has difficulty" in the next chapter). Very Trumpish. To Donald, if you don't lie to support his lies, you're his enemy.

The "My Doctor Loves Me" Lie

Susie Madrak on her website susiemadrak.com, writes, "Donald Trump's doctor released a medical report so silly that when we asked the American Medical Association about its language, their spokesman started to laugh."[16]

In December 2015, the Trump campaign released a letter from his physician, Dr. Harold Bornstein, attesting to the candidate's health. But something about the letter—in fact, many things—seem a little curious. The complete text of the letter follows so you can see for yourself, but first, let's discuss a few of these oddities.

In his statement regarding the letter, Trump refers to his doctor as Dr. Jacob Bornstein, who was actually Harold's father and died in 2010. He was Trump's doctor prior to 1980, more than 37 years ago. Dr. Harold Bornstein has been Trump's doctor since 1980. It seems a bit strange that Trump would get the name of his doctor of 35-plus years wrong, and it adds to the questions regarding the letter's legitimacy.

It's also odd that Jacob Bornstein's name is on his son's stationery years after his death, and decades after his retirement. Dr. Bornstein's stationery heading also includes his email address, which, for several reasons, is very unusual for a doctor. Also, the letterhead is the same font as the letter. This suggests the letter may have been written by somebody creating stationery for the project in word processing software as opposed to using a previous printed or developed letterhead.

The greeting of the letter is "To Whom My Concern." A grammatical and wording error like that would likely not be made by a doctor or his assistant. But it might be made by a presidential candidate with questionable grammar, and oh, does he have dubious grammar.

In the first paragraph of the letter, the doctor states, "Mr. Trump has had a recent medical examination that showed only positive results." This actually means he tested positive for heart disease, positive for diabetes, etc., although that was surely not the intended meaning. You wouldn't think any legitimate doctor would use the term positive results in that context. A layperson might.

Dr. Bornstein states that Trump's "physical strength and stamina are extraordinary." I wonder what test he did to come to this silly conclusion.

Trump's doctor reports that the candidate's cardiovascular status is excellent—again, not very "doctor-like" phrasing. "Actually, his blood pressure, 100/65, and laboratory test results were astonishingly excellent," states the doctor. Again, "astonishingly excellent" is not part of the usual lexicon of doctors but more the lexicon of a not-too-smart braggart.

Dr. Bornstein continues, "He has no history of ever using alcohol or tobacco products." A doctor could not definitively make such a statement. More commonly, a physician would state, "He has no reported history of alcohol or tobacco use."

The doctor closes his letter with, "If elected, Mr. Trump, I can state unequivocally, will be the healthiest individual ever elected to the presidency." Healthier than Millard Fillmore in 1849? He was a pretty healthy fellow—the first president who was a "health nut." He did not smoke or drink and was meticulous about measures he believed could affect his physical well-being. How does the doctor know the medical status of each of the previous 44 U.S. presidents when elected to office?

Dr. Bornstein signs the letter "Harold N. Bornstein, M.D., F.A.C.G. [Fellow of the American College of Gastroenterology]." But Dr. Bornstein is not an F.A.C.G. He has not been since 1995. His use of the F.A.C.G. title is fraudulent. When questioned on this matter, Bornstein said, "FACG is a title they sell for a fee. In reality, it has no value." Nonsensical, but in any case, the doctor didn't even pay that fee. He said he would keep using this title because it's part of his resume—yes, a fraudulent part of his resume.

The doctor's signature line includes the name of his hospital, Lenox Hill Hospital, and his "section" the "Section of Gastroenterology". But the hospital doesn't have a "Section of Gastroenterology"; it does, however, have a "Division of Gastroenterology". You would think a doctor on staff at Lenox Hill Hospital would know that. But Trump wouldn't. And the doctor is actually not on staff at the hospital (although he does have admitting rights).

Charles C. W. Cooke wrote a parody of the letter in the *National Review*. Mr. Cooke, writing about the "full report," states, "During a recent comprehensive medical examination, Mr. Trump revealed himself to be quite extraordinarily healthy. . . . His unfortunate wartime experiences aside, Mr. Trump has never suffered any physical ailments whatsoever. He has never coughed or sneezed or been forced to wipe grit from his eyes. He has never had the hiccups."[17]

In an August 26, 2016, interview on the *NBC Nightly News*, Dr. Bornstein was asked about his statement declaring Trump "the healthiest individual ever elected to the presidency." When asked how he could justify the hyperbole, Bornstein asserted, "I like that sentence, to be quite honest with you, and all the rest of them [presidents] are either sick or dead."[18]

Trump's doctor's letter has more of the braggadocious style of Donald Trump himself than the style of a professional medical doctor. It reads more like a recommendation letter than an objective medical report. It is written with the same awkward sentence structure and boastful style that Trump uses all the time. It seems careless and shows a surprising lack of knowledge about common medical terms and practices.

NBC also noted, "The doctor said he would not normally use such over-the-top language in a letter for a patient, but he made an exception for Trump—who just two weeks before had tweeted that the doctor's assessment would show 'perfection.' I think I picked up his kind of language and then just interpreted it to my own,' Bornstein said."[19] The doctor writes a letter under his own name but believes it appropriate to use the style of his patient. Does that seem right to you?

These observations clearly lead one to speculate that Trump either wrote the letter himself, wrote it with Dr. Bornstein, or inappropriately influenced his doctor regarding its content.

A note about Trump's health: I have no reason to think Donald Trump is not in good health. In fact, I suspect that he is. I think the reason for the apparent deception in Dr. Bornstein's letter is that merely being in good health is not sufficient for Trump. He needs people to believe he is in *great* health—astonishingly excellent health, even. Remember, Trump lies even when it's not necessary—even when it achieves nothing.

JACOB BORNSTEIN, M.D.
HAROLD N. BORNSTEIN, M.D., P.C.
101 EAST 78th STREET
NEW YORK, NY 100075-0301
TELE: (212) 988-6600 FAX: (212) 988-6602
e-mail: hbornst1@gmail.com
www.haroldbornsteinmd.com

December 4, 2015

To Whom My Concern:

I have been the personal physician of Mr. Donald J. Trump since 1980. His previous physician was my father, Dr Jacob Bornstein. Over the past 39 years, I am pleased to report that Mr. Trump has had no significant medical problems. Mr. Trump has had a recent complete medical examination that showed only positive results. Actually, his blood pressure, 110/65, and laboratory test results were astonishingly excellent.

Over the past twelve months, he has lost at least fifteen pounds, Mr. Trump takes 81 mg of aspirin daily and a low dose of a statin. His PSA test score is 0.15 (very low). His physical strength and stamina are extraordinary.

Mr. Trump has suffered no form of cancer, has never had a hip, knee or shoulder replacement or any other orthopedic surgery. His only surgery was an appendectomy at age ten. His cardiovascular status is excellent. He has no history of ever using alcohol or tobacco products.

If elected, Mr. Trump, I can state unequivocally, will be the healthiest individual ever elected to the presidency.

Harold N Bornstein, MD, FACG
Department of Medicine, Section of Gastroenterology
Lenox Hill Hospital, New York, NY[20]

Underlines indicate questionable parts of the letter.

The Students Love Him Lie

When speaking to students at Liberty University, a Christian college in Virginia, on Martin Luther King's birthday in January 2016, Trump bragged about the large number of people in attendance breaking a record. He even dedicated the record (whatever that means) to "the late, great Martin Luther King." He neglected to mention that the university mandates attendance at all its convocations.[21]

The Tax Return Lie

When questioned about releasing his tax returns, Trump claimed he could not do so because he was being audited. But the IRS said an audit does not prevent a person from releasing his or her tax return. When confronted about his statement, Trump said he meant he couldn't release his taxes because his accountants had advised him not to do so while under audit. If that's what he meant, that's what he should have said.

Trump commonly uses this trick when caught in a lie: he then tells you what he "really meant." By the way, even if it were true about his tax returns being under audit, he could release tax returns from previous years.

It's also interesting that in May of 2016, Trump professed he could not release his 2015 tax return because he was being audited. However, it is my understanding that if the IRS chooses to audit your return, it can take months or years before they contact you. In April 2016, his 2015 return was not being audited. It was too soon. Also, Trump refuses to release the IRS letter stating that he is being audited. Why do you think he won't do that?

One is led to conclude Trump continues to lie about releasing his tax returns because he's hiding something.

The Other Tax Lie

In his acceptance speech at the Republican National Convention, Trump said, "America is one of the highest-taxed nations in the world." This is simply untrue. In fact, when it comes to personal taxes, the United States is one of the *least*-taxed countries in the world. But Donald Trump never lets the truth get in the way. He doesn't think about whether a statement is true; he considers only if it serves his interest.

The Melvin P. Thorpe Award for Lying

Remember when Trump blamed a faulty earpiece for his answer to CNN about KKK leader David Duke's support of him? Then, after a poor showing in his second debate with Hillary Clinton, he blamed a bad mic. (He even suggested he had been given the bad mic on purpose.) I knew he was just making excuses, but somehow it all seemed a little familiar. I thought, and I thought, and I just couldn't figure it out. Then it hit me.

Do you remember tacky-dressing, wig-wearing Melvin P. Thorpe, the over-the-top reporter from *Watchdog News*? He was the character played by Dom DeLuise in the movie *The Best Little Whorehouse in Texas*. Thorpe confronts the side-stepping, double-talking Texas governor, asking him why the Chicken Ranch (whorehouse) continues to operate. The governor, looking to get off the hook, responds, "We seem to be having some acoustic problems in here." That's where I heard it before! It was the Texas governor responding to Melvin P. Thorpe in *The Best Little Whorehouse in Texas*.[22] Trump must have seen the movie, too. Tricky fellow.

Trump-Style Lying

Trump has his own lying style, his go to personal "bag of lies." It's the art of the lie.

1. Trump likes to lie big. As noted by Ronald Bailey on the website Reason.com in reference to Trump's "Big Lies," "the principle—which is quite true within itself—that in the big lie there is always a certain force of credibility." For most people, "it would never come into their heads to fabricate colossal untruths, and they would not believe that others could have the impudence to distort the truth so infamously."[23]

2. Trump tries to sell a lie by uttering it with certainty. Let's look at simply one example of many. In a July 31, 2016, interview with ABC's George Stephanopoulos on *This Week,* Trump declared that Russia would not move into the Ukraine. "He's not going into Ukraine, OK, just so you understand. He's not going to go into Ukraine, all right? You can mark it down. You can

put it down. You can take it anywhere you want."[24] Stephanopoulos then pointed out that Putin was already there.

How can he be so sure and so wrong? I marked it down, put it down, and took it anywhere I wanted, just as Trump suggested. Then I had to throw it away. He thinks lying with conviction makes him more believable (and he's probably right).

3. Trump likes to say it could be higher as part of his lie. So when speaking about the number of undocumented immigrants and he says there are, "30 million, it could be 34 million," he has employed this Trump-style lying technique. He gives you a number and then says it could be a higher, second number. It makes you think he looked into the matter and found a variance. It adds a little believability to his statement.

4. Trump likes to add a comment about others' thoughts or beliefs to his lies to make them more believable. So he says things such as, "as I think you know," "as I think I saw on your channel," "many people are saying," and "I've been given great credit for that." This tends to enhance his lie because it implies that what he is about to say is already well established.

The "as I think you know" enhancement is particularly interesting. It seems to me it is not merely a sign that Trump is lying, it's practically a guarantee. Every time I have heard him use the phrase, which is often, it followed what I know or think to be a lie.

Kurt Andersen, in an article in The Atlantic,[25] refers to this phenomenon as Trump style "vague source attribution."

Source Attribution–General
- A lot of people are saying …
- People think it's going to happen.
- Everybody's talking about it.
- They are saying …
- Everyone is now saying …

Source Attribution—Personal
- That's just what I had heard.
- I've heard that …

- What I've heard …
- I've been hearing …
- A lot of people tell me …
- I've seen this, and I've sort of witnessed it—in fact, in two cases I have actually witnessed it.

5. And then there's backtracking. When corrected by Stephanopoulos that Russia was already in the Ukraine, a reference to the Russian presence in Crimea, Trump responded, "OK—well, he's there in a certain way. But I'm not there. You have Obama there."[26] That's unintelligible but it is backtracking,

6. Trump often tells a lie and says he has proof that he will present later. He doesn't, and he will never offer any. As time passes and new issues arise, he is never held to account on the matter. It's a trick to make his lie seem more believable. If he claims he has proof, he can't be lying, right? Wrong. This is a common Trump tactic: he makes a false statement, says he has proof, then never presents it.

In October 2016, multiple women came forth to charge Donald Trump with inappropriate sexual conduct. Trump denied the charges. He claimed that he could prove their accusations were not true, but he never did. By the way, as part of Trump's denial, he stated that the women were part of a global conspiracy to extinguish his outsider movement.

It has regularly been reported that Trump's office doesn't respond to inquiries from members of the press who question something he has said. They do this because Trump doesn't want to have to explain his statement. He'd rather let the lie linger.

7. Trump thinks if he repeats a lie often enough people will believe it. The expression, "Tell a lie often enough, it becomes the truth" has been promulgated in a variety of ways and from several individuals. But the concept it conveys has been universally acknowledged. This seems to be a ploy that Donald Trump lives by and it seems to work for him.

8. Trump frequently follows a lie with "believe me." Don't.

9. Trump likes to tell a lie, to cover up a lie. If caught in a lie Trump finds new lies to support his old lies.

10. Accuse Trump of something and he'll claim the exactly the opposite. He wants you to think that if he'd go all the way to professing the reverse, the accusations must be false. For example:

Accusation	Trump Response
Trump mocked a disabled person.	"No one has done more for people with disabilities than me."
Trump isn't presidential.	"I am more presidential than anybody other than the great Abe Lincoln."
He's divisive.	"I am a unifier."
He's a racist.	"I am the least racist person you will ever meet." "No one has done so much for equality as I have."
He's a misogynist.	"Nobody has more respect for women than I do."
He's a braggart.	"I am the humblest celebrity." "I am very modest."

Donald Trump reasons that if he lies big, lies with certainty, attributes his lie to others, backtracks adeptly, says his has proof even if he doesn't, repeats his lies often, follows his lie saying "believe me", tells a new lie to support a previous lie, or proclaims the opposite of what's being said about him, his lies become more believable.

The " I'm Not Telling" Lies

The "I'm not telling" lie is a particular Donald Trump favorite. This entails Trump making something up, as usual; then, when challenged on his statement, he references an obscure source or explanation that he will not specify.

I'm Not Telling Lie #1

In September and October 2015, Trump repeatedly stated that President Obama wanted to accept 200,000 Syrian refugees even though the Obama administration had announced they planned to take in about 10,000. (When Trump lies, he does it big.) When asked how he knew this, he stated he had heard it—or, in other words, he made it up. A "I'm not telling" lie; see how this works?

I'm Not Telling Lie #2

On October 19, 2015, Trump told a rally in Anderson, South Carolina, that President Obama was considering an executive order to take away their guns. A simple lie. The next day on CNN's *New Day*, when asked by Alisyn Camerota how he knew that, Trump said he was told so. "I've heard that he wants to. And I heard, I think, on your network. Somebody said that that's what he's thinking about." He embellished his lie with "I think I heard it on your network"[27] to try to add validity to his statement, a common Trump ploy. No such consideration was reported on CNN as Trump suggested. Getting the hang of this "I'm not telling" thing?

Then, in the same interview, came more Trump-style lying, (see #3: Trump likes to add a comment about others' thoughts or beliefs to his lies to make them more believable). He continued in his response to Ms. Camerota, adding, "But nevertheless he was thinking about it. And I've heard it from numerous networks. And I've read it in the papers. You know. My source is the papers. So, they're pretty good sources."[28] Let's see, he heard it from numerous networks, and he read it in the papers. Well, then, it *must* be true.

Except he made it up. He didn't hear it from the networks or read it in the papers because President Obama never said what Trump claimed and it was not reported in the media. See how that works?

I'm Not Telling Lie #3

"When Mexico sends its people, they're not sending the best . . . They're bringing drugs, they're bringing crime. They're rapists. And some, I assume, are good people."[29] Possibly Trump's most infamous proclamation of his presidential campaign were these words regarding immigration.

In Trump's famous declaration regarding illegal Mexican immigrants, he stated that "Mexico sends" people across the border. This part of his statement is regularly overlooked because the rest has aroused such a strong reaction. But the assertion that the Mexican government is intentionally sending people across the border, as opposed to individuals choosing on their own to enter the United States, is baseless. Virtually all experts on this matter agree there is no evidence of this. Trump made it up.

When pushed on MSNBC's *Morning Joe* as to how he knew Mexico was sending rapists to America, Trump stated he had heard it from five different sources but refused to name any of them—a very classic "I'm not telling" lie.

The "I Made It Up" Lies

The "I made it up" lies are simply statements that Trump seems to make up out of nowhere. They are also known as the "I Lie for The Heck of It" lies.

"I Made It Up" Lie #1

During the March 3, 2016 Republican presidential candidate debate, Donald Trump repeated his claim that he could save the country $300 billion a year in Medicare costs by negotiating with pharmaceutical companies to lower drug prices. However, as pointed out by moderator Chris Wallace during the debate, Medicare spends only $78 billion a year on drugs. It is impossible to save $300 billion a year if you only have been spending $78 billion.

Trump's claim might lead you to believe that he and the smart people of his campaign carefully examined the matter, concluding they would be able to institute changes that would result in huge savings. Then we learn the truth: the numbers are nonsensical.

Trump's claim is so absurd that it's hard to figure out how he could have come to that conclusion. There seems to be only one explanation. Where did Trump get his facts? He plucked them out of thin air. He merely made it up. A presidential candidate on national television recklessly made up a number to try to deceive the American public.

"I Made It Up" Lie #2—The Lester Holt Lie

To prove his case that the presidential debates were rigged, Trump noted that Lester Holt, the host of the second debate, was a Democrat. He is not; he is a Republican. So why did Trump say he was a Democrat? He thought it would be useful. When Trump wants to make a point, he never lets facts get in the way.

"I Made It Up" Lie #3

When speaking about "illegal immigrants" on July 24, 2015, on MSNBC's *Morning Joe*, Trump said, "I don't think the 11 million—which is a number you have been hearing for many, many years; I've been hearing that number for five years—I don't think that is an accurate number anymore. I am now hearing it's 30 million; it could be 34 million, which is a much bigger problem."[30] Donald, it doesn't matter what you are hearing. What matters are the facts. And I don't believe you're "hearing" that anyway.

All credible sources, including the U.S. Department of Homeland Security, the Pew Research Center, and the Center for Migration Studies, estimate the number of illegal immigrants to be between 11 and 11.4 million. Even the Center for Immigration Studies, which argues against current "high levels" of immigration, estimates that there are only 11–12 million illegal immigrants. But 34 million sounds better when you're trying to rile up an audience. He frequently lies in this manner.

"I Made It Up" Lie #4

Speaking about John McCain on the July 19, 2015, edition of ABC's *This Week*, Trump said, "He's done nothing to help the vets." Trump couldn't say that if it weren't true, could he? Of course, he could. Trump has no idea what John McCain has done to help veterans.

There had been some criticism of McCain-sponsored legislation that some argued covered up the Veterans Administration scandal. But a claim that "he's done nothing to help the vets" is an extremely large stretch. In fact, it's a purely made-up lie. One example of the senator's many veterans-related efforts is the five caseworker advocates in his office who are devoted to aiding veterans who have problems with the Department of Veterans Affairs. McCain's office said they handled more than 2,000 such cases in 2015 alone.

A Bigoted Lie "I Made it Up" Lie

Following a June 2016 Trump rally in San Jose, California, violence erupted outside the venue. Reports indicated that Trump supporters were viciously attacked and injured by protesters. After the incident, Trump tweeted, "Many of the thugs that attacked the peaceful Trump supporters in San Jose were illegals. They burned the American flag and laughed at police."

Made up out of whole cloth. There were no reports on the legal status of the protesters and virtually no way Trump could have known their legal status. What did he do, have people go around and ask protesters if they were legal? But the truth never gets in the way of Donald Trump's agenda. Not only does he lie, but his lies serve to foster hatred toward undocumented Americans. However, it's important to remember that whoever assaulted the Trump supporters should be condemned and face any appropriate criminal consequences.

A Shameful, Self-Interested, Fearmongering "I Made it Up" Lie

In 1991, Trump was trying to subdivide his Mar-a-Lago property in Palm Beach, Florida, but had to overcome community and municipality objections. What to do? Well, part of his strategy was to frighten people.

A Trump associate put out the claim that the Unification Church was trying to buy the property. "If they don't like a subdivision of Mar-a-Lago, how will they feel when a thousand Moonies descend on Palm Beach every weekend?" the associate said. The statement was also released to the newspapers. But the "Moonies" themselves then reported they had absolutely no interest in Mar-a-Lago and called the statement "a deliberate fabrication." They added, "To use the Unification Church as a scare tactic in an attempt to compel Palm Beach officials to submit to the will of Mr. Trump and his associates is morally reprehensible."[31]

Trump used the same tactic when he opposed Native American owned casinos which compete with his casino interests. This invented declaration from Trump was part of his testimony before the House

Native American Affairs Subcommittee in Washington, D.C.: "Watch out. . . . Organized crime figures are slithering into Indian casinos around the country."[32] That's clearly a shameful, self-interested, fear-mongering "I Made It Up" lie. (For more detailed information on Trump's testimony see the chapter, "Trump the Terrible.")

The "I Got a Phone Call—-I Made It Up" Lie

Whenever Trump says, "I got a phone call" be skeptical, very skeptical. You see it's a Trump style lying technique. It doesn't sound like a lie, that's how he fools you, but usually it is. Who would ever just make up that someone called them? That would be kind of extreme. Enter Donald Trump.

A case in point. In July 2017 Trump spoke at the Boys Scouts annual National Jamboree. (You better sit down for this one.) In an interview with the Wall Street Journal he was asked why he thought there was a mixed reaction to his speech. Trump responded:

> That was a standing ovation from the time I walked out to the time I left, and for five minutes after I had already gone. There was no mix. And I got a call from the head of the Boy Scouts saying it was the greatest speech that was ever made to them, and they were very thankful. So there was—there was no mix.[33]

That's what he said. But it wasn't quite accurate. In fact, it simply wasn't true. It was pure fable. Michael Surbaugh, Chief Scout Executive for the Boy Scouts of America, corrected the record in an open letter to the scouting community:

> I want to extend my sincere apologies to those in our Scouting family who were offended by the political rhetoric that was inserted into the jamboree. . . . For years, people have called upon us to take a position on political issues, and we have steadfastly remained non-partisan and refused to comment on political matters . . . We sincerely regret that politics were inserted into the Scouting program.[34]

When Trump tells you "I've gotten lots of calls" on a matter don't believe it. It's just a variation of the "I Got a Phone call—-I Made It Up" Lie.

The "You're a Hypocrite—I Made it Up" Lie

This is another of my favorite Trump-style lies. The "you" in the "you're a hypocrite" lie is not Trump, of course: it's anybody who criticizes him. For a long time, I've observed Trump's accusations of hypocrisy regarding people who have criticized him and suspected Trump himself was lying. Then I found some evidence.

In 2005, Timothy O'Brien authored *TrumpNation: The Art of Being the Donald*. Trump claimed the book understated his wealth, thus damaging his reputation. O'Brien claimed that Trump was worth at best $250 million, while Trump said he was a billionaire. In 2006, Trump sued the author for more than $5 billion (yes, that's billion) in damages. Trump's lawsuit was dismissed. He appealed in 2011 and lost again. The appeals judges found there were no obvious reasons to doubt O'Brien's claim.

As part of the original lawsuit, O'Brien's lawyers deposed Trump regarding his net worth. During the deposition, Trump admitted to 30 lies (often giving a range of excuses) he had told over the years about his wealth, his debts, the cost of membership in one of his golf clubs, how many condos he had sold in one of his buildings, his speaking fees, a made-up story that O'Brien had been arrested once for stalking, whether he borrowed money from family members to avoid personal bankruptcy, etc.

Sometime later, O'Brien coauthored a story about Trump's impending casino bankruptcy. Trump called O'Brien to remind him that the author had tried to "extort" an autographed copy of one of his books, *How to Get Rich*, for his mother. This was not true. Trump was trying to discredit O'Brien and his assertions and make him look hypocritical. This time, Trump made his hypocrisy claim to perhaps the only person in the world who would know firsthand that it was untrue—the very person he was lying about. But he didn't care.

O'Brien told Trump he had certainly not asked for an autographed copy of his book for his mother (his mother had been dead for about 10 years). Trump's reaction to being caught in a lie was to switch to another subject without missing a beat. Trump is so oblivious to the shame of lying that he simply moves on. That's one reason he lies so much. He doesn't care if he gets found out; he'll either lie to cover up the first lie or just move on.

If you think back, you'll find Trump uses this hypocrisy technique regularly. If someone criticizes him or simply fails to endorse him, Trump will say he or she came to him for a job, or asked him for a donation, etc. And those assertions are usually made up. At first, I thought Trump's statements in such situations were merely irrelevant. Now I know they are both irrelevant and fabricated. As reported in *The Washington Post*, He has also routinely used alleged stories of his rivals begging him for something as a way to lash out against them...."[35]

By the way, in a statement to *The Washington Post* regarding O'Brien, Trump said, "I had great success doing what I wanted to do—costing this third-rate reporter a lot of legal fees."[36] Trump also bragged that he brought the lawsuit to make O'Brien miserable. The words of a small man.

An "I Lie for the Heck of It—I Made It Up" Lie

When someone lies to you, it provokes a number of emotions. But when someone lies to you for no apparent reason and does so when he or she might easily get caught, it leaves you bewildered. Some people, though not very many, lie for no reason. It's just the way they talk. They lie as easily as they speak.

For example, after his aborted March 2016 Chicago rally, Trump told several press outlets that he canceled the event after consulting with the Chicago police. But a Chicago Police Department spokesman said that Trump made that decision "independently." In fact, he said they did not even meet with Trump or the Trump campaign on this matter. If Trump had a reason for this lie, it is not apparent. But he doesn't need a reason. If he talks, he lies.

Another "I Lie for the Heck of It—I Made It Up" Lie

In an interview with Bill O'Reilly on August 22, 2016, Trump claimed he had met with a top Chicago police officer who told him he could stop Chicago crime in a week. A spokesman for the Chicago Police Department said no senior member of the department had met with Trump or anyone from his campaign. And the thought that someone could solve a city's crime problem in a week is irrational. But Trump figured no one would remember or care after the election.

An "I Made It Up/I'm Not Telling" Combination Lie

The "I Made It Up" Part: In a July 29, 2016 tweet, Trump wrote, "As usual, Hillary & the Dems are trying to rig the debates, so 2 are up against major NFL games. Same as last time w/Bernie. Unacceptable!"[37] He followed that in an interview on ABC News' *This Week,* stating, "I got a letter from the NFL saying, 'This is ridiculous. Why are the debates against—cause the NFL doesn't wanna go against the debates.'"[38]

But the political parties have no role in setting the dates for the debates. They are determined by an independent, bipartisan commission. And the NFL says it did not send a letter to Trump as he asserted. Trump made the whole thing up. He likes to do that. He lies by fabricating an issue and then uses that lie to slander Clinton. This man is a trip.

This is a bizarre Trump-style falsehood. Why bizarre? Well:

- As indicated, it's an "I made it up" lie. But what's the purpose of the deception? The only purpose I can see is simply to attack his opposition. But what an odd charge. The Democrats are trying to schedule debates to conflict with football. Those terrible sneaky Democrats.

- And then, how did he come up with the lie? Was he sitting around one day and said, "I've got an idea. I've been told the debates are on the same night as an NFL game. Why not blame the Democrats for this?" Bizarre thinking. I think his lie reveals much about him as a person. Trump prefers to lie and looks for opportunities to do so. No rhythm, no reason, just lies. He spends every day looking for lies he can tell.

- But didn't Trump know that the Democrats have nothing to do with the debate schedule? He should have. If he had, he wouldn't have made an assertion that could not be true. Or would he?

- Why involve the NFL in the lie? If the NFL decides to set the record straight, the lie would be exposed. And that's exactly what happened.

- Trump's claim seems even more odd because he says the NFL letter to him said, "This is ridiculous." That's not the professional tone that would be expected from the NFL. And why would the NFL write to Trump when someone else is responsible for the scheduling? Moreover, why would the NFL insert itself into a contentious presidential campaign by apparently siding with one of the candidates? And why would they document that in a letter?

The "I'm Not Telling" Part: After the NFL stated they didn't send him a letter, Trump's lie was revealed. But that's not a problem for Donald Trump. What did he do? He employed a classic Trump-style lying technique: tell a lie to cover up a lie. The Trump campaign put out a statement saying it was not a letter, but he had been told of the conflict by a source close to the league.[40] He attempted to cover up his lie with a new lie, claiming someone who knew someone informed him. Of course, he would not name the person. That's when it became an "I'm not telling" lie.

A source close to the league?
Image Source [39]

I think it's interesting how Trump tried to worm out of this lie. To contest those who had evidence to refute his lie, Trump claims to clarify his statement. It wasn't a letter from the NFL; it was information from someone close to the league. But he's not really clarifying his statement; he's changing it. If that was what he meant, why didn't he say so in the beginning? Trump puts forth his "clarification" only when evidence shows he was lying. He seems to do this all the time. He says he didn't lie; it was just a semantic difference. It's a Trump trick. Also, he makes sure to tell a cover-up lie that cannot be verified.

So there you have it: the absolute first documented case of a bizarre combination "I made it up/I'm not telling" lie. Congratulations to Donald Trump on this historic accomplishment.

"By a lie, a man…annihilates his dignity as a man."
– German philosopher Immanuel Kant[41]

Chapter 2
Trump the Bigot

"The land flourished because it was fed from so many sources—it was nourished by so many cultures and traditions and people."– Lyndon B. Johnson.[42]

I think Donald Trump is a bigot. In an earlier draft of this book, this chapter was called "The Bigotry of Donald Trump." I am hesitant to call anyone a bigot, and I thought that title was a touch softer than the format I use in most other chapters: "Trump the..." But as I did more and more research and as time passed, I became convinced Donald Trump is a bigot and a racist.

The bigotry of the 21st century is generally not as harsh or blatant as the bigotry of America's past. Nevertheless it still exists. And Trump is an old-school bigot. He tried to keep Blacks out of his apartment buildings; he has called Blacks lazy; he treats Black people differently when they are in his company; he makes bigoted comments about Black people; he demeans Muslims, Latinos, women, and others; and he is anti-Semitic. Donald Trump traffics in bigotry. His bigotry has been documented many times, in many contexts.

I think Trump stops short of the violent, hateful bigotry of hate groups, although hate groups (and bigots) do feel emboldened by him and he seems reluctant to speak out against hate groups. As president I fear he will mainstream bigotry. The ever-present bias he displays, in my opinion, warrants this chapter's title, "Trump the Bigot."

Did He Really Say That?

In an interview on ABC's *Good Morning America*, Trump was asked about the support he had received from white supremacist David Duke. George Stephanopoulos asked Trump if he was willing to renounce the support of all white supremacists. "Of course, I am. Of course, I am. I mean there's nobody that's done so much for equality as I have. You take a look at Palm

Beach, Florida, I built the Mar-a-Lago Club, totally open to everybody, the club that frankly set a new standard in clubs, and a new standard in Palm Beach, and I've gotten great credit for it. That is totally open to everybody. So, of course, I am."[43]

What a dishonest thing to say. Donald Trump says nobody has done as much as he for equality and gives as an example a country club he built that is open to everybody. He thinks no one has done more for equality than he because he doesn't run a "Whites only" club. What a great civil rights leader! (It should be noted that some have seen Trump's efforts in Palm Beach as fighting discrimination against Jews and African Americans. I do not.) And by the way, Donald, is there anything else on your list of "Things I did to fight discrimination"?

"There's nobody that's done so much for equality as I have." Abraham Lincoln, John Lewis, Jackie Robinson, Cesar Chavez, Susan B. Anthony, Malala Yousafzai, Rosa Parks, Elie Wiesel, Martin Luther King Jr., move over; Donald Trump has done the most for equality. Trump's predilection for making ridiculous statements borders on lunacy.

Donald and Marlee Matlin

In 2011, Academy Award-winning actress Marlee Matlin appeared on Trump's television show *The Celebrity Apprentice*. Matlin is deaf and has what some call "a deaf accent," the particular tonality with which many deaf people speak.

According to the *Daily Beast*, "One individual affiliated with the show revealed, '[Trump] would make fun of her voice. It actually sounded a lot like what he did [to] the *New York Times* guy,'"[44] a reference to when Trump seemingly mocked a disabled reporter during the campaign.

Several other sources affiliated with *The Celebrity Apprentice* said during Matlin's appearance on the show, Donald Trump mocked her hearing loss and speech pattern and seemed to get a real kick out of doing so. They said Trump would regularly ridicule and disrespect the actress. He is reported to have repeatedly called her retarded because of her deafness and deaf accent. Pure, unadulterated, unbelievable, cruel, medieval ignorance.

Again, according to *The Daily Beast* in their article on Trump and Marlee Matlin, "Due to extensive non-disclosure agreements signed by members involved with the production, every one of the sources asked to be quoted anonymously for fear of legal retribution."[45] That's how Trump rolls. He knows he does so much that is improper that he needs to keep his employees and associates, and others silent. He knows his conduct on the set of a TV show might be embarrassing if known by others, so he demands silence. Only a man whose conduct is so consistently improper would think to protect himself in this manner.

Donald, Randall Pinkett, and Rebecca Jarvis

In an interview for *US Weekly*[46], Trump was asked to describe the two Season 4 finalists, Randal Pinkett and Rebecca Jarvis, from his television show *The Apprentice*. He described Pinkett as lazy and Jarvis as beautiful. Pinkett is African American, Jarvis is White. And we know Trump thinks Black people are lazy (see "Atlantic City Bigotry" later in this chapter).

While it's beside the point, Pinkett attended Rutgers University, where he was an academic All-American and graduated summa cum laude; he was also captain of the men's track and field team. In 1993, he was named a member of the *USA TODAY* All-USA Academic Team. Pinkett is both a Rhodes Scholar and a Walter Byers Scholar. He has two master's degrees (from Oxford and MIT) and a PhD from MIT. He is the co-founder of the business consulting firm BCT Partners. He is the author of three books. Now that's a lazy guy.

Not only were Trump's comments seemingly bigoted they were also seemingly sexist. He description of Jarvis as beautiful seems to neglect her considerable achievements

While it's beside the point again, Jarvis is a graduate of St. Paul Academy and Summit School and the University of Chicago. She studied international economics and business at Sciences Po and Paris Dauphine University.

Jarvis was named one of Teen People's "20 Teens Who Will Change the World" in February 2000. She was recognized for raising over $750,000 for her own non-profit children's charity. She was also named as a "Point of Light" for her advocacy of disenfranchised children and teens.

Don Cheadle on Trump

Don Cheadle is an accomplished actor, writer, producer, director, and author. He is best known for his role as Paul Rusesabagina in the film *Hotel Rwanda*, for which he earned a Best Actor nomination for an Academy Award. He currently stars on Showtime's *House of Lies*, for which he won a Golden Globe Award in 2013.

Cheadle is a distinguished humanitarian. He is the co-founder of the Not on Our Watch organization, a group that focuses global attention on mass atrocities. Together with poker player Annie Duke, Cheadle organized an annual charity poker tournament, Ante Up for Africa.

In 2007, Cheadle, with George Clooney, received the Summit Peace Award, presented by the Nobel Peace Prize laureates, because of their work to raise money and attention to stop the conflict in Darfur that had claimed hundreds of thousands of lives. In 2007, Cheadle was awarded the BET Humanitarian Award for his numerous humanitarian efforts. In 2010, Cheadle was named U.N. Environment Program Goodwill Ambassador.

On March 4, 2017, Cheadle tweeted the following regarding Donald Trump: "Hated him since he asked my friend's father at the Doral pro-am if he'd ever 'f--ked a n----r' Did it for me."[47] Sickening.

Everybody Loves "The Donald"

Donald Trump's presidential candidacy was endorsed by the following:

- Richard Spencer, the director of the National Policy Institute, a white nationalist think tank

- Jared Taylor, editor of *American Renaissance*, a white nationalist magazine

- Michael Hill, head of the League of the South, a white supremacist secessionist group

Image Source[48]

- Brad Griffin, a member of League of the South and author of the popular white supremacist blog *Hunter Wallace*

- The American Freedom Party, an American political party that promotes white supremacy

- The *Daily Stormer*, an American neo-Nazi and white supremacist website

- David Duke, former KKK Imperial Grand Wizard and current white nationalist

Although others did not explicitly endorse his campaign, the trail of questionable supporters continues:

- Don Black, a former KKK Grand Dragon who runs the white nationalist website Stormfront.org, said he was skeptical of Trump but supports him.

- Rocky J. Suhayda, chair of the American Nazi Party, praised Trump's immigration policy and attitude and said a Trump presidency would be an opportunity for white nationalists.

The Crusader, the official paper of the KKK, endorsed Donald Trump
Image Souce[49]

Trump did say he was a great unifier, but I didn't know these were the folks he was going to unite. It looks like Trump has locked up the white nationalist vote.

Fred Trump and the Ku Klux Klan March

On Memorial Day 1927, the Ku Klux Klan marched in Queens to protest Protestant American citizens being "assaulted by Roman Catholic police of New York City." Donald Trump's father was one of seven men who were arrested that day (although he was not charged). A reported 1,000 Klansman were at the march. Those arrested were described as "berobed marchers"[51] in the *Long Island Daily Press*. Some other reports support the conclusion that Fred Trump was marching that day as a Klan member; other reports confirm his arrest but don't assert whether he was in the march or if he was a Klan member.

Donald Trump often says, "America First". So does the KKK.

Image Source[50]

Donald denied that his father was ever arrested, although it should be noted that Donald was not born until about 19 years after the incident.

Fred Trump, the Beach Haven Apartments, and Woody Guthrie

After World War II, hundreds of thousands of soldiers in need of affordable housing came home to New York City. In response, the Federal Housing Authority issued loans and subsidies to housing developers to construct public housing geared towards the returning soldiers. Donald Trump's father, Fred Trump, applied for and received financial support, and ended up making much of his wealth by building public housing. During those years, racism accusations related to Fred Trump's real estate ventures were regularly lodged against him.

Woody Guthrie was a singer/songwriter starting in the 1940s until his death in 1967. After serving in the Merchant Marine and the Army, Guthrie and his family moved into Fred Trump's Beach Haven apartment complex in Brooklyn in 1950, signing a two-year lease. Soon he realized that nearly all the apartments' residents were White, and he learned of Trump's unwillingness to rent to African Americans. This is from his writings:

"My worst enemy is my landlord that tries his best to make me and my family live a life of race hate just because he so quickly chose to live his own sad life that way."[52]

Guthrie also wrote the lyrics to a song about Trump and the Trumps' Beach Haven apartments. Here is an excerpt:

"Old Man Trump," words by Woody Guthrie, music by Ryan Harvey

I suppose that Old Man Trump knows just how much racial hate
He stirred up in that bloodpot of human hearts
When he drawed that color line
Here at his Beach Haven family project

Beach Haven ain't my home!
No, I just can't pay this rent!
My money's down the drain,
And my soul is badly bent!
Beach Haven is Trump's Tower
Where no black folks come to roam,
No, no, Old Man Trump!
Old Beach Haven ain't my home![53]

A Trump History of Housing Discrimination

In 1964, Maxine Brown, a nurse, applied for an apartment at Fred Trump's Wilshire Apartments in Queens, New York. According to an interview with the rental agent, Stanley Leibowitz, he brought the matter to the attention of Fred Trump, who told him to "Take the application and put it in a drawer and leave it there."[54]

Realizing how she was being treated, Ms. Brown filed a complaint with the New York City Commission on Human Rights. A hearing was convened at which Mr. Leibowitz was called to testify.

> Asked to estimate how many Blacks lived in Mr. Trump's various properties, he remembered replying: "To the best of my knowledge, none."

After the hearing, Ms. Brown was offered an apartment in the Wilshire, and in the spring of 1964, she moved in. For 10 years, she said, she was the only African American in the building.

Complaints about the Trump organization's rental policies continued to mount: By 1967, state investigators found that out of some 3,700 apartments in Trump Village, seven were occupied by African American families.[55]

After receiving a series of complaints, in 1972, the New York City Commission on Human Rights, the Urban League and other groups sent test applicants to Trump properties. As National Public Radio reported on their website:[56]

Back then, Sheila Morse worked as one of those testers. When a Black New Yorker was turned down for service and racial bias was suspected, Morse, who is White, would be dispatched to see if she received different treatment.

In this case, a Black man in search of an apartment in Brooklyn in 1972 saw a sign on a building: "apartment for rent."

He met with the superintendent, and the superintendent said, "I'm very sorry, but the apartment is rented — it's gone," Morse says. "So the gentlemen said to him, 'Well, why is the sign out? I still see a sign that says apartment for rent.' And the superintendent said, 'Oh, I guess I forgot to take it down.'"

When Morse went to the building to ask about the same apartment, she says, "They greeted me with open arms and showed me every aspect of the apartment."

Morse says she reported her experience to the Human Rights Commission, and then returned to the apartment building. After she was offered a lease, the Black man who had tried to rent the apartment entered the office with a city human rights commissioner, and the three of them confronted the building superintendent.

> "He said, 'Well, I'm only doing what my boss [Trump Management] told me to do — I am not allowed to rent to Black tenants,' Morse says."

The city and the Urban League then brought the matter to the attention of the Civil Rights Division of the U.S. Department of Justice (DOJ). After an investigation, they filed a suit against the Trump organization (Fred Trump & Donald Trump) charging them with racially discriminatory conduct at 39 different locations in New York City. A long history of racial bias at Trump properties was exposed.

According to court records, four superintendents and rental agents reported that housing applications were coded by race, and doormen were told to discourage prospective Black apartment-dwellers from even entering the building, claiming there were no vacancies or giving falsely inflated rent information. One agent said he was personally directed not to rent to Blacks.

A settlement was reached in the DOJ case; the Trump organization signed a consent decree and agreed to, among other conditions, actively recruit minorities for their properties. The DOJ called the settlement far-reaching. Since no admission of guilt was included in the settlement, Donald Trump naturally painted the agreement as favorable to him and his father.

Atlantic City Bigotry

Kip Brown, a former employee at Atlantic City's Trump Castle hotel, says, "When Donald and Ivana came to the casino, the bosses would order all the black people off the floor. ... It was the eighties, I was a teenager, but I remember it: they put us all in the back."[57] Why would the bosses want to hide the Black employees? I can come up with only two possible reasons. Either Trump didn't like being around Black people, or he would not be happy that Black people were working at his casino.

John R. O'Donnell, who was employed by Trump for three years, serving as president of Trump Plaza Hotel and Casino in his final year, says in his book *Trumped! The Inside Story of the Real Donald Trump*[58] that Trump made racial slurs against Black people.

"I think the guy is lazy," Trump said of a Black casino employee, according to O'Donnell. "And it's probably not his fault because laziness is a trait in blacks. It really is, I believe that. It's not anything they can control."[59] There can be no argument that this is a horrible, bigoted statement. It alone should have disqualified Trump from ever running for president.

O'Donnell writes that he advised Trump against publicly expressing those views. "Yeah, you're right," he quotes Trump as replying. "If anybody ever heard me say that . . . I'd be in a lot of trouble. But I have to tell you, that's the way I feel."[60]

Other employees at Trump's Atlantic City Casinos have also spoken of Trump's bigotry. As reported by the *Huffington Post*, "The New Jersey Casino Control Commission fined the Trump Plaza Hotel and Casino $200,000 in 1992 because managers would remove African-American card dealers at the request of a certain big-spending gambler. A state appeals court upheld the fine."[61]

"Racist Through and Through"

This from CNN, "Former President of Trump Plaza Hotel and Casino, Jack O'Donnell, said President Donald Trump has a long history of racism and is 'a racist through and through.'"[62]

Bigotry at the Beauty Pageant

Former Miss Teen USA Kamie Crawford tweeted on October 12, 2016: "...When I was 17, I met Mr. Trump for the first time as Miss Teen USA. As the first WOC [woman of color] to win the title in almost a decade—I was forewarned prior to meeting him that, 'Mr. Trump doesn't like black people. So, don't take it the wrong way if he isn't extremely welcoming towards you. If he is, then you just must be the "type" of black he likes.'"

"Sure enough, after I was warned about him, I saw him in action & witnessed him completely snub a black contestant at Miss Universe rehearsals. While she was practicing on stage (he) literally turned his back to the stage and made a face like he was going to vomit at the sight of her. Luckily for me—I was the 'type' of black he liked. He toted me around his buddies who were all there gawking at the Miss Universe girls." She went on to say Trump was not inappropriate with her, but she witnessed his "predatory" behavior with other contestants.[63]

It's interesting that Miss Crawford was warned that Trump "doesn't like black people." This suggests that his bigotry was well established among the pageant staff and he wasn't even aware enough to disguise his bigotry.

Tweet Bigotry

In November 2015, two days after some of his supporters kicked and punched a Black activist who disrupted a Trump rally, Trump tweeted a graphic. The image showed a masked, dark-skinned man with a handgun and the following statements regarding deaths in 2015 (see below). None of the statistics are accurate. For example, the graphic says that the percentage of Whites killed by Blacks was 81%, but the actual number is 15%. The source for his information, the so-called Crime Statistics Bureau, doesn't exist.

> Blacks killed by Whites – 2%
> Blacks killed by police – 1%
> Whites killed by police – 3%
> Whites killed by Whites – 16%
> Whites killed by blacks – 81%
> Blacks killed by blacks – 97%
>
> Source the "Crime Statistics Bureau – San Francisco"[64]

When confronted about his tweet the next day, Trump stated the statistics came from very credible sources. He made that up. The earliest tweet of these statistics, from November 22, 2015, seems to have come from a neo-Nazi individual and website, Non Dildo'd Goyim (@CheesedBrit). Some days later, Trump said that he didn't tweet it but rather retweeted it and that he can't check every statistic.

A Twofer

This is a 1989 doozy: "Black guys counting my money! I hate it. The only kind of people I want counting my money are short guys that wear yarmulkes every day."[65] Congratulations, Donald, you've offended two groups in one statement.

<u>"The Jews" #1</u>

On December 3, 2015, Donald Trump spoke to the Republican Jewish Coalition. He begins, "Thank you very much. You're just like me because my daughter happens to be Jewish. She has a great husband, Jared. Ivanka cannot be happier. The only bad news is I can't get her on Saturday night for a call. I can't speak to my daughter on Saturday, but that's OK."

He goes on: "Look, I'm a negotiator like you folks; we're negotiators . . . This room negotiates perhaps more than any room I've spoken to, maybe more..."

That's why you don't want to give me money. OK. But that's OK. You want to control your own politician, that is fine. Five months ago, I was with you."[66]

He has no clue. Let's break this down:

- Trump begins with a "joking" statement about his daughter being Jewish. Trump simplistically expects those in the audience to think anybody whose daughter is Jewish could not be prejudiced against them; he'll support them, so they're going to support him. But that's not how it works. It doesn't matter if you have a Jewish friend, a Jewish neighbor, or a Jewish relative. It doesn't make you more accepting of or friendly to Jews. Everybody should be accepting of and friendly to Jews. If you have a Jewish relative, you don't get extra credit; it proves nothing. But it does make one curious as to why you thought it necessary to tell me about Jews you know. Next time I meet Trump, I'm going to tell him my neighbor is a Presbyterian (Trump is a Presbyterian). Do you think then he'll support me?

  Trump's declaration regarding his daughter brings to mind the phrase, "Some of my best friends are Black". That expression has, over the years, become recognized as meaningless and even comical in its absurdity regarding the point it is trying to make. Having a "Black friend" proves nothing and doesn't verify you are not biased. The same is true if you have a Jewish daughter. Next, we'll hear Trump argue he is not a misogynist because he has a female wife.

- "Recognizing" that Jews like to negotiate like him is not endearing, as I think Trump intended. It's stereotyping and bigoted.

- Saying that Jews want to use their money to control politicians is offensive, stereotyping, and bigoted.

"The Jews"#2

And then there was this comment in March 2016 to the American Israel Public Affairs Committee: "I didn't come here tonight to pander to you about Israel." (Oh, I doubt that's true). Later in the same speech: "I love the people in this room. I love Israel. . . . My daughter Ivanka is about to have a beautiful Jewish baby."[67] (See? I told you he came to pander.)

"The Jews" #3

As Trump put it in 1989, "Who the f--k knows? I mean, really, who knows how much the JAPs will pay for Manhattan property these days? (*TIME*, January 1989)"[68] (Note: "JAP" is a derogatory term to describe Jewish women).

The Israel Day Parade

In speaking to the American Israel Public Affairs Committee, Trump proclaimed, "In spring of 2004 at the height of the violence in the Gaza Strip, I was the grand marshal of the 40th Salute to Israel Parade, the largest single gathering in support of the Jewish state.

"It was a very dangerous time for Israel and frankly for anyone supporting Israel. Many people turned down this honor." (I don't believe that.) "I did not. I took the risk and I'm glad I did."[69]

And he made a similar statement to the Republican Jewish Coalition: "I was the Grand Marshall of the Israeli Day Parade at a very dangerous time when people said don't do it. I walked up Fifth Avenue. I was looking for lots of trouble but I said no way I'm not going to do it. It was a rough time. It was

2004 and it was a tremendous successful parade—maybe the most successful parade that they ever had."[70] Here we have a typical Trump made-up lie, mixed with a typical Trump senseless boast.

Blame the Muslim

Some conservatives have accused Huma Abedin, an aide to Hillary Clinton, of being linked to the Muslim World League and to the Muslim Brotherhood, both extremist organizations. Donald Trump, when asked about this in April 2016, kept the allegations going when he suggested examining where Abedin and her mother worked.

Abedin was born in the United States but raised in Saudi Arabia. She previously worked as the assistant editor of an academic journal, the *Journal of Muslim Minority Affairs*. It was founded by her father and edited by her mother. It is not a radical Muslim publication, as has been promulgated.

When the assertions regarding Abedin were raised in the Senate, Senator John McCain defended her, stating the claims regarding Abedin's ties to Muslim extremist groups were without basis or merit. It is bigoted to imply someone is sympathetic to terrorists simply because he or she is a Muslim or because he or she was raised in Saudi Arabia. It is bigoted to assume that if you work for a Muslim publication, you are suspect. Trump has continued the bigotry of equating Muslims with terrorism.

> "The bosom of America is open to receive not only the opulent and respectable stranger, but the oppressed and persecuted of all nations and religions; whom we shall welcome to a participation of all our rights and privileges, if by decency and propriety of conduct they appear to merit the enjoyment."
>
> — George Washington[71]

Keeping Out the Muslims

You already know about this one.

"This Way We Can Track Who They Are and Where They Are"

Donald Trump has suggested creating a database of Muslims, forcing them to carry identification cards, and implementing heavier surveillance on mosques. Weren't identification cards based on religion required in Nazi Germany?

Keeping Out the Mexicans

You already know about this one, too.

Very Scary

Ethnic cleansing is the attempt to purge, through deportation, displacement, or even mass killing, members of an unwanted ethnic group in order to establish ethnic uniformity. Ethnic cleansing campaigns have existed throughout history, all across the globe. It would be unfair and inaccurate to say that Donald Trump is pursuing a policy of ethnic cleansing. However, the similarities between his positions and the early events of historical ethnic cleansing efforts are disturbing.

An overwhelming majority of Trump's supporters endorse his plan to deport undocumented Mexican immigrants. That's scary. A poll[72] revealed 36% of Trump supporters think the practice of Islam should be banned in the United States (no religious freedom for Muslims). Similar ideas gave rise to ethnic cleansing in Germany, in the former Yugoslavia, in Bosnia, and in Rwanda. In all these countries, ethnic cleansing started with the demonization of an ethnic group and the deportation of members of that group.

"The Danger of the Single Story"

Chimamanda Adichie is a Nigerian writer who gave a TED talk called "The Danger of a Single Story." As described by *The New York Times* writer David Brooks, "It was about what happens when complex human beings and situations are reduced to a single narrative . . . Her point was that each individual life contains a heterogeneous compilation of stories. If you reduce people to one, you're taking away their humanity."[73]

From the TED talk, "The consequence of the single story is this: It robs people of dignity. It makes our recognition of our equal humanity difficult. It emphasizes how we are different rather than how we are similar . . . . "[74]

The single story robs of us of a true understanding of people and fuels misunderstanding and prejudice. American politics can be a breeding ground for the "single story" and Donald Trump's campaign has been a sanctuary for it (Muslims are terrorists, Mexicans are rapists, etc.) And when he clings so hard to his single story, and continually speaks of it and when he never offers any other story, he becomes a purveyor of prejudice.

The Real Story

"The land flourished because it was fed from so many sources—it was nourished by so many cultures and traditions and people."– Lyndon B. Johnson.[75]

"I Would Never Mock a Person That Has Difficulty"

At a South Carolina rally, Trump seemingly mocked journalist Serge Kovaleski, who has arthrogryposis, a disease that limits the flexibility of his arms. As Trump referred to Kovaleski, he jerked his arms and held his hands in a fashion similar to the appearance of arthrogryposis sufferers, an apparent reference to the reporter's physical appearance. But Trump denied that he was mocking a disabled man.

It is hard to imagine a man running for president mocking people's physical characteristics and disabilities. But then there is Donald Trump. How does Trump respond to such accusations? He states that his buildings are handicapped accessible. Not much of an as being handicap accessible is required by law.

Although most seem to conclude Trump was indeed mocking Mr. Kovaleski, and I tend to agree, there is some indication he may not have been.

The case he wasn't mocking: It should be noted that Trump's explanation of his gestures at the rally was that he was simply trying to portray a confused individual searching for a response. I did find a video of him making similar motions when deriding someone's confusion (he does a lot of mocking) , but that similarity doesn't convince me. He may occasionally have made like gestures to simulate someone's confusion, but in light of the evidence presented below, I don't believe that is the explanation behind what he did regarding Mr. Kovaleski.

<u>The case he was mocking</u>: Some days after the rally, Trump stated, "If Mr. Kovaleski is handicapped, I would not know because I don't know what he looks like." But while seemingly mimicking Mr. Kovaleski at the event, Trump said, "Now the poor guy. You gotta see this guy,"[76] a clear reference to Mr. Kovaleski's physical appearance. Why would you say, "You gotta see this guy" if you yourself had never seen him? You probably wouldn't—unless you were lying. Moreover, Trump has used the expression, "You gotta see this guy" before, specifically in reference to someone he has seen.

Mr. Kovaleski has said he interviewed Trump in his office and interacted with him about a dozen times in the 1980s and 1990s and even spent a day traveling with him on the Trump Shuttle. He says they were on a first-name basis for years. Because of Mr. Kovaleski's distinctive appearance due to his condition, it is not credible that after 12 interactions, Trump doesn't know what Mr. Kovaleski looks like.

Andrew Gluck was a reporter and financial columnist at the *New York Daily News* with Kovaleski in the late 1980s. He coauthored stories about Trump with Kovaleski and confirms Kovaleski's assertions regarding his relationship with Trump and the fact that the two were on a first-name basis.

To add to it all, Trump put out a malicious statement about Kovaleski to try to further obviate the truth. In his statement, Trump declared, "Serge Kovaleski must think a lot of himself if he thinks I remember him from decades ago—if I ever met him at all, which I doubt I did. He should stop using his disability to grandstand and get back to reporting for a newspaper that is rapidly going down the tubes."[77] Donald Trump is simply without decency. For the record, Mr. Kovaleski has never mentioned nor made reference to his disability regarding this matter.

Making this disrespect all the more believable, Donald Trump has frequently mocked people's physical characteristics. In August 2015, Trump said Megyn Kelly had "blood coming out of her wherever."[78] He has called singer Bette Midler "ugly" and "grotesque," author/columnist Arianna Huffington "unattractive both inside and out," former Connecticut governor Lowell Weicker a "fat slob," Marlee Matlin "retarded," and comedian Seth Meyers "a stutterer." During the presidential campaign, he made disparaging remarks about or references to the physical appearance of Carly Fiorina, Heidi Cruz, Marco Rubio, and Rand Paul.

Inspiring America's Youth

In February 2016, students at a high school in Indiana held a cutout showing Trump's face and chanted, "Build a wall; build a wall,"[79] during a basketball game against a high school that has a large number of Latino students. Remember that song "Greatest Love of All," and the line "I believe the children are our are future, teach them well and let them lead the way." Trump is good at teaching the children—teaching them hate.

Virginia parent Evelyn Momplaisir posted this on Facebook: "I just got a call from my son's teacher giving me a heads-up that two of his classmates decided to point out the 'immigrants' in the class who would be sent 'home' when Trump becomes president. They singled him out and were pointing and laughing at him as one who would have to leave because of the color of his skin. In the third grade…in Fairfax County…in 2016. In the United States of America."[80] School officials have confirmed the incident.

Inspiring America's Adults

Trump's bigotry and hatred has encouraged bigotry and hatred in others. While Donald Trump is not the cause of others' bigotry, he does inspire it. His rhetoric often emboldens others in a terrible way. A long list of examples has been chronicled.

As reported in the *Christian Science Monitor* in August 2015, two months after Trump's statement regarding Mexico sending us rapists, two Boston men walking home from a baseball game used a metal pole to beat a homeless Latino man who is a legal U.S. resident; they also urinated on his face. State troopers who arrested the two men reported that one said, "Donald Trump was right, all these illegals need to be deported." Trump, when told of the alleged assault, said it was the first he had heard of it and added, "I think it would be a shame… I will say that people who are following me are very passionate. They love this country and they want this country to be great again. They are passionate."[81] This is not the response of someone with an ounce of decency.

Two days later, Trump tweeted, "Boston incident is terrible. We need energy and passion, but we must treat each other with respect. I would never condone violence." Even his attempted backtracking two days later falls far too short of the mark. He seemingly commends the energy and passion of the two men, yet he mentions virtually nothing about how vile it is to hate people because of their ethnicity.

In August 2015, Trump had security physically remove Univision television anchor and reporter Jorge Ramos from his press conference after Ramos started to ask a question without being called on. Once escorted into the hall by security, a Trump supporter approached Ramos and said, "You were very rude. It's not about you. Get out of my country."[82] As if it matters, Ramos is an American citizen. Ramos was later allowed back in the press conference.

In December 2015, William Celli was arrested because, days earlier, he had yelled, "I'm going to kill you all" outside the Islamic Society of West Contra Costa County (California). After a search of Celli's house, a suspicious device was found and detonated. Celli had made a series of xenophobic, Islamophobic, and pro-Trump Facebook posts in the months prior to the incident. In one post, he stated regarding Trump, "I'll follow this MAN to the end of the world."[83] Clearly, he feels trump support his extreme views

In February 2016, Trump, commenting about a protester at a Las Vegas rally, said he'd like to punch him in the face. A few weeks later at a North Carolina rally, a Trump supporter sucker-punched a Black protester in the face as he was being led out of the building. Monkey see, monkey do. When asked by a reporter why he punched the protester, the Trump supporter said, "Number one, we don't know if he's ISIS. We don't know who he is, but we know he's not acting like an American, cussing me. . . . Yes, he deserved it. The next time we see him, we might have to kill him. We don't know who he is. He might be with a terrorist organization."[84]

Outrageous. But one aspect of the disturbance has been overlooked. The Trump supporter repeatedly used the word "we." I think this suggests he feels he was acting on behalf of Trump and Trump supporters—or at least with their blessing. What has Donald Trump unleashed on us?

CBS journalist Sopan Deb covered the Trump campaign from the beginning. While covering the March 2016 Trump rally in Chicago, Deb was filming a handcuffed man who was bloodied, lying on the ground, and surrounded by police, who then arrested him. Suddenly, Deb was grabbed from behind and thrown to the ground. He was handcuffed, detained, and later charged with resisting arrest.

Deb claimed he was simply filming the unfolding events. He says he did not resist police, and he properly identified himself as a member of the press. Video of the incident seems to support his claims.

Later Deb tweeted, "I've never seen anything like what I'm witnessing in my life." Deb is of Indian descent but has never been to India or to the Middle East. He has repeatedly been singled out at events. In January 2016, he tweeted, "a Trump supporter just asked me at Reno event if I was taking pictures for ISIS. When I looked shocked, he said, 'Yeah, I'm talking to you.'"[85]

In March 2016, a video was posted on Facebook showing a man yelling, "Kill Muslims! Kill them all!" and "Bury the Muslims!" to a group of men preaching on the sidewalk in Grand Rapids, Michigan. As he walks away, he turns and yells, "Trump, Trump, Trump."[86]

Also, in March 2016, a Muslim student and a Hispanic student in Kansas were reported to have been attacked by a man who chanted, "Trump, Trump, Trump" and shouted, "brown trash, go home."[87]

In April 2016, at a Starbucks in Washington, D.C., a Muslim woman wearing a hijab was harassed and assaulted by a woman who called her "a worthless piece of Muslim trash" and a "terrorist." She told the victim she was "planning to vote for Donald Trump in the hope he would send all you terrorist Muslims out of this country."[88] After leaving the area, the woman returned and poured a liquid over the Muslim woman's head. Part of the incident was caught on Starbucks' surveillance video.[89]

Beginning in April 2016, crude anti–Hillary Clinton buttons, T-shirts, and bumper stickers began appearing at Trump rallies and other places. At a New Hampshire Trump rally, a man in the front held up a bumper sticker that read, "Trump That B—ch." Trump reacted: "What the hell was that, I'm wondering," while smiling and making faces, adding, "This could only happen at a Trump rally."[90] He made no comment to condemn the vulgarity. To the contrary, he appeared to be proud of the supporter. Hatred, sexism, and nasty rhetoric: coming to a Trump rally near you.

In June 2016, during an Arizona Trump rally, a man went on a tirade against an older Latino man, repeatedly doing the Nazi salute. At one point, he shouted at the man, "Go f--king make my tortilla, mother--ker and build that f--king wall, for me! Trump! I love Trump! F--k you, I love my country!" A video of the incident is on YouTube.[91]

Inspiring Anti-Semitism

In April 2016, Julia Ioffe's, a Jewish journalist, wrote a profile article of Melania Trump which appeared in GQ magazine. Within 24 hours she received a flood of anti-Semitic, vitriolic, and threatening messages, including death threats, apparently from Donald Trump supporters.

Ioffe also received a phone call from an anonymous individual who played a Hitler speech. She received another call from "Overnight Caskets." On Twitter, users posted photos of her face superimposed on a photo of an Auschwitz prisoner and a cartoon of a Jewish man on his knees being shot in the head. Another picture showed Ioffe in a gas chamber and a smiling Trump outside the chamber in a Nazi uniform. I can't imagine anything much more revolting than these images. I have copies of them, and I considered including them in this book. I could not bring myself to do so.

The Daily Stormer, a white supremacist website, denigrated Ioffe in a blog post titled, "Empress Melania Attacked by Filthy Russian Kike Julia Ioffe in GQ!"

On May 4, 2016, Wolf Blitzer of CNN asked Trump if he would denounce the anti-Semitic death threats against Ioffe. Trump refused to do so, saying he was unaware of them and adding, "I don't have a message to the fans. A woman wrote an article that was inaccurate."[92] He refers to the perpetrators of this filthy hate as his "fans" and makes no response condemning their actions.

Image Source[93]

After the South Carolina primary, writer Bethany Mandel, who is Jewish, posted a tweet regarding the number of anti-Semitic supporters of Donald Trump. The response to that tweet included Mandel being called a "slimy Jewess" and told that she "deserves the oven." On Facebook, she received death threats.

Adam Yauch, a member of the Beastie Boys, died of cancer at age 47 in 2012. He was Jewish. In November 2016, a memorial park honoring Yauch was defaced with swastikas and the words "Go Trump" (see photo).

What Would Ronald Reagan Say?

Trump professes his admiration for Ronald Reagan. But when Reagan saw bigotry, he spoke out. These are just a few of Reagan's many elegant statements regarding hate and bigotry: [94]

- "We must never remain silent in the face of bigotry. We must condemn those who seek to divide us. In all quarters and at all times, we must teach tolerance and denounce racism, anti-Semitism, and all ethnic or religious bigotry wherever they exist as unacceptable evils. We have no place for haters in America -- none, whatsoever."

- "No one group in this country is better than another. No one race or religion or sex or color is better than another. And no region is better or worse than another. It's time we erased the last vestiges of intolerance, bigotry, and unkindness from our hearts. Decency demands this and so does our history."

- "And let me say there is no place in the Republican Party for those who would exhibit prejudice against anyone. There's no place in our party for the kind of bigotry and ugly rhetoric that we've been hearing outside our party recently. We have no room for hate here, and we have no place for the haters."

- "Racial discrimination and religious bigotry have no place in a free society."

- "And let me add, in the party of Lincoln, there is no room for intolerance and not even a small corner for anti-Semitism or bigotry of any kind. Many people are welcome in our house, but not the bigots."

- "I was raised in a household in which the only intolerance I was taught was intolerance of bigotry."[95]

When Donald Trump saw bigotry, he declared:

- "I don't have a message to the fans." [96]

You Know You're a Bigot When...

It's very unusual for someone to be asked directly, "Are you a bigot?" It is even more unusual for a candidate for president of the United States to be asked directly, "Are you a bigot?" (I would speculate David Duke and George Wallace were the last.) During his campaign, Trump was asked this very question by ABC's Barbara Walters, Fox's Chris Wallace, CNN's Anderson Cooper, and CNN's Don Lemon, to name a few.

Bigotry, Stupidity, or Both?

Trump once offered a unique idea regarding his television show, *The Apprentice* while on the Howard Stern radio show. "On *The Apprentice* there was a concept, okay, thrown out by some person, nine blacks against nine whites," Trump told Stern. "And it would be nine blacks against nine whites, all highly educated, very smart, strong, beautiful people, right? Do you like it?"[97] Bigotry, stupidity, or both?

How Could He Be a Racist…

Here is Trump's response when asked on *Fox & Friends* about accusations he is a racist. "Well, you know, when it comes to racism and racists, I am the least racist person there is. And I think most people who know me would tell you that. I am the least racist, I've had great relationships. In fact, Randal Pinkett won, as you know, on *The Apprentice* a little while ago, a couple of years ago. And Randall's been outstanding in every way. So I am the least racist person." [98]

Here's some more proof he's not a racist. According to Trump:

- He loves "the" Hispanics. The Hispanics are good people. Many Hispanics work for him.

- He loves "the" Blacks. The Blacks are good people. Many Blacks work for him.

- He loves "the" Muslims. The Muslims are good people. Many Muslims work for him.

Now I guess that puts that racist and bigotry stuff to rest.

Proving He's Not a Racist

Not being a racist is not something you prove; it is something you are.

End the Bias Against Trump

When speculating as to why he is so frequently audited by the IRS, Trump offered, "Well, maybe because of the fact that I'm a strong Christian, and I feel strongly about it and maybe there's a bias." Does he think that all those auditors at IRS are saying, "Let's audit the strong Christian, Trump"?[99]

Hate vs. Civility

In October 2016, a GOP office in Hillsborough, North Carolina, was firebombed. Vandals assaulted the office, throwing a Molotov cocktail through one of the building's windows and painting "Nazi Republicans leave town or else" on an adjacent building.

In response, local Democrats started a GoFundMe page to raise funds to rebuild the office. The following was posted on the GoFundMe page:

> As Democrats, we are starting this campaign to enable the OrangeCounty, North Carolina Republican office to re-open as soon as possible.

> Until an investigation is undertaken, we cannot know who did this or why. No matter the result, this is not how Americans resolve their differences. We talk, we argue, sometimes we march, and most of all we vote. We do not resort to violence by individuals or by mobs.

> So, let's all pitch in, no matter what your party affiliation, in and get that office open again quickly. [100]Can you imagine the Trump campaign ever doing something like that? You can stop laughing now. I can envision Trump saying that if he had built the building it would have withstood the firebombing.

Then or Now: On September 15, 1963, a bomb placed by members of the Ku Klux Klan under the 16th St. Baptist Church in Birmingham, Alabama, went off, killing four girls and injuring 20 others. Addie Mae Collins, 14, and Denise McNaire, 11, were in the church choir; Carole Robertson, 14, and Cynthia Wesley, 14, were church ushers.

Two days later, Eugene Patterson, the editor of the Atlanta Constitution, wrote, "A Negro mother wept in the street Sunday morning in front of a Baptist Church in Birmingham. In her hand she held a shoe, one shoe, from the foot of her dead child. We hold that shoe with her. Every one of us in the white South holds that small shoe in his hand." He went on, calling out, "We – who go on electing politicians who heat the kettles of hate." That was said on September 16, 1963— and, sadly, is still true today.

Chapter 3
Trump the Hypocrite

Hypocrite[102]

[hip·uh·krit] *noun*

1. a person who pretends to have virtues, moral or religious beliefs, principles, etc., that he or she does not actually possess, especially a person whose actions belie stated beliefs.

2. a person who feigns some desirable or publicly approved attitude, especially one whose private life, opinions, or statements belie his or her public statements.

No tale of Donald Trump would be complete without a review of his hypocrisy. Most people are hypocrites from time to time. For Donald Trump, it's a lifestyle. And the stark, blatant nature of his duplicity is at a level unmatched.

Hypocrisy #1

Donald Trump infamously remarked that John McCain is "not a war hero." Trump said, "He's a war hero because he was captured. I like people that weren't captured, okay? I hate to tell you. He's a war hero because he was captured, okay?"[103] Donald Trump wasn't captured. Oh yeah; he didn't serve in the military. He had a boo-boo on his foot.

Donald Trump says he received a medical deferment because of bone spurs on his foot. When asked which foot had the bone spurs, he replies that he can't remember. Sounds fishy to me. (The Trump campaign says it was on both feet.)

As Trump biographer Wayne Barrett told the New York Daily News on the subject of Trump's medical exemption, "I doubt it was a serious medical issue . . . Up to that time, he was an active athlete. It was bull----t." And on the subject of the draft, "It appears he was actively looking for some justification to evade it."[104]

Hypocrisy #1a

Donald Trump uttered his words regarding John McCain in July 2015. Trump also called McCain a "dummy" because he graduated near the bottom of his class at the U.S. Naval Academy—outrageous comments about a former POW who spent five years in captivity and 23 years in the Navy serving his country.

These comments that are even more outrageous when you look at what Trump said about the senator during McCain's presidential run. "He's a tough guy, he's a smart guy, he's a very, very bright guy. He's a very, very, he's just a quality human being . . . . He is a man worthy of respect. And this country no longer has respect. What we need more than anything else is just that word: respect."[105] Which is it, Mr. Trump?

Hypocrisy #2

In the first Republican debate of the 2016 presidential campaign, Megyn Kelly asked Trump if he lacked the temperament to be president because of offensive remarks he had made about women. She pointed out that he had referred to them as "fat pigs, dogs, slobs, and disgusting animals." That apparently angered Trump, and over the days and months that followed, he regularly attacked Kelly and criticized her journalistic ability. In effect, he went to war with her.

His first and most criticized response to Kelly was on CNN, where he complained, "She gets out and she starts asking me all sorts of ridiculous questions and you know, you could see there was blood coming out of her eyes, blood coming out of her... wherever. In my opinion, she was off base."[106] He followed that by later calling her a "lightweight reporter,"[107] a "bimbo," and "overrated."[108] He didn't think she was a lightweight reporter; he just said it because he was angry at her for asking him a question he didn't like. Among his many tweets denigrating Kelly were, "I liked The Kelly File much better without @megynkelly. Perhaps she could take another eleven-day unscheduled vacation!"[109] and "The bimbo back in town. I hope not for long."[110]

But back in 2011, Trump was interviewed by Megyn Kelly about, ironically, a proposed presidential debate the two of them were to co-host. Trump was critical of the skills of many journalists and suggested he could do a better job than most of them. Kelly asked him if he thought he was a better moderator than her. Trump replied, "No. I could never beat you. That wouldn't even be close. That would be no contest." He added, "You have done a great job, by the way. And I mean it."[111]

One interesting aspect of this story: Donald Trump was annoyed that Kelly asked him about his tendency to refer to women as fat pigs, dogs, slobs, and disgusting animals. He said she was off base. Then he called her a bimbo. Anybody see the pure hypocrisy in that?

Before announcing his candidacy, Trump apparently tried to woo Kelly. In an interview with *Vanity Fair*, she reported, "he would send me press clippings about me that he would just sign 'Donald Trump'. And he called from time to time to compliment a segment. I didn't know why he was doing that."[112] But that was before Kelly asked a question that he didn't like. Which is it, Donald? He says she's a great reporter when it suits his needs and a bimbo when that suits his needs.

Hypocrisy #3

What does it say that Donald Trump was slow to disavow David Duke, a white supremacist former Grand Wizard of the Ku Klux Klan, but quick to denounce Pope Francis, the leader of the Catholic Church?

Hypocrisy #4

Donald Trump doesn't want to release his tax returns. The speculation is they contain revelations that would be damaging to him. Maybe it's that he didn't pay any federal income tax in the last few years, that he doesn't make charitable contributions, or that he has questionable foreign business dealings.

Trump knows exactly how he can quiet the critics. If there's nothing wrong, just release the returns and the whole thing goes away. Isn't that the advice he gave President Obama concerning his birth certificate? What's good for the goose . . . unless you're a hypocrite.

Hypocrisy #5

Donald Trump has boasted that if elected, nobody would be able to buy influence with him (e.g., through political contributions). But he regularly acknowledges that as a businessman, he made large contributions to many candidates, presumably to gain influence.

This is from the August 6, 2015 Republican presidential debates, "I will tell you that our system is broken. I gave to many people. Before this, before two months ago, I was a businessman. I give to everybody. When they call, I give. And do you know what? When I need something from them two years later, three years later, I call them—they are there for me."[113]

According to Trump, it's okay to *buy* political influence but not to *sell* political influence. Huh?

Hypocrisy #5a

Trump boasts that he's an outsider. But he acknowledges that he has donated millions of dollars to hundreds of Democratic and Republican candidates over many years. He donated to gain influence with them, and he says it worked. Doesn't that make him a pretty big insider?

Hypocrisy #6

Trump derides the philandering of Bill Clinton, but he has long been known as a womanizer. He had a well-known affair with Marla Maples for several years while married to Ivana. In his book *The Art of the Comeback*, Trump revealed, "If I told the real stories of my experiences with women, often seemingly very happily married and important women, this book would be a guaranteed best-seller."[114] People in glass houses shouldn't throw stones.

Hypocrisy #7

He harshly criticizes Carrier Air Conditioners for planning to move its plant in Indiana to one in Mexico, and Ford and Nabisco for opening factories in Mexico—but the ties, shirts, suits, cuff links, etc. of the Trump Signature Collection are made in China, Bangladesh, Honduras, Indonesia, and Mexico.

Hypocrisy #8

Trump, referring to former Mexican President Vicente Fox, who stated Mexico will not build that "f-----g wall" said this, "This guy used a filthy, disgusting word on television, and he should be ashamed of himself, and he should apologize, OK?"[115] Here's Trump at a 2011 Las Vegas rally: "Listen, you motherf--kers, we're gonna tax you 25%"[116] (Tea Party rally, Las Vegas, April 28, 2011)

Flip-Flopping

A flip-flop is a particular type of hypocrisy. The reason Donald Trump is such a hypocrite is the same reason he consistently lies: he has no interest in the truth. His hypocrisy stems from what's best for Trump. If it's best for Trump to say something today, but it is in his interest to say the opposite a month later, that's what he'll do. Here's a chart summarizing some of Trump's many flips and flops (compiled in part from an article in *The Huffington Post*).[117]

What He Says Now	What He Said Then
Trump, speaking about Hillary Clinton: "She has no natural talents to be President" (Sacramento rally, June 1, 2016)	Trump, speaking about Hillary Clinton: "Very talented, very smart. She's a friend of mine, so I'm a little bit prejudiced. She's a very, very capable person…" (*Anderson Cooper 360°*, CNN, March 16, 2007)
Ted Cruz to Trump: "Donald, true or false, you said the government should pay for everyone's health care." Trump: "That's false." (Republican primary debate, February 26, 2016)	Trump: "Everyone's got to be covered. I'm going to take care of everyone. The government's gonna pay for it, but we're going to save so much money on the other side." (60 Minutes, September 27, 2015)

Trump: "Hillary Clinton was the worst secretary of state in the history of the United States" (interview posted on NBCNews.com, July 8, 2015)	Trump: "I know her very well. I know her husband very well. I like them both, and they're just really terrific people. I like them both very much, but I think you'll be looking at the record of Hillary Clinton and how did she do as secretary of state—probably above and beyond everybody else and everything else" (interview posted on NBCNews.com, August 11, 2013)
Trump: "We would be so much better off if Gaddafi were in charge right now." (Republican primary debate, February 25, 2016)	Trump: "Gaddafi in Libya is killing thousands of people.... We should go in; we should stop this guy, which would be very easy and very quick." (Donald Trump video blog, February 2011)
Trump: "I don't know anything about David Duke. I don't know anything about what you're even talking about with white supremacy or white supremacists." (*State of the Union*, CNN, February 28, 2016)	Matt Lauer: "What do you see as their biggest problem with the Reform Party just now?" Trump: "Well, you got David Duke, just joined, a bigot, a racist, a problem." (*Today*, NBC, February 14, 2000)
George Stephanopoulos of ABC News asked Trump what his tax rate is, and Trump replied, "It's none of your business." ("Donald Trump Refuses to Reveal His Tax Rate: 'It's None of Your Business,'" abcnews.go.com, John Santucci, Veronica Stracqualursi, May 13, 2016).	Trump: "If I decide to run for office, I'll produce my tax returns, absolutely." (TV3's Ireland AM, an Irish television show, May 2014) "Trump: "I would release tax returns, and I would also explain to people that as a person that's looking to make money, you know, I'm in the this. And if I won, I would

	make money for our country. [...] So the answer is yeah, I would do it." (interview with radio host Hugh Hewitt, February 25, 2015)
Trump: "They said I want Japan to nuke. I want Japan to get nuclear weapons. Give me a break." (Sacramento, California, rally, June 2016)	Trump: "It's not like, gee whiz, nobody has them. So North Korea has nukes. Japan has a problem with that. I mean, they have a big problem with that. Maybe they would in fact be better off if they defend themselves from North Korea." When asked by Chris Wallace, "With nukes?" Trump replied, "Including with nukes, yes, including with nukes." (*Fox News Sunday*, April 2016)
Trump: "They're here illegally. You take them, they have to go back." (interview with Fox News' Bret Baier, November 2015)	Trump: "We have to show some compassion. You can't just throw everybody out. How do you throw somebody out who's lived in this country for 20 years?" (*Fox & Friends*, 2012)
Trump: "She's married to a man who got impeached." (Speech in Spokane, Washington, May 7, 2016)	Trump: "Look at the trouble Bill Clinton got into with something that was totally unimportant. They tried to impeach him, which was nonsense." (Interview with CNN's Wolf Blitzer, 2008)
In an interview with George Stephanopoulos, Trump asserted that "I have no relationship with Putin. . . . I don't think I've ever met him. . . . I have never	In 2013, Trump said that "I do have a relationship" with Putin, and in 2014, he said, "I spoke indirectly and directly with President

spoken to him on the phone." (ABC's *This Week*, July 3, 2016)	Putin."(National Press Club, May 27, 2014) In 2015, Trump said, "I got to know him very well because we were both on *60 Minutes*. We were stablemates." (Republican primary debate, November 10, 2015)
"No group in America has been more harmed by Hillary Clinton's policies than African Americans [...] No group. No group. If Hillary Clinton's goal was to inflict pain to the African American community, she could not have done a better job. It is a disgrace." (Trump rally in Michigan, August 18, 2016)	In a 2011 interview on Albany, New York's Talk Radio 1300, Trump said it was a "very sad thing" that "Hillary Clinton had done so much for the black population, so much and got very few votes," referring to her showing in the primaries versus Barack Obama.

Give Me a Break

Donald J. Trump
@realDonaldTrump

Can you believe that, with all of the problems and difficulties facing the U.S., President Obama spent the day playing golf. Worse than Carter.

8:03 PM · Oct 13, 2014

Grand Hypocrisy

These next tweets demonstrate that Trump's statements reflect only his self-interest. That makes his every assertion meaningless. The first tweet is from election night 2012. The second tweet was from nine days after Trump's own election, in which he lost the popular vote but won the electoral college.

Donald J. Trump
@realDonaldTrump

The electoral college is a disaster for a democracy.

11:45 AM - 6 Nov 2012

Donald J. Trump
@realDonaldTrump

The Electoral College is actually genius in that it brings all states, including the smaller ones, into play. Campaigning is much different!

8:40 AM - Nov 15, 2016

Chapter 4
Trump the Bully

bully[118]

[boo·lee] *noun*

1. a blustering, quarrelsome, overbearing person who badgers and tries to intimidate others; the behavior is often repeated and habitual.
2. calling names, spreading rumors, threatening behavior, and making fun of others are all bullying behavior.

Bullying often takes the form of slurs, rumors, put-downs, jokes, innuendo, demeaning comments, gestures, threats, and other written, oral, physical, or electronically transmitted messages or images.

Yep, that's him. Look at the last sentence in the definition. Bullying often takes the form of slurs (e.g., calling Elizabeth Warren "Pocahontas"); rumors (e.g., Ted Cruz's father is associated with John F. Kennedy assassin Lee Harvey Oswald); put-downs (calling Marco Rubio "Little Marco"); jokes (jokes about Hillary Clinton not satisfying her husband); innuendo (calling New York Sen. Kirsten Gillibrand a "flunky" who "would do anything for" campaign contributions); demeaning comments (calling Miss Universe "Miss Piggy"); gestures (mocking a disabled reporter); threats ("Be careful, Lyin' Ted, or I will spill the beans on your wife"); and other written, oral, physical, or electronically transmitted messages or images (any one of hundreds of Trump tweets).

Donald Trump is an enormously effective bully. His wealth, personality and lying fuel his bullying. When Trump goes up against you and starts throwing out lies about you, he's a very tough adversary. Some may question such lies, but many will question the target of his lies instead. It's not a fair fight. Trump is always a dirty fighter and he never plays by the rules. Once he decides you are not supporting him enough, he'll embark on a ruthless smear campaign. Trump loves a good smear campaign. It must surely be a helpless feeling to have to defend yourself against pure and extreme fabrications. Ask President Obama.

> ## smear campaign[119]
>
> [smir kam·peyn] *noun*
>
> 1. a planned attempt to harm the reputation of a person or company by telling lies about them.
>
> 2. a smear campaign, also referred to as a smear tactic or simply a smear, is an effort to damage or call into question someone's reputation, by propounding negative propaganda.

Everybody is afraid of Donald Trump. His 16 opponents for the Republican nomination were afraid of him. His employees are afraid of him. Contestants in his beauty pageants were afraid of him. Contestants on *The Apprentice* were afraid of him. Billy Bush was afraid of him. Women who won't come forward regarding his inappropriate conduct are afraid of him. His two ex-wives are afraid of him. So are reporters who cover him and the media in general, his campaign staff, people he does business with—the list goes on and on. They're all scared of Donald Trump. He pounds his victims, but he also maliciously intimidates without even trying. The fear of these groups and individuals have is warranted because Trump is a ruthless intimidator like no other.

Donald Trump is a classic bully and always one without remorse. Nobody epitomizes bullying more than Donald Trump. People submit to his bullying in large numbers.

Trump Sues

Donald Trump is quite a litigious fellow. A business mogul such as Trump may have more cause to bring or defend lawsuits than most—but come on. He constantly threatens to sue people and institutions that do things he doesn't like, all to get back at or intimidate people. Why not? He has the money to intimidate people with his threats and lawsuits. Some of Trump's lawsuits are against reporters and others who criticize him. He tries to silence his critics with million-dollar lawsuits. He uses lawsuits and the threat of lawsuits as a tool to coerce and torment.

USA Today reported that Trump and his businesses have been involved in at least 3,500 legal actions during the past 30 years.[120] Trump doesn't like businesses that compete with his or municipalities that have regulations or practices that adversely affect his companies. So, he sues.

Palm Beach International Airport is just a few miles from Mar-a-Lago. In 2015, Trump sued Palm Beach County for $100 million because of the "disturbance" caused by planes from the county's airport flying over his resort. Trump claimed the planes caused "a direct and substantial invasion of the property by excessive, unreasonable, unwarranted, and uninvited noise, vibrations, fumes, pollution, and residue, which cause direct physical damage to Mar-a-Lago." He called the county and airport's efforts "deliberate and malicious."[121]

The excessive damages he sought are part of Trump's manipulative, bullying style. He accused the county of purposely flying over his estate to maliciously disturb the peace at Mar-a-Lago. I'm serious. I didn't make this up, I promise. I understand that this may not sound believable, but it's true. This is what this small man—and big bully—did.

Trump wants the jets to be rerouted to fly over other people's homes instead of his resort, and he wants the county (and, in turn, the taxpayers of Palm Beach County) to pay him $100 million for the damages the planes' path have caused him. For years Trump argued that "the noise and fumes were ruining his investment, and that the decent thing for the county to do was to move the airport farther west." He called the airport director a "moron" and "the worst airport director in the country."[122]

Trump's election as president seems to have made his lawsuit moot because federal security concerns resulted in planes being diverted from flying over Trump's estate.

Trump seems to like suing the City of Palm Beach and Palm Beach County. The 2015 suit brought against Palm Beach County regarding airport disturbance was one of three he brought over the years concerning that issue. In 2006, he sued Palm Beach over the size of flagpoles allowed by the city (see the chapter "Trump the Thief"). In 1992, he sued the city, seeking $50 million because they would not approve his plans to subdivide his estate. Trump filed other suits against the city as well.

The website FiveThirtyEight.com documented many of Trump's lawsuits and threatened lawsuits during the presidential campaign.[123] According to the website, in 2015 alone, Trump threatened to sue:

- Univision over the Miss USA pageant (he did sue)
- The National Hispanic Media Coalition after it called one his speeches a "bigoted, racist, anti-Latino rant"
- The Club for Growth, a D.C.-based nonprofit, over negative ads
- StopTrump.us over selling anti-Trump shirts
- The Culinary Workers Union and Bartenders Union for saying Trump spent the night at the unionized Treasure Island casino-resort instead of his own hotel (he did sue)
- John Kasich over negative ads
- New Day for America, a super PAC, over negative ads
- Mike Fernandez, a Jeb Bush donor, over negative ads

In 2016, Trump threatened to sue:

- *The Washington Post* for writing an article about how one of his casinos filed for bankruptcy
- Ted Cruz over voter fraud in the Iowa caucuses
- Ted Cruz for not being a natural-born citizen
- Ted Cruz, yet again, for attack ads
- The Republican Party over a dispute about Louisiana delegates
- The Associated Press for publishing an article about the handling of a Trump-branded condo development in Panama
- David Cay Johnston, if he didn't like what Johnston reported
- *The Washington Post* for libel
- Tony Schwartz, co-author of Trump: *The Art of the Deal*, for negative statements Schwartz made to the *New Yorker*
- The *New York Times* for publishing an article on Trump's tax returns
- The *New York Times* for publishing an article about two women who accused Trump of sexual assault
- Nearly a dozen women for accusing him of sexual assault

And here are a few more threats that emerged during the campaign but were not included by FiveThirtyEight.com:

- A British student nightclub after they used Trump's image for a Halloween poster
- Restauranteur José Andrés for backing out of his plan to open a restaurant in the Trump International Hotel
- The *Huffington Post* and *Rolling Stone* to put them out of business
- Actor Tom Arnold after he claimed he had video of Trump using racist, inflammatory language on *The Apprentice*
- The U.S. Golf Association, if it moved the 2017 U.S. Women's Open away from Trump National Golf Club
- *The Daily Beast* for reporting that Trump's ex-wife had accused him of rape
- Movie theaters, reporters, or anyone who promulgates the allegations of bullying and intimidation made in the film *You've Been Trumped Too*

Here are just a few of Trump's older notable lawsuits and threatened lawsuits:

- In 2013, Trump sued comedian Bill Maher after Trump provided his birth certificate to prove he was not the son of an orangutan, which Maher had joked he might be. Maher had said he would donate $5 million to charity if Trump could prove he was not the son of an orangutan. When Maher didn't donate the money, Trump sued. He later dropped the suit.

- In 1995, Trump sued New York State when a state-sponsored video game called Quickdraw, based on the casino game Keno, was introduced. Trump saw the game as a threat to his Atlantic City casinos where Keno was played, although he claimed his primary concern was that the game would bring a tremendous amount of crime and destroy businesses.

- In the 1980s, Trump sued the *Chicago Tribune* because a writer for the paper had expressed doubt that Trump would be successful with his plans to build a tower in New York that would be taller than Chicago's Sears Tower.

Donald Trump is obsessed with revenge. He is a petty man and a malicious, spiteful, mean spirited predator who lives for the opportunity to go to battle.

Trump to Spend the Rest of His Life Destroying These Five People

In a blog post on his website, Sir Richard Branson, business leader and the Virgin Group founder, said that some years ago, Trump had invited him to lunch or dinner. After sitting down to the meal, Trump began speaking with a vengeance about how he would get back at five people whose institutions had refused to lend him money after his bankruptcies in the 1990's.

Branson wrote, "He told me he was going to spend the rest of his life destroying these five people" and noted Trump "didn't speak about anything else." Branson said the incident left him "disturbed and saddened."[124]

Here's what is so terribly wrong with Trump's conduct in this scenario:

- He sees enemies where none exist—Trump felt the five individuals who would not lend him money had wronged him. But I suspect they simply made a financial decision in their or their company's interest. Trump's distorted view of the world sees these five as enemies. This is typical narcissistic behavior. Trump sees others' behavior, if it is not in his interest, as negative and as a personal attack on him. He feels he must respond and will often do so with vengeance and contempt.

- He rejoices in revenge and in deriding people—Trump decides to go after the five because he likes going after people. As he says, in his book, *Think Big: Make It Happen in Business and Life,* "When people wrong you, go after those people, because it is a good feeling and because other people will see you doing it. I love getting even."[125] Trump would get a good feeling "destroying these five people."

- Trump says he wants to destroy the "no-loan five" seemingly because he is bizarrely and extremely heartless, callous, and contemptuous. He lacks any degree of empathy.

Threat #1

In March 2016, an anti-Trump super PAC in Utah featured an ad with Melania Trump posing nude for *GQ*. Although the super PAC was independent of the Cruz campaign, Trump blamed Cruz. The truth is that Cruz had no responsibility or involvement regarding the ad but that didn't matter to Trump. He tweeted, "Lyin' Ted Cruz just used a picture of Melania from a G.Q. shoot in his ad. Be careful, Lyin' Ted, or I will spill the beans on your wife!"[126] Trump loves to make vague threats, even against the wives of presential candidates.

Threat #2

After hearing that John McCain echoed Mitt Romney's much-publicized March 2016 criticisms of him, Trump told CBS News' chief White House correspondent, Major Garrett, "Oh, he did? Well, that's not nice. He has to be very careful." When asked why the Arizona senator would need to be careful, Trump replied, "He'll find out."[127] Another vague threat.

Threat #3

Here is a Trump tweet threat from October 2015: "The @WSJ Wall Street Journal loves to write badly about me. They better be careful, or I will unleash big time on them. Look forward to it."[128] Another vague threat of looming vengeance.

Threat #4

On February 22, 2016, Trump tweeted, "I hear the Rickets family, who own the Chicago Cubs, are secretly spending $'s against me. They better be careful, they have a lot to hide!"[129] Trump was referring to the fact that the Ricketts family had donated to a PAC opposing him. Fred Hiatt of *The Washington Post* asked Trump what he meant by "they should watch out." Trump replied, "Well, it means that I'll start spending on them. I'll start taking ads telling them all what a rotten job they're doing with the Chicago Cubs. I mean, they are spending on me. I mean, so am I allowed to say that? I'll start doing ads about their baseball team. That it's not properly run or that they haven't done a good job in the brokerage business lately."*[130]*

Trump thinks it's okay to go after someone simply because he or she doesn't politically support him.

Threat #5

In January 2016, Trump repeatedly denounced the *New Hampshire Union Leader* and its publisher, Joseph W. McQuaid, after the paper endorsed Governor Chris Christie of New Jersey for president. He called McQuaid a "bad guy," "a liar," "a psycho," and a "dirty dog."[131] He further accused McQuaid of seeking to get advertising and political favors in exchange for an endorsement. McQuaid denied the assertions. If you endorse someone other than Trump, he comes down viciously on you. Ask him about a newspaper's endorsement of another candidate, and he'll respond by disparaging the paper. You see, all the good newspapers endorse him, and the bad ones endorse someone else.

Bullying Tenants

In 1981, Trump purchased a building on Central Park South in New York City. He intended to knock it down and then build condos on the site. When he tried to evict tenants in the rent-controlled building, many fought back. Trump employed a series of intimidation maneuvers to tried to get the tenants out. The tenants accused Trump of cutting off heat and hot water, stopping building repairs, and general harassment.

Catalina Meyer, an elderly woman in the building battling cancer and emphysema, and her husband felt particularly harassed. In court papers she pleaded, "I am a very sick woman battling for my life. I have begged for reasonableness. The landlord will not be reasonable."[132]

Then Trump pulled out his big guns. He placed ads in newspapers offering to house homeless New Yorkers in his building. In vintage Trump fashion, he also sued tenants for $150 million when they complained about the building. Eventually the tenants and Trump reached a court settlement.

More Trump Enemies

If you do something in any way critical of or against Trump, he gladly responds. He gleefully searches for new enemies to fight. Some people are vindictive and go after people who have harmed them. Trump is doubly vindictive because he'll go after anybody who doesn't unflaggingly love and praise him. You can be a big supporter, but if you do one thing that displeases him, he'll pounce. Even if that one thing is not your fault, he's frequently inclined to see you as worthy of his scorn. Trump has had more fights with more people during his campaign than can be counted on several hands. And he seemingly enjoys every one of them.

During the campaign, Trump went after a disabled news reporter; John McCain; Univision anchor Jorge Ramos; Megyn Kelly; Joe Scarborough; Mika Brzezinski; Ted Cruz's wife and father; George H. W. Bush; George W. Bush; a Latino judge; the news media; Paul Ryan; Bill Clinton; the Republican "establishment;" the *New York Times*; *The Washington Post*; former Miss Universe Alicia Machado; billionaire Carlos Slim; Gold Star parents Khizr and Ghazala Khan; New York State Attorney General Eric Schneiderman; 12 women who accused him of sexual assault; and a Flint, Michigan minister, to name a few. Why? Because it made him feel good. He lives to attack, disparage, and intimidate anyone who doesn't pray at the Temple of Trump. "Sometimes, part of making a deal is denigrating your competition."[133] The words of a small man.

This Is Just Sick

It was at the first Republican primary debate in 2016 that the Trump–Megyn Kelly brouhaha first surfaced, sparked by Trump's anger over Kelly's debate question regarding his treatment of women. The following night, Don Lemon of CNN was set to interview Trump by phone. Megyn Kelly stated in her book: "I heard later that Trump had insisted his interview with Lemon air opposite our show at 9:00 p.m., as opposed to at 10:00 p.m., when Don usually anchors. CNN acquiesced and gave Trump a 30-minute phoner, commercial-free. (*The Kelly File* crushed them in the ratings that night.)"[134]

Trump was trying to slate his interview to air opposite Kelly's show to hopefully cut into her ratings. It's astonishing that anybody could be that vindictive and that petty. Who thinks like that?

vindictive[135]
[vin·dik·tiv] *adj*

1. disposed to seek revenge; vengeful.
2. having or showing an unreasonable desire for revenge.
3. intended to cause anguish or hurt; spiteful; cruel.
4. showing malicious ill will and a desire to hurt; motivated by spite; characterized by spite or rancor.

The "Pull You In/I'm in Charge" Handshake

If you see Trump extending his hand for a handshake, brace yourself. Donald Trump's handshaking style reflects his bullying behavior. When Trump shakes your hand, he wants to remind you that he's in control. He wants to declare his dominance.

So here's what he does. He grips your hand, yanks your arm, and pulls you in. He pulls you toward him, which may put you a little off balance. It leaves your arm extended, reaching out to him, and close to his body. He'll also often hold his grip for an extended period to further assert his power and status. This handshake behavior has been noted by many observers, to the extent that I came across one article online entitled, "How to Defend Yourself Against A Trump-Style Handshake"[136] and another, "Expert Analyzes Trump Handshake, Says He's Seeking The 'Upper Hand.'"[137]

The Words of a Decent Man?

From his book, *Trump: How to Get Rich*, "For many years I've said that if someone screws you, screw them back. . . . When somebody hurts you, just go after them as viciously and as violently as you can."[138]

Chapter 5
Trump the Thief

Donald Trump is a thief and a con man. He is a millionaire who will cheat you out of a dime. His unrestrained greed has a tremendous impact on his conduct. He will cheat and deceive three times a day to feed his greed. He will cheat and deceive in ways you have never heard of. He is obsessed with cheating to feed his personality and his greed.

The line "greed is good" drew lots of attention when proclaimed by Gordon Gekko (played by Michael Douglas) in the film *Wall Street*. It could have also come from Donald Trump. Donald Trump makes Gordon Gekko look like a philanthropist; he has reached new heights of greed that Gekko could only dream of.

"Just Don't Pay" Scam

Trump steals money. He frequently does it by not paying his bills. Wait, wait, wait, wait. You mean to say a business mogul and presidential candidate steals money from people by not paying his bills? That can't be true.

But it is. What type of decent human being would do that? An easy question: a decent human being *wouldn't*.

This has not happened only a few times. If you google "Trump doesn't pay his bills," you'll see story after story of Trump failing to repay debts or obligations. It seems that not paying bills is common operating practice for Donald Trump and his companies. It's an extension of his dishonest, bullying personality.

I'm not a businessman. And I certainly don't run in the same circles as Donald Trump (surprise you as that might). But I know personally of three or four stories of Trump not paying his bills from friends and acquaintances of mine. And there are hundreds of stories in the public domain of Trump's thievery. Take, for example, Trump's New York City headquarters, Trump

Tower. As writer Mark Sumner put it, "The big glass lobby around the Trump Tower? Yeah, Trump didn't pay for that. Or the carpet. He stiffed his plumber. Shorted the painters."[139]

Records indicate that more than 250 subcontractors weren't paid in full or on time for work performed while building Trump's Taj Mahal casino in Atlantic City. These contractors' claims total $69.5 million. What excuse did Trump provide for not paying them? He "wasn't happy with the work." In fact, he's regularly "not happy with the work." But it's usually a false claim to set the groundwork for swindling a contractor or vendor.[140]

Here's how the typical Trump con works. Trump reaches an agreement or contracts for goods and services. He agrees to pay a certain amount for those goods or services. Then he doesn't pay. In cases where he is making payments as the work progresses, he'll often withhold the last payment(s). Simple, huh?

Contractors can accept not getting paid, accept a lesser payment, or decide to go to court. Trump knows facing his company in court would be an expensive and overwhelming choice for many businesses, particularly smaller ones—often more expensive and overwhelming than the company can bear. In essence, he simply bullies them into acquiescing to the theft.

If contractors decide to seek resolution in court, the anticipated or actual legal fees may exceed the amount of money owed them. These contractors are left with virtually no options to collect the money they're owed. Companies can go bankrupt fighting Trump because he has cheated them out of so much money or because the cost of the protracted court battle overwhelms them. I would speculate that Trump looks to do business with smaller companies so he can stiff them, knowing the expense of a legal battle may be beyond their means. These David vs. Goliath legal battles reflect Trump's greedy, coldhearted, devious, scheming, callous nature.

Sometimes Trump does end up in an actual court battle, where he'll delay and delay, or seek a settlement at less than he owes.

Trump's cruel exploitation of these businesses frequently brings hardship and pain to individuals and companies, and he doesn't care. If he can crush someone's small business, to Trump, it's a victory. To him, it's all sport. It's all a calculated plan to cheat people, and he rejoices in it.

Trump is so notorious for his unscrupulous business practices that some people in the construction trades compensate. They add 10%, 20%, or more to any Trump bid to allow for his cheating. They call it compensating for "the Trump discount," which is Trump's practice of rarely paying the full sum he owes on a bill.[141] To Trump cheating people is a way of life. If you ever play tic-tact-toe with him don't turn your back.

Deadbeat Trump and the Chandeliers

In 2004, Donald Trump purchased three crystal chandeliers for his Mar-a-Lago estate from 82-year-old Nicolas Jacobsen's Classic Chandeliers. Jacobsen, a small business owner in Florida, agreed to sell the fixtures to Trump for $34,000. Jacobsen claimed Trump initially tried to have him waive the sales tax. Trump paid approximately $17,000 as a deposit.

When the installation of the chandeliers was complete, Trump refused to pay the balance owed. After an article on the conflict appeared in the *Palm Beach Post*, Trump called the article's author and berated him. Typical Trump. Any criticism triggers his wrath, even if you are simply a journalist reporting a story.

As the reporter later detailed, "You want a story?" Trump shouted. "I'll give you a story. This guy [Jacobsen] did a terrible, terrible job. He was late with the chandeliers. He didn't have the proper equipment to install them. His bills were too high. He had to use my people to install them. We're going to end up in court because he's just trying to get free publicity. I'm not going to pay him what I owe him. That's it. I'm not paying."[142]

Again, typical Trump, using an accusation of poor-quality work to justify nonpayment. And, of course, his attempt at righteous indignation is a classic Trump technique to cover up his lies and wrongdoing.

Jacobsen denied Trump's claim of shoddy work. After the story ran, Jacobsen told the *New York Daily News* that he had received 22 calls from other merchants who claimed Trump had failed to pay them as well. The day that story ran, Trump brought a civil suit against Jacobsen for breach of contract. The next day, a Trump attorney sent Jacobsen a letter threatening a libel suit over his comments to the *Daily News*. He demanded that Jacobsen turn over the names of the 22 merchants who had called him.

Some days later, the attorney reiterated Trump's intention to file a libel suit. But he told Jacobsen he could settle the lawsuits by taking back the chandeliers and refunding any payments received, or by accepting half the remaining amount owed on the bill. Jacobsen would also be required to write an apology letter to Trump—a ridiculous demand—for his comments to the media and say he'd lied about Trump's desire to dodge sales taxes. Trump also demanded that Jacobsen state in his letter that he "never told anyone at the newspaper that 22 people had called and told you that Mr. Trump had stiffed them."[143]

Notice the last part of this. Jacobsen did not lie about the sales tax, and Jacobsen did tell the reporter the 22 merchants had called him. Trump made up a double lie about those things and then tried to coerce and bribe Jacobsen into telling it. There's something particularly abhorrent about all this—it's bad enough that he lies without provocation, but he also tries to coerce others to be just as deceitful in his interest.

Rather than giving in, Jacobsen countersued, calling Trump's lawsuit "nothing but fabricated allegations, falsehoods, and outright lies" and an attempt to use the court system to avoid "paying what they owe."[144]

The case went to mediation and was finally settled in early 2007 with Jacobsen accepting a reduced payment of approximately one-third of what he was owed. As Trump had intended all along, he wore down Mr. Jacobsen (who was 85 at the time of the settlement). Jacobsen could not afford, financially or otherwise, to continue with a lawsuit that seemed to have no end. In the end, Trump was successful at cheating and taking advantage of an 85-year-old small businessman. Trump is a cruel mogul.

Trump and the Paint Shop Owner

Trump refused to pay Florida painter Juan Carlos Enriquez, owner of The Paint Spot, for work he had done at the Trump National Doral Golf Club. He owed Mr. Enriquez $32,000. What type of millionaire tries to cheat a contractor out of $32,000? The nonpayment led to a court case. The great Trump organization was going to go up against a painter.

In court, the general contractor for work done at the Doral club stated that a decision was made not to pay Enriquez because Trump had "already paid enough." Very revealing. The judge in the case ordered Trump's Doral to be foreclosed on and sold, with $30,000 plus reimbursement of considerable court fees being paid from the proceeds to Enriquez. You go, judge.

Trump's attorneys filed a motion to delay the sale, and the case continued. If Enriquez were to lose Trump's appeal, he would lose his $30,000 and possibly be responsible for Trump's very hefty legal costs, which could bankrupt him. (Note: in April 2016, the matter was settled in court with Enriquez to receive over $300,000 to cover his loss and his court costs.)

Real Estate Broker Sues Trump

As a real estate developer, Donald Trump has frequent dealings with real estate agents who market, sell, or lease his properties. Rana Williams was one of these real estate agents. She claimed to have sold hundreds of millions of dollars' worth of properties for Trump. In 2013, she sued Trump for $735,212 in commissions that she said were due her. Williams revealed Trump had decided to pay her less than the agreed amount based on his whim alone. The case was settled in 2015 with the terms confidential.

Mortgage Broker Sues Trump

As reported by the *Chicago Tribune*, in October 2005, Jennifer McGovern was hired by Trump Mortgage as a broker. In May 2006, she sold a property that earned her a $238,000 commission, per her employment contract. Trump refused to pay her. Instead the company offered her $10,000, retroactively changing the terms of her contract. When she refused to accept the $10,000, she was fired. [145]

Trump's Lawyers Sue Trump

Ironically, law firms that represented Trump in cases where he withheld payments can find themselves in lawsuits to collect money due to them for that representation. That's right, Trump didn't pay the lawyers who represented him for not paying contractors.

- William Scherer is a Fort Lauderdale lawyer and GOP fundraiser who once represented Trump in a legal matter. In 1994, Scherer sued Trump for $5,000 the millionaire had cheated him of by not paying a bill—which was already a reduced rate. Scherer called Trump a deadbeat. He won the case.[146]

- Morrison Cohen LLP, which represented Trump in a suit regarding payments to a contractor, sued (in a counter suit) Trump regarding his payments to them. The suit alleged nonpayment of nearly half a million dollars. It was settled in 2009 for an unknown amount.[147]

- "The Atlantic City law firm of Levine Staller saved one of Trump's companies tens of millions of dollars in taxes—and then sued the company, Trump Entertainment, after the business tried to pay Levine Staller $1.25 million less than the firm was owed."[148] A judge ordered Trump to pay up.

- Cook, Heyward, Lee, Hopper & Feehan also sued Trump for over $94,000 in unpaid legal fees. From the court records: "[Donald Trump's] attempt to avoid paying our firm seems to me to have been just part of a larger pattern of running up bills, refusing to meet his obligations, and then trying to negotiate drastically reduced payments," according to David D. Hopper, the firm's president."[149] The case was settled out of court.

Trump and a Friend of a Friend of a Friend #1

This is from an email forwarded to me by a friend as part of a casual conversation. The story is thirdhand or so, but it's documented in a series of emails and I trust the source.

"Rather than sharing or linking to one of the many stories about Trump, I decided to share my own experience. In 2004, I was working with a small company to help their sales and marketing, and I came across an opportunity to sell products to the Trump Casino in Atlantic City.

"In the process of preparing quotations, we talked to other vendors that had more Trump experience and were warned about the likely outcome of getting a contract with the Trump Corporation. They suggested we should add 20%, or whatever the final payment would be, to our price because we would probably never get our final payment. It wouldn't matter how good the product or our service was, they would come up with a reason not to pay.

"We were told that Trump knows small businesses can't afford to fight his army of lawyers, so this is a common practice by Trump. They went on to say how he is a major cause of putting small companies into bankruptcy or at least causing them significant financial problems, depending on the size of the order they got from him. With this information, we did not continue to pursue doing business with Trump.

"I know my story is insignificant compared to the many other, more dramatic and sad stories being reported by the small businesspeople that did get contracts and were unjustly cheated out of payments. And as recently reported on the news, Trump has some 1,200 lawsuits pending, not to mention the many thousands from the past and those small businesses that couldn't afford to file."

Trump and a Friend of a Friend of a Friend #2

This is the response by Bob (not his real name) to the email in the previous section. It is part of the same email forwarded to me. The story is again thirdhand or so but documented in a series of emails. I have not used the real names of the people involved.

"This is identical to a story that neighbors of our friends Susan and Mike told. The neighbors have a printing business in [city redacted] and did a small job for a 'Trump Enterprises' representative that came into their shop. The job was for only around $800. He delivered the product and never got paid. When he was able to connect by telephone, the representative said, 'We weren't happy with the job, so we've decided not to pay. You can take us to court.' The neighbor said (to me), 'What am I gonna do, get a lawyer for an $800 bill?'

So the moral of the story is that Trump is actually right when he says he's created thousands of jobs. He just doesn't pay people in those jobs for their products and services."

Mr. G.

Some months back, I overheard a conversation in a hospital between a doctor and an 86-year-old patient, Mr. G. The doctor performed a brief mental status screening and asked the patient if he knew where he was. "In the hospital," he replied. Then the doctor asked Mr. G. if he knew the date. He answered quickly and sharply with the correct date. Then the doctor asked Mr. G. if he knew who the president was. Loudly and even more quickly, he answered, "Donald Trump."

Then Mr. G. enthusiastically elaborated. He told the doctor how he had known Donald Trump, his brother, and his father. He told how he knew them when Donald Trump was just starting out in Manhattan, when Donald's brother died, and when Donald was building housing in Queens. He said one day, Donald came down to his Queens construction site and "bought" lunch for all the workers at a small nearby luncheonette. He said the owner of the luncheonette gladly accommodated Trump and was happy for this unexpected boost in business. But then the other shoe dropped. After getting the lunches the Trump people refused to pay. They simply told the owner, "We're not paying." Trump had decided that he, the millionaire business mogul, would essentially steal from a hardworking luncheonette owner. Mr. G. ended his story by revealing that it was he who owned that luncheonette.

This story interested and surprised me for a few reasons. First was the random chance that I, the author of a book entitled *Donald Trump Is the Worst Person in the World,* would overhear such a story. Second was the total inhumanity of Trump. If a teenager in the community had ducked out of paying his lunch bill, he might have ended up arrested. But the mighty bully Donald Trump walks away.

The third reason I found the story interesting was the allure of Mr. G. This 86-year-old man told his story with charm, clarity and a touch of pride. But there was one additional twist to the story. Mr. G. ended his tale by saying he had voted for Trump. Go figure.

Trump the Corrupt: The Story of Trump University

Trump University was a scam. Trump University, Trump's real estate training program, defrauded students, bilking them out of millions.

In a lawsuit brought against Trump University, Ronald Schnackenberg, a former salesman for the institution, testified that the school, "was only interested in selling every person the most expensive seminars they possibly could." He also attested, "I believe that Trump University was a fraudulent scheme and that it preyed upon the elderly and uneducated to separate them from their money."[150]

Three lawsuits brought against the school resulted in Trump agreeing to pay $25 million in damages.

Chapter 6
Trump the Braggart

"God opposes the proud but gives grace to the humble."

– The Bible[151]

---

braggart[152]
[brag·ert] *noun*

1. a person who boasts loudly or exaggeratedly; bragger.
2. someone that talks a lot about his or her own accomplishments in a way that will make him or her look better to others.

A man who tells everyone how rich and successful he is all the time is an example of a braggart.

syn: blowhard, big mouth, windbag, show off

Some people say Donald Trump is a braggart. Actually, most people say Donald Trump is a braggart. His bragging is unusual, extreme, and grotesque. But you decide for yourself. Here are some Donald Trump quotations about Donald Trump, broken down by theme.

The "Nobody but Me" Quotations

"Nobody reads the Bible more than me."

"Nobody loves the Bible more than I do."

"Nobody has more respect for women than I do."

"Nobody's ever been more successful than me."

"Nobody is more pro-Israel than I am."

"Nobody but Donald Trump will save Israel."

"Nobody builds walls better than me."

"Nobody knows jobs more than I do."

"On trade, there's nobody more conservative than me."

"There is nobody more against Obamacare than me."

"There's nobody bigger or better at the military than I am."

"Nobody understands politicians like I do."

"No one would be tougher on ISIS than Donald Trump."

"No one has done more for people with disabilities than me."

"No one has done so much for equality as I have."

"Nobody in the history of this country has ever known so much about infrastructure as Donald Trump."

"Nobody knows more about taxes than I do, maybe in the history of the world."

"I know more about courts than any human being on Earth."

"I'm the king of debt…. Nobody knows debt better than me."

"I know more about [energy] renewables than any human being on Earth."

"I know more about Cory [Booker] than he knows about himself."

The "I Am Best, Most, or Only" Quotations

"I am the best builder."
"I am the most successful person ever to run for president."

"I am a unifier."

"I am the least racist person there is."

"I am the only one who can fix our southern border."

"I am the only one who can fix immigration."

"I am the most militaristic person on that stage."

"I am the worst thing that ever happened to ISIS."

"I am the law and order candidate."

"I am the only one who can beat Hillary Clinton."

"I am the worst thing that ever happened to the establishment."

"I am more presidential than anybody, other than the great Abe Lincoln."

"I am the only one who can make America truly great again."

"I am the best to win the general election."

"I'm very highly educated."

"I know words, I have the best words."

"I'm more honest and my women are more beautiful."

"If you get ratings, you're king, like me. I'm a king."

"I'm the most pro-gay candidate."

"I'm the most conservative when it comes to the military."

"I think I'm the most conservative person there is."

The "I Went, I Have, I Would, I Will" Quotations

"I went to one of the best schools."

"I have the world's best memory, and everybody knows that."

"I have the best [golf] courses in the world."

"I have proven to be far more correct about terrorism than anybody.
It's not even close."

"I would build a great wall."

"I will be the greatest jobs president God ever created."

"I will be so good at the military your head will spin."

"I will help the veterans like no one else."

And One More Lulu

"Peace all over the world would be the best deal.
And I think I would know how to do it better than
anybody else, but peace all over the world."

And the Coup de Grâce

"I am the least racist person you will ever meet."

"I am the humblest celebrity."

"I am very modest."

That's 54 different things that Trump says nobody is better at than he. Wow. (Compiled from articles in the Huntington Post,[153] from an article on the Axios website,"[154] and from other sources.)

An observation about Trump's self-compliments: He doesn't merely say "I'm good"; he has to say, "I'm the best." He can't say, "I am," but must say, "I am the most." He can't say, "I can," but has to say, "I'm the only one who can" or "nobody else can." He likes to say, "and everyone knows that" to enhance the boast further. (He has the world's best memory, and "everybody knows that.")

Not only does he boast about the credit he has gotten for various "accomplishments," but his massive ego always has him saying he's gotten "great" credit. And we all know great credit is better than just plain old credit.

Trump is the king of self-promotion. As noted by journalist Wesley Pruden, "The Donald never met a superlative he didn't like, himself as the ultimate superlative most of all."[155]

The Trump Tower Is Huge

In a very telling account of Trump hyperbole and blatant self-inflation, the *Business Insider* describes the folly of the Trump Tower model. In 1979, as Mr. Trump examined a model of the soon to be Trump Tower, he noticed another building near him was taller than his, as evident in the model. He was not having that.

"'My building looks a little small,' he said, according to Norman Brosterman, the model maker's assistant at the time. Assured the scale was accurate, Mr. Trump had an inspiration on his next visit to the architectural workshop.

"'Can you make my building taller?' Mr. Trump asked. No, he was told. 'Well, can you make the G.M. building shorter?' Mr. Trump marked the G.M. building at his preferred height with a pencil. Mr. Brosterman sawed off the top third, leaving Trump Tower—in the one-thirty-second-scale model, at least—the tallest in the neighborhood."[156] Trump was content.

Trump had to employ bizarre deception in order for his building to be seen as taller. The lying ways of a petty braggart.

Something Else Is Huge

Only Donald Trump would brag about the size of his penis on national TV during a presidential debate.

humble[157]
[həm·bəl] *adj*

1. not overly proud or arrogant, modest.
2. not thinking you are better than other people.
3. having or showing a consciousness of one's defects or shortcomings.
4. a person may have accomplished a lot but doesn't feel it is necessary to brag about it.

syn: modest, respectful, soft-spoken, unassuming

"No man will make a great leader who wants to do it all himself, or to get all the credit for doing it." — Andrew Carnegie[158]

Chapter 7
Trump the Crude

Donald Trump has publicly called people dopes, losers, scum, ugly, grotesque, dummy, an overrated clown, a slob, a low-class slob, a fat slob, stupid, a total joke, a big fat pig, a waste, a little bit of a maniac, highly neurotic, a fool, an idiot, very dumb, a moron, a zero, a bimbo, and a lightweight. That's no way for a president or a presidential candidate to speak. In fact, that's no way for an adult to speak. Come to think of it, children shouldn't speak that way either. If your child spoke like that, you would discipline him or her.

Trump's language and his proclivity for name-calling are ugly and tell you more about him than the people he is disparaging. There's not much explanation necessary on this topic. But for the record:

Crude Utterance #1–-My Hands

"[Rubio] hit my hands. Nobody has ever hit my hands, I've never heard of this before. Look at those hands, are they small hands?" Trump said at the Republican presidential debate in Detroit. "And he referred to my hands, 'if they're small something else must be small.' I guarantee you there's no problem, I guarantee it."[159] Now, if you think this was an overheard remark between two men drinking beer and watching a football game, you are wrong. Trump said this on purpose, out loud, at the March 2016 presidential primary debate with millions of people watching. A man, just shy of his 70th birthday, bragging about the size of his "hands"—crude, classless, and embarrassing.

Crude Utterance #2—Nasty

"'You know what she just said?' he asked. 'Shout it out, because I don't want to say it. You're not allowed to say that,' he continued. 'I never expect to hear that from you again.' Trump paused, looked out at his election-eve audience and leaned into the microphone, 'She said he's a p----y'" referring to Ted Cruz.[160] Crude and vulgar.

Crude Utterance #3—Hillary

In April 2015, Trump tweeted, "If Hillary Clinton can't satisfy her husband, what makes her think she can satisfy America?"[161] Another typically revolting Trump remark. (I couldn't decide whether to include this reference in this chapter or later in the chapter "Trump the Lewd", so I included it in both.)

Crude Utterance #4—Hillary Again

In December 2015, while speaking about Hillary Clinton, Trump said, "She was favored to win, and she got schlonged, she lost. I mean she lost."[162] *Schlong* is a slang Yiddish term for male genitalia. Trump can be crude in multiple languages.

Crude Utterance #5—Hillary One More Time

In December 2015, Trump called Hillary Clinton "disgusting" for apparently using the restroom during a commercial break at the Democratic debate. "I know where she went. It's disgusting. I don't want to talk about it," he added. "No, it's too disgusting. Don't say it; it's disgusting."[163]

Crude Utterance #6—Look at That Face

In September 2015, when speaking about Carly Fiorina Trump declared, "'Look at that face!'. He then added "Would anyone vote for that? Can you imagine that, the face of our next president?!" That outburst, however, wasn't enough. He went on, "I mean, she's a woman, and I'm not s'posedta say bad things, but really folks, come on. Are we serious?"[164]

Crude Utterance #7—Rosie

This doozy, as reported by CNN, targets one of Trump's favorite enemies, Rosie O'Donnell, "'She announced last week that she suffers from depression,' Trump told an audience at the Learning Annex in 2007. 'They called me for a comment, and rather than saying "I have no comment" or "isn't that too bad oh, that's so bad," I said, "I think I can cure her depression,"' — most of you heard this. 'If she stopped looking in the mirror, I think she'd stop being so depressed.'"[165] I can't imagine how any man, let alone a candidate for president of the United States, could make such a disgusting statement, let alone make it publicly. What goes through the mind of someone who speaks like that?

Crude Utterance #8—Negotiable Assets

"I would never buy Ivana any decent jewels or pictures. Why give her negotiable assets?"[166]

Crude Utterance #9—A Glass of Wine

As reported in the *The Daily Beast*, "'Trump "boasts about having poured a whole bottle of wine down Marie Brenner's back after she wrote a story on him that he hated,' *New York Magazine* reported in 1992."

"Well, it wasn't a bottle, actually—it was a glass," Brenner stated to *The Daily Beast*. "I didn't even notice it was happening, because like everything with Donald, it was a stealth maneuver. It came from behind."[167]

Crude Utterance #10—A Piece of …

In a 1991 interview with *Esquire* magazine, Trump said, "You know, it doesn't really matter what [the media] write as long as you've got a young and beautiful piece of ass."[168]

Crude Utterances #11 to 16 Ivanka (Crude, Creepy, and Disturbing)

#11) On the television show *The View*, Trump was asked how he would feel if his daughter Ivanka posed for *Playboy* magazine. He answered, "I don't think Ivanka would do that inside the magazine, although she does have a very nice figure. I've said if Ivanka weren't my daughter, perhaps I'd be dating her."[169]

#12) Ivanka was a host at the 1997 Miss Teen USA pageant. Donald Trump sat in the audience next to Brook Antoinette Mahealani Lee, Miss Universe at the time. "Don't you think my daughter's hot? She's hot, right?" Ms. Lee reports Trump asking her. "I was like, 'Really?' That's just weird. She was sixteen. That's creepy."[170]

#13) On a 2013 episode of *The Wendy Williams Show*, Wendy asked Ivanka, "What's the favorite thing you have in common with your father?" to which she replied, "Either real estate or golf." Williams then put the same question to Donald, and he responded, "Well, I was going to say sex, but I can't relate that to her,"[171] pointing to Ivanka. Crude, creepy, bizarre, disgusting, disturbing, and inexplicable. And what's additionally bewildering is that he apparently doesn't realize how creepy his words really are.

#14) In 2003, Trump appeared on Howard Stern's radio show, where he said, "You know who's one of the great beauties of the world, according to everybody? And I helped create her. Ivanka. My daughter, Ivanka. She's 6 feet tall; she's got the best body."[172] To make comments like that once would be terrible, but now we're up to four times Trump has made lewd remarks about his daughter. And counting.

#15) *Washington Post* columnist Richard Cohen reported this Trump remark, "Is it wrong to be more sexually attracted to your own daughter than your wife?" Ivanka was 13 years old at the time. (The quote was deleted from the column before it was published.)[173]

#16) Paul Solotaroff in a *Rolling Stone* interview reported this quote from Trump, "Yeah, she's really something, and what a beauty, that one. If I weren't happily married and, ya know, her father …"[174]

And add this to the list of creepy Trump remarks about Ivanka. Trump took a number of what many would say are inappropriate pictures with his daughter.

Crude Utterance #17—Tiffany Also

Oh, and here's one more, this time regarding Trump's other daughter, Tiffany. "In a 1994 episode of *Lifestyles of the Rich and Famous*, Trump spoke about the attributes Tiffany, (then a one year old), had inherited from him and his second wife, Marla Maples. 'I think that she's got a lot of Marla, she's really a beautiful baby,' Trump said. 'She's got Marla's legs. We don't know whether or not she's got this part yet, but time will tell,' he added, holding his hands in front of his chest to represent breasts."[175]

Crude Utterance #18—Paris Hilton

Again from the Howard Stern radio show this Trump admission, "I've known Paris Hilton from the time she's 12. Her parents are friends of mine, and, you know, the first time I saw her, she walked into the room and I said, 'Who the hell is that?' ... Well, at 12, I wasn't interested. I've never been into that. They're sort of always stuck around that 25 category."[176]

Crude Utterance #19—"The Face of a Dog"

According to newspaper columnist Gail Collins, "During one down period, I referred to him [Trump] in print as a 'financially embattled thousandaire' and he sent me a copy of the column with my picture circled and 'The Face of a Dog!' written over it."[177] That's how Donald Trump rolls.

Crude Utterance #20—Treat 'Em Like"

On women: "You have to treat 'em like s--t."[178]

Crude Utterance #21—Megyn

Donald Trump has commented on Megyn Kelly's menstrual cycle (see the "Hypocrisy #2" in the chapter "Trump the Hypocrite").

Crude Quiz #1—Who Said It?

Below are crude utterances from two famous Americans: Donald Trump and 70's sitcom character Archie Bunker. See if you can match the quotation to the person who said it (the answers follow). It's time to play, "Who Said It?" (Imagine catchy quiz show music playing in the background.)

1. "The only kind of people I want counting my money are little short guys that wear yarmulkes every day."

2. "I don't have a racist bone in my body."

3. "I was talking about the Bible, which has nothing to do with the Jews."

4. "I'm not racist! I'll be the first to say it; it's not their fault. . . ."

5. "I have a great relation with the blacks."

6. "Born stupid" and "a dummy."

7. "A dummy who is lost!"

8. She is "crude, rude, obnoxious and dumb—other than that, I like her very much!"

9. "Why don't you go to sleep and dream about the tragedy that is your life?"

10. "His chest is all puffed out like Raquel Welch."

11. "I don't have a lot of time for listening to television."

12. "I have never seen a thin person drinking Diet Coke."

13. "There's nothing wrong with revenge—it's the best way to get even."

14. "Tiny children are not horses."

15. "The country is going straight into the dumper."

16. "This whole thing with the energy and everything, this is a conspiracy."

17. "If you can't get rich dealing with politicians, there's something wrong with you."

18. "The pope is like the civil service; the guy is in for life."

19. "The concept of shaking hands is absolutely terrible, and statistically I've been proven right."

20. "Bing bing, bong bong bong, bing bing."

Numbers 3, 4, 9, 10, 13, 15, 16, and 18 were said by Archie Bunker; the rest were said by Donald Trump. How'd you do?

- If you scored 19 or more correct: Congratulations, you really know your Donald Trump and Archie Bunker utterances.

- If you scored 15 to 18 correct: Pretty good, you understand the difference between Donald Trump and Archie Bunker better than most Americans.

- If you scored less than 15 correct: Don't feel bad, you're like most Americans; you can't tell the difference between Donald Trump and Archie Bunker.

Crude Quiz #2—Which Bully Said It?

"Sorry losers and haters, but my IQ is one of the highest—and you all know it! Please don't feel so stupid or insecure. It's not your fault." Which famous bully said this?

a. Biff to Marty McFly in the movie *Back to the Future*
b. The Wicked Witch of the West in the *Wizard of Oz*
c. Johnny in *The Karate Kid*
d. Nelson in *The Simpsons*
e. Donald Trump

Answer: Oh, you know.

Crude Quiz #3—Who's He Talking About?

Trump's passion for name-calling and making derogatory comments in general, are one the most prominent characteristics of his public image. Ignorant people call people names. I waited throughout the campaign for someone to lower themselves to his level and respond to Trump name-calling with, "I know you are, but what am I?" No one did.

Trump's name-calling is an extension of his bullying. Here's a Trump "crude quiz" you can play with your friends. Try copying this chart and scrambling the order of the names. Then challenge your friends to match the quotation to the individual Trump was talking about. The list comes from an article in the *New York Times*.[179]

What He Said	Who He Said It About
"A fat slob who couldn't get elected dogcatcher."	Former Connecticut governor Lowell Weicker
"You were born stupid" and a "dummy."	Michelle Malkin, a Fox News contributor
"A dummy who is lost!"	Russell Brand
"I thought [name omitted], his delivery frankly was not good." "He's a stutterer."	Seth Meyers
"Your performance was terrible in that the show lacked mood, temperament, and just about everything else a show needs for success. I knew it would fail as soon as I first saw it and your low ratings bore me out."	Martha Stewart
"Unattractive both inside and out. I fully understand why her former husband left her for a man—he made a good decision."	Arianna Huffington
A "big, fat pig" and, you guessed it, a "loser."	Rosie O'Donnell

"I like his acting, but in terms of when I watch him doing interviews and various other things, we're not dealing with Albert Einstein."	Robert De Niro
"And I promise not to talk about your massive plastic surgeries that didn't work."	Cher
"Failed on the border. He should be forced to take an IQ test before being allowed to enter the GOP debate."	Former Texas Governor Rick Perry
"Reminds me of a spoiled brat without a properly functioning brain."	Senator Rand Paul
"A bitch."	Condoleezza Rice
"They're scum." "They're horrible people. They are so illegitimate. They are just terrible people."	The press
"A total clown," and "a low-class slob."	Frank Luntz, Republican political consultant and pollster
"A clown."	Two-time Purple Heart recipient and former Secretary of Defense Robert Gates
"Obvious moron."	Former CIA director and Secretary of Defense Chuck Hagel

A "moron."	Political commentator George Will
A "moron."	Television journalist Chuck Todd
"Irrelevant dope" and "total whack job."	Tony Schwartz, co-author of *Trump: The Art of the Deal*
A "total lowlife" and a "sleazebag"	Former New York State Attorney General Eric Schneiderman
"Pocahontas."	Massachusetts Senator Elizabeth Warren
"Retarded."	Actress Marlee Matlin
"Uncle Tom."	Rapper Lil' Jon
"Piglet."	Khloe Kardashian
"The face of a dog."	Columnist Gail Collins
"Crazy," "very dumb," "insecure," "hostile," "a mess," "a clown," "irrelevant," "neurotic," "wild with hate," "not very bright," "unwatchable," "low-rated," "having lost their way," "having a mental breakdown," and "having a small audience."	Joe Scarborough and Mika Brzezinski, hosts of MSNBC's *Morning Joe*

"Never says anything good and never will," "shouldn't be on the air!, should be fired!," "sick," "so biased," "unfair," "dummy," "Fox News should can him," "no credibility," "a loser," "dopey," "shouldn't be allowed to do [his] biased commentary," "establishment flunky," "should get a life," "just totally bombed," "a loser," "an establishment dope," "has made so many mistakes," "part of the Republican establishment problem," "an all-talk, no-action dummy!," "total fool," "dopey," "purposely mischaracterized my statement," "dummy," "moron," "biased dope," "dope," "didn't win one race," "total loser," "a clown with zero credibility," "made a fool of himself in '12," "has zero cred," "irrelevant clown, sweats and shakes nervously," and "clown." (Author's note: Due to space restrictions, this list had to be limited to the above.)	Karl Rove, political commentator and former deputy White House chief of staff

That last one is a humdinger. That's a lot of insults, you might say. But no, not really. You see the total list compiled by *The New York Times* includes 281 people, places, and things Donald Trump has insulted on Twitter alone. That is from June 15, 2015 to September 2016, but the newspaper is continually updating the list. Classy guy, that Donald Trump.

Chapter 8
Trump the Ignorant

"Stupid is as stupid does." – Forrest Gump

There's nothing there. No substance, no policies, no knowledge, and worst of all, he doesn't care. He thinks he can wing it when it comes to running for president of the United States. Donald Trump is the least qualified individual to ever run for president.

Get Tough

The campaign philosophy of Donald Trump was, if you have no substance, simply repeat "you'll be tough." As he has said, he'd be tough with illegal immigrants. He would be "very, very *tough* on borders." We have to be *tough* with Mexico. We have to be *tough* with China because they take advantage of us in trade deals. Trey Gowdy was not *tough* with Hillary Clinton. Bernie Sanders is not *tough* because he allowed someone from Black Lives Matter to take the microphone from him. The individual to replace John Boehner must be *tough*. Trump says he would be *tough* on ISIS, *tough* on crime in Chicago, and *tough* with Iran by tripling sanctions. Speaking of terrorists on US soil, "I would handle it so *tough*, you don't want to hear."[180] The title of Trump's 2011 book is *Time to Get Tough: Making America #1 Again*.

But ask Donald Trump a *tough* question, and he whines you're being unfair, or you don't like him (see Megyn Kelly, Jorge Ramos, *New York Times*, and others). The emperor has no clothes.

I'm Speaking with Myself

During the campaign Trump pledged to hire the greatest minds, the smartest people to be part of his administration. But he didn't mean it; he's not smart enough to do that. It just sounded good.

The Trump campaign apparently hired very few policy advisors. When asked on MSNBC to name the advisors he consults with regarding foreign policy, he said, "I'm speaking with myself, No. 1, because I have a very good brain, and I've said a lot of things."[181] That's Trumpspeak. Let's take a closer look at that response.

Trump doesn't really use foreign policy advisors. He talks to himself about foreign policy, and he does so for three reasons:

1. He talks to himself.
2. He has a very good brain.
3. He has said a lot of things.

Raging stupidity. It should be against the law to be that dumb and run for president.

A Quiz

Who talked approvingly about lining up 50 prisoners and shooting and killing them with bullets dipped in pig's blood?

a. Former Iranian despot Saddam Hussein   b. Charles Manson
c. Islamic extremist Jihadi John   d. Osama bin Laden
e. Former Libyan dictator Muammar Gaddafi   f. Jack the Ripper
g. Donald Trump

Answer: Donald Trump

It's Going to Be Terrific

Trump's campaign website related very few policy positions. Then, as now, he thinks he can just go into an interview, debate, or rally, and just wing it. That's why his answers to questions frequently talk around the issue to disguise the fact that he doesn't have an answer (see the chapter "Trump the Bizarre").

Trump often gives very vague general responses to questions to conceal that he has very few policy ideas (more Trumpspeak). For instance, he has frequently promised to repeal and replace Obamacare with something "terrific." That was his policy. That's a frequent ploy of Trump—say it will be great. Don't explain, don't give details, just say it will be great. Or it will be terrific. Or it will be "the best" or "amazing." And for anything he doesn't like, he simply says it was "a disaster."

On the January 31, 2016 edition of ABC's *This Week with George Stephanopoulos*, Trump was asked how he would replace Obamacare. He responded, "We're going to work with our hospitals," he said. "We're going to work with our doctors. We've got to do something. . . . We'll work something out. That doesn't mean single-payer." Trump was faking it. In the United States of America, where health care is such an important and contentious issue, a presidential candidate's position on healthcare is "we'll work something out." First, he said it would be "terrific"; then it's "we'll work something out."[182]

Finally, in March of 2016, Trump announced his healthcare plan, and I use the word "plan" loosely. It was not, in fact, terrific. At the time, journalist Peter Suderman observed, "It is not really a plan at all. Instead, it is a bunch of words somewhat related to health policy that his campaign is calling a plan. Those words demonstrate not only that Trump does not understand health care policy, but that he cannot be bothered to hire anyone who does to work with him. Even more than that, Trump's willful ignorance on this issue and others suggests that his entire campaign is rooted in near-total disregard for expertise."[183]

Henry Aaron is a senior fellow in economic studies at the Brookings Institution. He very articulately makes the point in *U.S. News & World Report* that "one cannot help feeling a bit silly taking seriously the policy proposals of a person who seems not to take policy seriously himself."[184]

You Would Think He Would Know That

At CNN's March 2016 town hall, moderated by Anderson Cooper,[185] Trump was asked to name the top three functions of the United States government. "Well, the greatest function of all by far is security for our nation. I would also say health care, I would also say education." Cooper asked, "And federal healthcare run by the federal government?" Trump responded, "Healthcare — we need healthcare for our people. We need a good — Obamacare is a disaster. It's proven to be…"

Cooper: "But is that something the federal government should be doing?"

Trump: "The government can lead it, but it should be privately done." He said it was one of the top three functions of the federal government; an instant later, he asserted that the federal government should only lead. What does that mean, "the government should lead"? Without being more specific, it means nothing. honesty

Trump's inclusion of education in his response is even more peculiar since he has said he wants to cut back or abolish the federal Department of Education. The man contradicts himself because he has no intellectual honesty. Cooper, attempting to clarify Trump's positions, asked, "So that's not part of what the federal government's . . ." Trump replied, "The federal government, but the concept of the country is the concept that we have to have education within the country . . . " Is that the "concept of the country"? Stupid is as stupid does.

Tweeting Ignorance

Donald J. Trump
@realDonaldTrump

It's freezing outside, where the he - - is "global warming"??

7:00 PM · May 6, 2016

I Love Abe

In an April 2016 interview with Bob Woodward of *The Washington Post*, Trump was asked what made Abraham Lincoln succeed. "Well", Trump replied, "I think Lincoln succeeded for numerous reasons. He was a man who was of great intelligence, which most presidents would be. But he was a man of great intelligence, but he was also a man that did something that was a very vital thing to do at that time. Ten years before or 20 years before, what he was doing would never have even been thought possible. So, he did something that was a very important thing to do, and especially at that time."[186]

Norm Crosby would be proud. With the grammar of an underachieving third-grader, Trump's reply defies explanation. At one point, he states, "He was a man who was of great intelligence…. But he was a man of great intelligence." It appears he doesn't know the meaning of the word "but." "But" is "used for joining two ideas or statements when the second one is different from the first one or seems surprising after the first one" (macmillandictionary.com, 9/6/2016). Trump used it to join two ideas that are the same. So, if we adopt Trump-style grammar, you could say, "I'm feeling tired, but I'm feeling tired," or "I'm going to make America great again, but I'm going to make America great again."

After reading his response, if I asked what he said, you couldn't tell me. In fact, you probably couldn't even tell me what the question was. At times, the man is just not coherent.

Is He Smarter Than a 5th Grader?

The simple answer is no, at least when it comes to his English skills and speaking style. Donald Trump is linguistically challenged and probably the most inarticulate individual to ever run for the presidency.

Trump's vocabulary is very limited. His speech pattern is particularly simple. He tends to use monosyllabic words, typically using words such as "good," "bad," "great," and "very," or expressions such as "not good." "If I'm elected president, we will win again. We will win a lot. And we're going to have a great, great country, greater than ever before,"[187] Trump declared at the December 15, 2015 Republican debate. Trump's use of simple and ill-suited words tends to confuse the listener. He overuses pronouns that also confuse, because you can't tell what noun he is referencing. And Trump continually repeats himself, often in the same sentence. In listening to Trump speak, you can easily get lost and confused several times in rapid succession.

To return to the Trump statement noted in the preceding section, here's an example of "Trumpspeak" from when NBC's Chuck Todd questioned Trump on whom he talks to for military advice (with my comments in brackets): "Well, I watch the shows. I mean, I really see a lot of great—you know, when you watch your show, and all of the other shows, and you have the generals, and you have certain people—." Now let's break this down.

"Well, I watch the shows." (What do you mean *the* shows?)

"I mean, I really see a lot of great. . ." (Great what? Finish a thought before you move on to another thought.)

"You know, when you watch your show, and all of the other shows. . ." (What *other* shows?)

"And you have the generals. . ." (*The generals,* what generals?)

"And you have certain people. . ." (Then what? Finish the thought.)[188]

The Flesch–Kincaid readability test reveals the grade level of a document. When the August 2015 Republican primary debate text was run through the test, it revealed Trump's content was at a fourth-grade level, the lowest of the 10 candidates at the debate. His comments from an August 11 news conference in Michigan the following week got a third-grade score.[189]

The Political Studies Association completed a study to "identify the readability and simplicity of Donald J. Trump's speech."[190] They analyzed the spontaneous speech (from transcripts) of six presidential candidates mostly from interviews, some from Presidential debates, and one from a Town Hall meeting. The analysis revealed that a fourth-grade level of education (9 or 10-year-olds) is required to understand Trump's language. The chart that follows summarizes the results

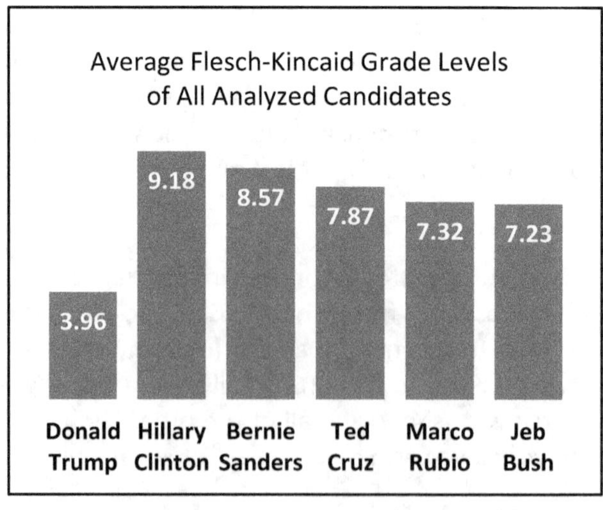

Donald, Louie, and Me

On the August 15, 2015 edition of NBC's *Meet the Press*, when asked whom he talks to for military advice, Trump replied, "Well, I watch the shows. I mean, I really see a lot of great—you know, when you watch your show, and all of the other shows, and you have the generals, and you have certain people—."[191] It's not too comforting to know that a candidate for the presidency of the United States gets his military information from the same place my neighbor Louie and I do.

Donald Trump the Digresser

In his usual speech and conversation, Trump is prone to meandering and digressing. As stated previously, he continually interrupts himself without completing his original thought. In an article by Andrew Romano, that originally appeared on Yahoo.com, former Clinton White House speechwriter Jeff Shesol describes it this way: "Trump's speech is a constant stream of 'asides' and 'by the ways.'" He continues, "He feels absolutely no obligation to finish a thought or complete a sentence."[192] Very well put.

This example also from the same article,

> How to Talk Like Trump
> Rule #1: Interrupt yourself—a lot.
>
> One of the things with the, our Japanese relationship—and I'm a big fan of Japan, by the way; I have many, many friends there; I do business with Japan—but, that, if we are attacked, they don't have to do anything.[193]

OK, here's a challenge. Read this, also from Andrew Romano's article, put it down, then tell me what Donald Trump said. I don't think you will be able to. Here it is. Apparently one sentence of 285 words. One news source identified it as the longest sentence ever.

"Look, having nuclear — my uncle was a great professor and scientist and engineer, Dr. John Trump at MIT; good genes, very good genes, OK, very smart, the Wharton School of Finance, very good, very smart — you know, if you're a conservative Republican, if I were a liberal, if, like, OK, if I ran as a liberal Democrat, they would say I'm one of the smartest people anywhere in the world — it's true! — but when you're a conservative Republican they try — oh, do they do a number — that's why I always start off: Went to Wharton, was a good student, went there, went there, did this, built a fortune — you know, I have to give my, like, credentials all the time because we're a little disadvantaged — but you look at the nuclear deal, the thing that really bothers me — it would have been so easy, and it's not as important as these lives are (nuclear is powerful; my uncle explained that to me many, many years ago, the power and that was 35 years ago; he would explain the power of what's going to happen and he was right — who would have thought?), but when you look at what's going on with the four prisoners — now it used to be three, now it's four — but when it was three and even now, I would have said it's all in the messenger; fellas, and it is fellas because, you know, they don't, they haven't figured that the women are smarter right now than the men, so, you know, it's gonna take them about another 150 years — but the Persians are great negotiators, the Iranians are great negotiators, so, and they, they just killed, they just killed us." (The End)

Once again if I asked you what he said you couldn't tell me. Pure rambling nonsense.

7-Eleven

At an April 2016 rally in Buffalo, New York, Trump said, "Because I was down there, and I watched our police and our firemen down at 7-Eleven, down at the World Trade Center right after it came down. And I saw the greatest people I've ever seen in action."[194] Hey, Donald, 7-Eleven is a convenience store, not a national tragedy and day of remembrance.

The "Stupid Donald Trump Statements" Game (Four adults or children over 5 years of age necessary to play)

Here's a game to play at your next party. As you know, Donald Trump has been known to say stupid stuff. Ask your friends to put a check in the box next to the Donald Trump proclamation they think is the dumbest. Total the results and then have fun debating everyone's responses.

- ☐ There's nobody that's done so much for equality as I have.
- ☐ I know more about ISIS than the generals do. Believe me.
- ☐ I am very modest.
- ☐ Look at those hands. Are they small hands?
- ☐ I am more presidential than anybody, other than the great Abe Lincoln.
- ☐ I am a unifier.
- ☐ I like people who weren't captured.
- ☐ All I did is point out the fact that on the cover of the *National Enquirer* there was a picture of him and crazy Lee Harvey Oswald [President Kennedy's assassin] having breakfast.
- ☐ An 'extremely credible source' has called my office and told me that @BarackObama's birth certificate is a fraud.
- ☐ I've said if Ivanka weren't my daughter, perhaps I'd be dating her.
- ☐ I have a great relation with the blacks.
- ☐ Tiny children are not horses.

Things Donald Trump Has Said

- If you're 21 years old, you pay $12 a year for insurance.

- Puerto Rico is an island surrounded by water, big water, ocean water.

- Windmills cause cancer.

- Global warming was created by and for the Chinese.

- Ebola would stop people from shaking hands and that is a good thing

- Bodies are like batteries and have a finite lifespan, so we don't need to exercise.

- Finland doesn't have wildfires because they spend a lot of time ranking and cleaning and doing a lot of things.

Chapter 9
Trump the Religious Charlatan

"Nobody reads the Bible more than me."[195] – Donald Trump

I could respect Donald Trump's religious beliefs if he were a religious man. But he is not. I could respect his beliefs if he believed in God but was admittedly not particularly religious. But he does not. I could respect his beliefs if he were an atheist. But he is not. But if Donald Trump were a man who professed to be a man of faith but was not, I could not respect that. And in my view, he is precisely that.

I hate to be in the position of commenting on someone's religious honesty. But when a presidential candidate invokes his commitment to God and then exploits those declarations (and faith in general) for his personal gain, I feel moved to voice an opinion. Donald Trump is a religious charlatan.

From time to time, Trump makes statements regarding his religiosity. But, here, as in the rest of his life, he lies. He is a religious phony. Religion may be part of his image, but it is not part of his reality. Faith is what he portrays, it is not part of who he is. His values are not Christian values, in fact they are the antithesis of them. He waves the flag of Christianity but only that, not much more. He exploits Christianity. What follows is some evidence that Donald Trump is a religious charlatan.

I Love My Bible #1

In a 2015 interview on Bloomberg TV, Trump was asked for his favorite Bible verse. He responded, "I wouldn't want to get into it because to me it's very personal."[196] An excuse to cover up that he couldn't think of any Bible verses. (I think he got that from Sarah Palin's response of, "I've read most of them," when asked by Katie Couric what newspapers and magazines she reads.)

Days later, Trump relented to requests for his favorite passages in the Bible by sharing, "Proverbs, the chapter 'never bend to envy.'" Yeah, now he can answer the question—after having time to research it. But he still couldn't get it right. This actual quote does not appear in the Bible. Later, Trump aides said he was referring to Proverbs 24:1-2: "Be not thou envious against evil men, neither desire to be with them. For their heart studieth destruction, and their lips talk of mischief."[197] Another cover-up gone bad.

Despite Trump's faux pas regarding his pronouncements about the Bible, he sticks to his phony claims of piety.

I Love My Bible #2

When speaking before students at the Virginia's Liberty University, a Christian college, in January 2016, Trump quoted from the Bible, which he has proclaimed is his favorite book, referencing "Two Corinthians" instead of "Second Corinthians," the latter being the standard nomenclature. You can't really love your Bible if you don't know the common correct way to reference passages. When questioned the next day, he said he'd seen it used both ways. He hadn't. A lie to cover up his error, which had revealed a previous lie. Now the pathology is beginning to show.

I Love My Bible #3

The mission of Catholic Online is to accurately represent the Catholic religion, both past and present. The organization provides Catholics "comprehensive, educational and timely information about Catholicism, and provides a range of easy methods to integrate their faith into their daily lives.[198]"

In February 2016, Kenya Sinclair, in an article on Catholic Online[199] wrote about Trump's claim that John Kerry, "… did not read *The Art of the Deal*, and that he 'probably didn't read the Bible either'. What a hypocrite. Trump's joke led to his claim that 'Nobody reads the Bible more than me'— a statement that sent millions of critics into fits of laughter."

By the way, the headline for this article was, "'Nobody reads the Bible more than me': Trump's claim is a laughingstock."

Oops

"Before the 2016 Iowa caucus, Trump attended a church service in Iowa as part of his outreach to evangelical Christians. But the church he attended was a mainline Protestant denomination that supports gay marriage. At an Iowa church service before the Iowa caucus, Trump put money in the communion plate, mistaking it for the offering plate."[200]

Forgive Me

In July 2015, Trump attended the Family Leadership Summit in Ames, Iowa, sponsored by several Christian organizations. At the event, moderator Frank Luntz asked Trump whether he had ever asked God for forgiveness. Trump replied, "I am not sure I have, I just go and try to do a better job from there. I don't think so. I think, if I do something wrong, I think I just try to make it right. I don't bring God into that picture. I don't."[201]

In January 2016, Trump doubled down on his previous statement regarding forgiveness, telling CNN, "Why do I have to repent or ask for forgiveness, if I am not making mistakes? . . . I work hard, I'm an honorable person."[202]

The Bible says, "for all have sinned and fall short of the glory."[203]

I Love My Church

During the Family Leadership Summit, Trump stated, "I go to church, and I love God, and I love my church." He has also said that he is a "Presbyterian Protestant" and a member of Marble Collegiate Church on Fifth Avenue in Manhattan, one of the oldest Protestant congregations in North America. In response, the church said in a statement, "Donald Trump has had a longstanding history with Marble Collegiate Church, where his parents were for years active members and one of his children was baptized. However, as he indicates, he is a Presbyterian, and is not an active member of Marble."[204]

What Jesus Said/What Donald Trump Said

The following is from an article in the *Huffington Post*:[205]

Jesus: "Love your enemies, bless those who curse you, do good to those who hate you."
Trump: "When people wrong you, go after those people, because it is a good feeling and because other people will see you doing it. I always get even."

Jesus: "Those who exalt themselves will be humbled, and those who humble themselves will be exalted."
Trump: "Sorry losers and haters, but my I.Q. is one of the highest - and you all know it! Please don't feel so stupid or insecure, it's not your fault."

Jesus: "I have not come to call the righteous, but sinners to repentance."
Trump: "Why do I have to repent, why do I have to ask for forgiveness if [I'm] not making mistakes?"

Jesus: "Blessed are the meek, for they shall inherit the earth."
Trump: "I fully think apologizing is a great thing. But you have to be WRONG . . . I will absolutely apologize sometime in the hopefully distant future if I'm ever wrong."

One Pastor's Take

John Pavlovitz is a blogger and a pastor at North Raleigh Community Church in North Carolina. These are some of his statements regarding Donald Trump as he posted on his website[206]:

- His life [Trump] showed an open contempt for most of the things the Jesus of the Gospels lived and preached: humility, generosity, respect, empathy, kindness, peace.

- It's exactly the kind of greedy, bloated, bitter, violent, self-centered, myopic existence that Jesus spent his life calling us to reject. So no, I don't know the President's heart or his inner confession of faith, but I have eyes and they see no love or benevolence or compassion—and that does matter to Jesus.[207]

What Did the Pope Say?

"A person who thinks only about building walls, wherever they may be, and not building bridges, is not Christian," Pope Francis said speaking about Trump's proposals to stop illegal immigration. (Trump responded, calling the Pope disgraceful for "questioning a person's faith."[208])

Trump on the Religion of Others

While Trump's claims regarding his religious faith seem disingenuous, he continually questions not only others' religious commitment, but the validity of their religion as well. During the campaign, he questioned the faith of Ted Cruz, Mitt Romney, Hillary Clinton, John Kerry, President Obama, and Ben Carson.

In January 2016, Trump said this regarding Ted Cruz who is a Southern Baptist and a pastor's son: "Just remember this—you gotta remember, in all fairness, to the best of my knowledge, not too many evangelicals come out of Cuba, okay?"[209] That's a bigoted and stupid thing to say.

Speaking at a rally in March 2016, Trump said, "'Do I love the Mormons? OK, I love the Mormons,'" a statement met by cheers. He then added, "By the way, Mitt Romney is not one of them . . . Are you sure he's a Mormon? Are we sure?"[210]

In June 2016, speaking to a group of evangelical leaders in New York, Trump said, "We don't know anything about Hillary in terms of religion. Now, she's been in the public eye for years and years, and yet there's no — there's nothing out there. There's like nothing out there. It's going to be an extension of Obama but it's going to be worse, because with Obama you had your guard up. With Hillary you don't, and it's going to be worse."[211]

Though it's beside the point, Clinton is a practicing Methodist, who is well versed on the Bible and frequently speaks about the role her faith plays in her life.

As described earlier, in February 2016, Trump commented regarding Secretary of State John Kerry's piety when he said, "Obviously, Kerry did not read *The Art of the Deal*. Probably didn't read the Bible, either."[212]

Once again, it shouldn't matter, but Kerry is a devout Catholic and has spoken often about the role of faith in his life, much of it part of the public record. Here's a side note regarding Donald Trump's hypocrisy. Senator John Kerry is a practicing Catholic and a former altar boy. He attends Mass on a regular basis. He often quotes the Bible (and accurately) particularly as it directs him in his role as an elected official. As a young man Kerry considered becoming a priest. When serving in Vietnam he often wore a rosary around his neck when going into battle.

On the other hand, Donald Trump is a religion phony. He doesn't attend church, never quotes the bible and is not capable of doing so without someone providing him the quote. He seemingly is ignorant to the teachings and traditions of his professed religion.

The following is an example of the glowing hypocritical ways of Donald Trump. He, a religious phony, decides to criticize John Kerry, a faithful practicing Catholic, for his religious commitment. That's absurd. It's like an overweight man criticizing a thin man for being fat. Trump dwells in never seen levels of hypocrisy and lunacy.

In October 2016, Trump said this regarding Ben Carson: "I'm Presbyterian. Boy, that's down the middle of the road, folks, in all fairness. I mean, Seventh-Day Adventist, I don't know about. I just don't know about."[213]

In 2011, Trump spoke about President Obama on Fox News. "He doesn't have a birth certificate. He may have one, but there's something on that, maybe religion, maybe it says he is a Muslim. I don't know. Maybe he doesn't want that."[214] A thinly veiled attempt to scare people by suggesting Obama might be Muslim.

On February 20, 2015, Trump's Muslim bigotry was alive and well when he tweeted, "I wonder if President Obama would have attended the funeral of Justice Scalia if it were held in a Mosque? Very sad that he did not go!"[215]

Little is more offensive than a man of little faith questioning the commitment of people of great faith. This is religious hypocrisy.

Chapter 10
Trump the Philanthropic Phony

Charity—Trump Doesn't Believe in It

Philanthropy in the United States is astonishing and has particularly flourished in recent years. The extremely large number of generous philanthropic works that flood our country and our world is remarkable. Americans are concerned about the welfare of others and act accordingly. The results of these activities permeate the landscape and greatly improve the quality of life for millions. Athletes, celebrities, sports and entertainment companies, corporations, business leaders, and wealthy individuals seem to, as a matter of course, set up charitable foundations or otherwise support charitable efforts. Most Americans in general very charitable, demonstrating their goodness daily. But not Donald Trump.

Trump doesn't believe in charity. I know that sounds like an odd thing to say. You thought everybody believed in charity; maybe some more than others, but *everybody* believes in doing good. Trump doesn't. While so many Americans have compassion and love in their hearts, which motivates them to act on their concern for others, Trump's heart is cold and cares only about Trump. The idea of supporting those in need never enters his mind unless it's to enhance his business or other interests.

The Donald J. Trump Foundation

Donald Trump established the Donald J. Trump Foundation (a family foundation) in 1988 (what took him so long?). The Trump Foundation's vision and practices are very different from those of other foundations, whether family run or otherwise. The Trump Foundation's limited charitable giving is often illicitly related to his self-serving business, personal, and political interests. It's self-dealing disguised as charitable giving. Most charities have purposes—giving to medical research, or giving to improve the environment, or supporting efforts to fight poverty. They reflect the charity's concern regarding societal problems. Not the Trump Foundation. According to a recent IRS Form 990 filing for the foundation, it does not have "restrictions or limitations on awards such as by geographical areas, charitable fields, kinds of institutions, or other factors."[216] By itself, this policy is not problematic, but combined with the foundation's giving history, the foundation's illegitimacy begins to emerge.

Since 2008, according to his foundation's tax return, Trump has not contributed a penny of his own money to his foundation. *The New York Daily News* reported, "By contrast, in 2012 alone (according to a *Forbes* review of their philanthropies), Bill and Melinda Gates donated $1.9 billion to charity, Warren Buffett donated $1.8 billion to charity, George Soros donated $763 million to charity, Mark Zuckerberg donated $519 million to charity, and former New York City Mayor Michael Bloomberg donated $370 million to charity",[217] most of that to their own foundations. Although a purpose of a family foundation is to provide an avenue for the benefactor's contributions to charitable efforts, it might be possible that Trump made personal donations directly to charities. However, there is no evidence of that. As reported in the *New Yorker*, "Back in April [2016], Fahrenthold and Rosalind S. Helderman reported that they couldn't find a single cash donation to charity that Trump personally had made over the previous five years."[218] You rarely see Trump's name associated with a charity or with a community's relief efforts responding to a tragedy. He may sometimes boast of a particular charitable effort, but usually it is an empty boast.

Trump's foundation pales when compared to the foundations of other business leaders:

- Jeff Skoll, the founder of eBay, has set up a center for social entrepreneurship at Oxford University. He has also given the charitable Skoll Foundation $250 million worth of eBay stock, which the foundation uses to make grants of more than $30 million per year.

- Michael Bloomberg contributes around $140 million every year, usually anonymously, toward education, public health, arts, and social services in New York.

- Since 1999, Michael Dell and his wife, Susan, have contributed more than $1.2 billion toward education and child development programs in Texas, and they gave $5 million to help Hurricane

Katrina storm victims. They also contributed to microfinance lenders in the six biggest cities of India, making an effort to lift millions of slum dwellers out of poverty. The Michael and Susan Dell Foundation is dedicated to improving the lives of children.

- Warren Buffett has committed $31 billion to the Bill & Melinda Gates Foundation, which sponsors efforts to improve education in the United States and health and standards of living worldwide. He has also allocated billions to family foundations that support various causes worldwide.

Remember, since 2008, Trump has given nothing to his own foundation. To compare the Trump Foundation to the foundations of other wealthy business leaders is like comparing a pick pocket to Mother Theresa. Donald Trump is a high-tech pick pocket.

Another way of saying this is: other foundations give money; the Trump Foundation takes money.

Most foundations have staff to run the charity, along with an active Board of Directors, as appropriate. A no staff charitable foundation is almost a fraud by definition, particularly if it is a large foundation. IRS documents show there to be five Trump Foundation board members: Donald, his three oldest children, and Allen Weisselberg, who is CFO of The Trump Organization. However, as of this writing, the Board of Directors has not met since 1999 (that's a long time without a meeting) and Weisselberg did not know he was on the board. The board did not set policy or criteria for choosing grant recipients; and it did not approve of any grants [219]

Donald Trump makes all foundation grant decisions[220], a very suspect arrangement in itself. This facilitates him using the foundation as a slush fund to pay his personal, political, and business expenses, to scratch the back of people who have scratched or will scratch his back and to otherwise serve his personal needs. The foundation lists two addresses for their offices on various documents, but I can't figure out how you can have no staff but still have offices. Who sits in the offices?

How substantial can the Trump Foundation be with no staff, a questionable and inactive board of directors, and little or no time and financial

contribution from Donald Trump? The Trump Foundation seems to simply be a desk with a checkbook in one of its drawers
From *Wikipedia*:[221]

> The Donald J. Trump Foundation is a New York-based private foundation founded and chaired by President of the United States Donald Trump. It has been a source of controversy, criticism, and scrutiny. The foundation has been fined for making political contributions and admitted engaging in self-dealing practices to benefit Trump, his family, and businesses.

> . . .

> Trump may have used Trump Foundation grants to advance his presidential campaign, in violation of rules barring charities from engaging in political activity. Trump distributed at least some of the funds publicly at "Donald Trump for President" political rallies, displaying large-size donation checks that included his campaign slogan "Make America Great Again" or a link to a campaign website.

> . . .

> In each of 1995 and 1999, the Trump Foundation granted $50,000 to the National Museum of Catholic Art and Library. A 2001 report by *The Village Voice* stated, after visiting the museum in East Harlem, that the facility had "next to no art" and no official connection to the Catholic Church, despite having had a 10-year track record of soliciting large-scale donations for its collection. The *Voice* and, later, *The Washington Post*, concluded that Trump may have directed the grants to the museum to curry favor with the museum's then chairman, Eddie Malloy, who was also head of the Building and Construction Trades Council of Greater New York. The Council had worked on behalf of one of the unions of workers who worked on Trump construction projects.

> . . .

Trump may have strategically directed money from the Trump Foundation to support his presidential campaign. In one case, the grants were used specifically to pay for newspaper ads. In October 2016, RealClearPolitics reported that Trump directed significant amounts of foundation money to conservative organizations, possibly in return for political support and access. [222]

Trump finds numerous ways to use his foundation to cheat, misuse funds, steal, and avoid personal income taxes. *Wikipedia* lists over 50 different what they call "legal and ethical controversies." I call it cheating, misusing funds, stealing, and avoiding personal income taxes. Some of his practices are quite imaginative. If only he would use that energy for good instead of evil.

This is why I say Trump doesn't believe in charity. He doesn't care about others, so he doesn't care about providing comfort or support to others. He diverts money intended for charitable purposes for his own personal or business use. Given the opportunity, Trump would steal from the church collection plate. He will exploit any charity to enhance himself. The Trump Foundation is not a real foundation. His foundation is no more than a way to keep up appearances and to put money in his own pocket. It's a front that enables Trump to channel funds into his own pocket. It's clear to me that the Trump Foundation is a farce and a scam. Trump said he plans to dissolve his foundation in order to avoid "even the appearance of any conflict with [his] role as president.[223]" Poppycock. That's not the reason he's dissolving his foundation. He doesn't care about charity, so he can readily dissolve his foundation to give the appearance of being ethical. That's the reason.

Donald Trump's name should be prevalent among many of the community institutions and charitable efforts in his hometown New York. It is not. He has not been a voice for any particular cause. That's because, in the case of Trump, his focus is on emblazoning his name on steaks, vodka, and cologne.

The Trump Foundation/Mar-a-Lago

Here's an intriguing story about a despicable Trump theft and the incredible deception that came along with it. It is a story of lies, deceit, intimidation, greed, manipulation, and unscrupulous actions. It is one of a number of times Trump reportedly used Donald J. Trump Foundation funds to pay his personal and business expenses, as reported by David A. Fahrenthold of *The Washington Post* in a series of articles. Hundreds of the foundation's grants and contributions that were not included in Fahrenthold's story are, to me, still destined for Trump's personal or political benefit.

Here's how Trump scammed and bullied both the City of Palm Beach and donors to his foundation. In 2006, Donald Trump wanted to construct an 80-foot-high flagpole to display on his Mar-a-Lago estate in Palm Beach, Florida, which would be in violation of town zoning regulations that call for a maximum height of 42 feet. Trump knew the proposed flagpole would not comply with the rules, so he erected it without applying to Palm Beach for a building permit or variance. The scheme begins.

Palm Beach ordered him to take down the flagpole and fined him $1,250 - per day (some reports say $250 per day) for every day the flagpole remained. Trump, in turn, filed a $25 million lawsuit against Palm Beach, claiming that the town was selectively enforcing its rules and infringing on his constitutional right to free speech. He sought $25 million in damages because he couldn't erect a flagpole as tall as he wanted. The lawsuit and the size of the damages sought were to try to coerce the city. Lawsuits, as we've seen, are Trump's favorite rip-off/bullying technique. The con continues.

Trump argued in court that he couldn't bring his flag and pole into compliance because, according to the lawsuit, "A smaller flag and pole on Mar-A-Lago's property would be lost given its massive size, look silly instead of making a statement, and most importantly would fail to appropriately express the magnitude of Donald J. Trump's and the Club's members' patriotism."[224] Idiocy. Let's examine his ludicrous arguments.

- "A smaller flag and pole on Mar-A-Lago's property would be lost given its massive size, look silly instead of making a statement." A US flag flying on a 42-foot flagpole, which would probably be the tallest in the city of Palm Beach, would not be lost or look silly. And even if it did, "looking silly" is not a valid reason to violate building codes.

- "A smaller flag and pole on Mar-A-Lago's property . . . would fail to appropriately express the magnitude of Donald J. Trump's and the Club's members' patriotism." One's patriotism is not measured by the size of his or her flag (just as one's sexual prowess is not measured by the size of his or her hands).[225]

In his statements to the media, Trump framed the issue as being one of his standing up to anti-American, anti-flag, anti-patriotic forces. "The town council of Palm Beach should be ashamed of itself," Trump proclaimed. "They're fining me for putting up the American flag. This is probably a first in United States history."[226] Typical Trump manipulative deceit, a simple ruse. The plot thickens.

Frank Cerabino, a writer for the *Palm Beach Post* saw it similarly, "The whole incident had nothing to do with patriotism but was part of a pattern of Trump's use of lawsuits to bend local authorities to his will—dredging up excuses to sue them for exorbitant amounts of money, then offering to drop the suits in exchange for agreements that provide him with significant business advantages."[227] Yep. Trump might call it "the art of the deal." I call it a con.

After being ordered by the court to come to some agreement, the two sides did reach a settlement. The town agreed to waive all fines against Trump and to "review its ordinances and codes dealing with flagpoles and flags during the next zoning season," and Trump agreed to "drop his lawsuit, lower the height of his flagpole from 80 to 70 feet, obtain a permit for the pole and move it farther inland, and (in lieu of the fines) donate $100,000 to charity."[228] Trump complied. Well, not really. Here comes the bait and switch.

Trump made the donation to charity but did so using funds from his foundation. In other words, he used money others had donated to charity to bail out himself, a millionaire, and pay his personal business obligation. Now he can get credit for a donation to charity— because on the surface it seemed reasonable, even admirable. But Trump effectively manipulated the county and the court and as a result he avoided paying any fine out of his own pocket. There it is—scam complete

To misuse money intended for the needy and other charitable purposes is truly low. For a millionaire to misuse money meant for the needy and other charitable purposes is worse. But that's what Donald Trump has done. He is a disgrace of a human being.

The Trump Foundation—Smile

One of the more blatant Trump swindles entailed his spending $20,000 of foundation funds in 2007 for a six-foot-tall portrait of himself, apparently to hang at the Trump National Golf Club Westchester. In 2014, Trump purchased another painting of himself, paying for it with $10,000 in Trump Foundation funds. In 2012, Trump bought a Tim Tebow Denver Broncos helmet for $12,000, paid for with money from his foundation. *Washington Post* reporter David A. Fahrenthold has documented these "thefts."[229]

The Trump Foundation and the Florida Attorney General

Fahrenthold also reported that in 2013, the Trump Foundation violated tax laws when it made a $25,000 donation to the campaign of Florida Attorney General Pam Bondi. At the time, Bondi was considering an investigation of Trump University. It appeared that Trump was obviously trying to influence Bondi not to launch that investigation and, in fact, Bondi did not pursue the allegations of impropriety. So Trump took $25,000 that had been donated to his foundation, supposedly for charitable use, and instead used it for political purposes to apparently unduly influence an elected official to not investigate his fraudulent university. That's like paying off a judge and doing so with stolen money from a local charity. Trump's aides professed the donation was all an administrative error, that the money was supposed to come from his personal account. This is how corrupt Trump is. He says his apparent bribe was not supposed to come from a charitable foundation. It was an error. His bribe was supposed to come from his personal funds. There was no proof Trump's payment to Bondi was a bribe, but it strongly looks that way to me. Trump's foundation was assessed an IRS penalty for unlawful use of foundation funds for the Bondi donation.

The Trump Foundation and the Private School

Now, if you search hard, you may find donations that the Trump Foundation has made to some reputable organizations and seemingly for legitimate charitable purposes. But they seem to be infrequent and very small—particularly when compared to the foundations of other wealthy businessmen. And in most cases, I would probably question Trump's impetus for the support as I think a closer examination might reveal questionable activity.

An example of this is the foundation's grants to the Columbia Grammar and Preparatory School. The Foundation made grants of $50,000 to the school in 2012 and 2014, 2015, and 2016. Donald Trump's son, Baron attended this school until 2017 when he began attending a school in Washington DC. The Columbia Grammar and Preparatory School website lists its tuition for the 2018-19 school year at $50,690[230], which apparently is a small increase over the previous year. The Trump Foundation has made $50,000 grants to the school four times, all in years that match his son's enrollment.

And since Trump doesn't contribute to his own foundation, most donations are made with other people's money, others who have donated to his foundation. Now Trump has used this trick often and not only to divert $50,000 from his foundation but also to divert amounts as low as $7. Consider:

"Donald Took $7 Out of His Charity to Pay for His Son's Boy Scout Membership Fees — I Can't Make This Stuff Up"

That's the title of an article that appeared on medium.com.[231] I liked it, so I borrowed it. It fit. To explain: in 1989, the Trump Foundation made a $7 contribution to the Boy Scouts. That seems like a particularly small and strangely odd amount. At that time, the cost to register a child in the Scouts was, you guessed it, $7. Also, at that time, Don Jr. was 11 years old—the age young boys are eligible for the Boy Scouts.

Let me see if I have this right. A millionaire takes money donated to help people in need, to pay for his soon-to-be millionaire son's $7 scouting registration. I could pay that with the loose change in my top dresser drawer. This millionaire steals from charity to pay it.

I am ashamed to be of same species as this man.

Conning Other Charities

One favorite scam of Trump's is to get charities to contract for an event at one of his clubs or properties and then overcharge them. On the surface, it appears he is helping a charity, but he is not. Sometimes he'll even offer them a small donation from his foundation to increase the appeal. You would think he would consider reducing or waiving the cost for a charity, but instead Trump exploits them. He will do the same for Republican party events, steering them to one of his properties and then overcharging them. Donald Trump never met a scam he didn't love.

An example of this practice is described in the Forbes magazine article, "How Donald Trump Shifted Kids-Cancer Charity Money Into His Business." The article details how an Eric Trump charity event paid the Trump organization $1.2 million for use of the Trump National Golf Club in Westchester County for use of the property. "Golf charity experts say the listed expenses defy any reasonable cost justification for a one-day golf tournament."[232]

It should be noted that despite this example, Eric Trump has reportedly donated millions of dollars to the St. Jude Children's Research Hospital over a number of years. But in this case, it was apparently after Donald Trump took his cut.

The Fake Philanthropist

Donald Trump wants you to think is a generous philanthropist. He is not. He puts on a facade to cover up his greed and lack of charity. He'll sometimes announce a donation but never actually make the contribution. He'll brag about the millions of dollars he gives to charity, an exaggeration or an outright falsehood. There are even reports that he didn't follow through on the pledges he made to charity on his television show, *The Celebrity Apprentice. The Washington Post* tracked all the "personal" gifts that Trump promised on the show — during 83 episodes and seven seasons — but could not confirm a single case in which Trump actually sent a gift from his own pocket. It should be noted that most of the pledged donations seemed to have been paid, but not personally by Trump, as he had often promised. "In some cases . . . Trump's 'personal' promise was paid off by a production company. Other times, it was paid off by a nonprofit that Trump controls, whose coffers are largely filled with other donors' money."[233]

This next Trump absurdity, from another story in *The Washington Post*, is an illustration of the real nature of "Trump the Philanthropist."[234] After reading this escapade, the thought comes to mind, "Who does that?"

Here's a problem Donald Trump faced. Trump was approached to make a donation to a charity for children. But remember, he doesn't believe in charity. Trump wanted to get credit and publicity for making a sizeable donation to the charity. What to do? Trump came up with a solution. Don't give a donation but make it look like he did:

> In the fall of 1996, a charity called the Association to Benefit Children held a ribbon-cutting in Manhattan for a new nursery school serving children with AIDS. The bold-faced names took seats up front.
>
> There was then-Mayor Rudolph W. Giuliani (R) and former mayor David Dinkins (D). TV stars Frank and Kathie Lee Gifford, who were major donors. And there was a seat saved for Steven Fisher, a developer who had given generously to build the nursery.
>
> Then, all of a sudden, there was Donald Trump.
>
> "Nobody knew he was coming," said Abigail Disney, another donor sitting on the dais. "There's this kind of ruckus at the door, and I don't know what was going on, and in comes Donald Trump. [He] just gets up on the podium and sits down."
>
> Trump was not a major donor. He was not a donor, period. He'd never given a dollar to the nursery or the Association to Benefit Children, according to Gretchen Buchenholz, the charity's executive director then and now.
>
> But now he was sitting in Fisher's seat, next to Giuliani.

Frank Gifford turned to me and said, "Why is he here?" Buchenholz recalled recently. By then, the ceremony had begun. There was nothing to do.

"Just sing past it," she recalled Gifford telling her.

So they warbled into the first song on the program, "This Little Light of Mine," alongside Trump and a chorus of children — with a photographer snapping photos, and Trump looking for all the world like an honored donor to the cause.

Afterward, Disney and Buchenholz recalled, Trump left without offering an explanation. Or a donation. Fisher was stuck in the audience. The charity spent months trying to repair its relationship with him.

"I mean, what's wrong with you, man?" Disney recalled thinking of Trump, when it was over.[235]

More of the Fake Philanthropist

Barbara Res, a longtime Trump employee, asked Trump to support a gala where she was to receive an award from the Professional Women in Construction. It was usual practice for the awardee's employer to make a sizeable contribution to the event by buying tables or being a sponsor. But not Trump.

Trump bought one $100 ticket at the door. Then he announced to Lenore Janis, president of the organization, "I have a few things that I want to say. I will need the microphone," She refused him, but he wouldn't accept that so he found someone else who said it would be OK. "He got up there and for 15 minutes he blew his own horn," giving the appearance he had made a big contribution to the organization.[236]

Chapter 11
Trump the Lewd

Let me see if I have this right. Trump says he kisses women without their consent. Numerous women say he kissed them without their consent. Trump says the women are lying. Got it.

---

sexual harassment[237]

[sex·u·al ha·rass·ment] *noun*

1. behavior characterized by the making of unwelcome and inappropriate sexual remarks or physical advances in a workplace or other professional or social situation.

2. uninvited and unwelcome verbal or physical behavior of a sexual nature especially by a person in authority toward a subordinate (as an employee or student).

Here's some of the evidence, story after story, of Donald Trump's unwanted sexual advances, sexual assault, lewd sexual conduct, offensive language to and about women, womanizing, and general disrespect for women (limited because of space constraints).

Respecting Woman Trump Style

Donald Trump has called women dogs, slobs, pigs, a piglet, dummies, stupid, a bitch, disgusting animals, bimbos, and Miss Piggy. Oh, and Trump says, "Nobody has more respect for women more than me."[238]

A Womanizer and Adulterer – He Told You

Here's the reason I know Donald Trump is a womanizer and serial adulterer: He told me. He told everybody. Trump has a long history of admitting and bragging about his reputation as a "ladies' man" and womanizer. If Trump sees a woman who interests him, the fact that she may be married is inconsequential. The fact that he is married certainly is inconsequential.

In his book *The Art of the Comeback*, Trump revealed, "If I told the real stories of my experiences with women, often seemingly very happily married and important women, this book would be a guaranteed best-seller."[239]

In the March 2000 issue of *Gear* (a now defunct magazine), Trump claimed that his long list of ex-lovers was a sign that he would make a good president.

In 1998, during the Monica Lewinsky scandal, Trump was asked by MSNBC's Chris Matthews about his interest in running for office. Trump compared himself to President Bill Clinton remarking that his own history might be a problem. "Can you imagine how controversial I'd be?" Trump asked. "You think about [Clinton] with the women—how about me with the women? Can you imagine?"[240] In fact, Trump's main criticism of Clinton was regarding the women he was linked to. "The whole group, Paula Jones, Lewinsky, it's just a really unattractive group. I'm not just talking about physical."[241]

During his marriage to his first wife, Ivana, Donald was rumored to be involved with several different women. Ivana named Marla Maples as the "other woman" in Trump's divorce proceedings in 1991. Before she became the second Mrs. Donald Trump, Ms. Maples was Trump's mistress in an affair that is said to have begun as long as five years before he finally divorced Ivana. It was an affair Trump did not hide from the public or, apparently, from Ivana.

When Trump was deposed in his divorce proceedings, he invoked the Fifth Amendment 97 times, primarily in response to questions about other women.

Trump is reported to have met his current wife, Melania, when he was in the company of another woman. He waited for his date to go to the restroom and then asked Melania for her phone number.

According to people.com,[242] Karen McDougal, the 1998 Playboy Playmate of the Year, reportedly told friends she had had a consensual affair with Trump for 10 months or so starting in 2006. At the time, he was married to Melania.

Salma Hayek and "The Donald"

In an article on the website buzzfeednews.com ("Salma Hayek: I Denied Trump A Date, So He Planted A National Enquirer Story About My Height") actress Salma Hayek tells her story about Donald Trump. "When I met that man, I had a boyfriend, and he tried to become his friend to get my home telephone number," she stated, describing the meeting Trump early in her career. "He got my number and he would call me to invite me out.

"I told him I wouldn't go out with him even if I didn't have a boyfriend, [which he took as disrespectful]. Shortly thereafter, someone planted a story with the *National Enquirer* saying that he wouldn't go out with me because I was too short."[243] Trump has been known to have a close relationship with the *National Enquirer*.

Trump extended his womanizing to an even more depraved level when he sought revenge and planted a story in the *National Enquirer*. That's scary and that's disgusting.

Trump and Nancy O'Dell

In the infamous *Access Hollywood* tape, Trump discussed his attempt to seduce a woman, whose name was not given in the video but was later determined to be television personality Nancy O'Dell. "I moved on her, and I failed. I'll admit it," Trump is heard saying. "I did try and f--- her. She was married," He continues, "And I moved on her very heavily. In fact, I took her out furniture shopping. She wanted to get some furniture. I said, 'I'll show you where they have some nice furniture.' I moved on her like a b---h, but I couldn't get there. And she was married," Trump said. "Then all of a sudden, I see her, she's now got the big phony tits and everything. She's totally changed her look."[244]

Trump and the Olympian

As reported in *New York Magazine* in November 1992, Trump said that German Olympic ice skater Katarina Witt was: "Wonderful looking while on the ice but up close and personal, she could only be described as attractive if you like a woman with a bad complexion who is built like a linebacker".[245] How charming.

The Donald Goes to the Movies

Here's a quote from Trump speaking about the movie *Pulp Fiction*, "My favorite part is when Sam has his gun out in the diner and he tells the guy to tell his girlfriend to shut up: 'Tell that b---h to be cool! Say: "B---h be cool!" I love those lines."[246] That speaks volumes.

Creepy Trump and Lady Di

Trump is said to have had a passion for Princess Diana. In 1995, Trump offered Diana complimentary membership in his Mar-a-Lago Club (she declined). After her divorce, Trump sent her massive bouquets of flowers. TV journalist Selina Scott, a friend of Lady Di, has since revealed that Diana had said that she felt stalked by Trump and that he gave her the creeps. In 1997 on his radio show, Howard Stern asked Trump, "You could've nailed her, right?" Trump responded, "I think I could've."[247]

Trump, Vendela Kirsebom, and the White House Correspondents' Dinner

In 1993, Donald Trump was a guest of *Vanity Fair* editor Graydon Carter at the White House Correspondents' Association dinner. Swedish model Vendela Kirsebom, also a *Vanity Fair* guest, was seated next to Trump at one of the publication's two tables. Carter related, "After 45 minutes, she came over to my table, almost in tears, and pleaded with me to move her. It seems that Trump had spent his entire time with her assaying the 'tits' and legs of the other female guests and asking how they measured up to those of other women, including his wife." She told Carter that Trump was "the most vulgar man I have ever met."[248]

Kirsebom later told the *Huffington Post*, "He did talk about other women's breasts and the size . . . . If you were flat-chested, you are not really worth anything—tons of derogative talking about women. If a woman would be successful, it would definitely be because she had bigger breasts. Stupid stuff that made no sense to me whatsoever and made me very upset. . . . I remember feeling like it was very, very uncomfortable," She added, "I tried to kind of steer conversation over to other things, but I felt that it always got back to this type of conversation."[249]

The Fat Picture

After she joined Donald Trump's real estate business, Louise Sunshine found herself struggling to maintain her weight. Donald Trump seized on that as he kept a "fat picture" of Sunshine in his desk and would pull it out to show her anytime he was unhappy with her[250].

They Felt All Wrong

At the end of his marriage to Ivana, Trump told various New York newspapers that his wife's breast implants "felt all wrong." He alluded that this was one of the reasons he was pursuing a divorce from her.

Sex and *The Apprentice*

The Associated Press interviewed more than 20 former crew members, editors, and contestants on Trump's reality television show *The Apprentice*. They documented numerous reports of Trump displaying lewd and sexist conduct, degrading women with sexist language, rating female contestants by the size of their breasts, asking female contestants to wear shorter dresses and show cleavage, and talking about which ones he'd like to have sex with. In portions of the show's boardroom sessions that were not broadcast, Trump would ask male contestants to rate the attractiveness of their female competitors.

Former *Apprentice* producer Katherine Walker has said that Trump frequently remarked about female contestants' bodies and speculated about which of them would be "a tiger in bed."[251]

"If there was a break in the conversation, he would then look at one of the female cast members, saying 'you're looking kind of hot today, I love that dress on you,' then he would turn to one of the male cast members and say 'wouldn't you sleep with her?' and then everyone would laugh," said a former crew member who spoke to the Associated Press on condition of anonymity because of a nondisclosure agreement. "There would be about 10 or 12 cameras rolling and getting that footage, which is why everybody was like, this guy just doesn't care.

"We were in the boardroom one time figuring out who to blame for the task, and he just stopped in the middle and pointed to someone and said, 'You'd f--- her, wouldn't you? I'd f--- her. C'mon, wouldn't you?'"[252]

And this from Richard Hatch a 2011 contestant on the show, ""Watching him in the boardroom making sexual comments to Marlee Matlin, to all of the women on the Apprentice, it was obvious that that's just a part of who he is... It was obvious and it was grotesque. It was blatant and it was frequent. He did it with Lisa Rinna; He did it with Marlee Matlin. He did it with whomever happened to be there at the time."[253]

Former crew members of the show also reported that Trump frequently made lewd comments about one of the camerawomen, saying that she "had a nice rear - comparing her beauty to that of his daughter, Ivanka."[254]

Sex, *The Celebrity Apprentice*, and Gary Busey

In 2011, actor Gary Busey appeared on *The Celebrity Apprentice* and, according to five staff on the show, assaulted a female show employee. As described by the victim of that assault, "We were smoking cigarettes outside, and Busey was standing next to me. And then at one point, he grabbed me firmly between my legs, and ran his hand up my stomach, and grabbed my breasts," she added. "I didn't know what to do. So I made this joke that, 'Oh, I've never been sexually harassed by a celebrity before!' Then he grabbed my hand and put it [over] his penis, and said, like, 'I'm just getting started, baby.'" She continued "Then my friend jumped in between [me and Busey] and put his hand on Busey's chest."[255] Trump later confronted Busey as part of the show. The staff member recalled Trump saying, "'Gary, did you do a bad thing . . . [and] got your hands where they're not supposed to be,' *The Apprentice* staff member recalls Trump as saying, and then adding that the two of them were 'yukking' it up as Trump was supposedly disciplining him. Another staffer said Trump called Busey a 'bad boy, a very bad boy.'"[256]

In an interview, the victim of the assault said that Trump "would say 'gross things all the time' during *The Apprentice* and that the atmosphere of Trump Tower was 'a disgusting place to work' due to the high frequency of sexual harassment. '[Trump] is, and always has been a joke—I can't believe anyone now is taking him seriously,' she continued. 'He's a monster.'"[257]

Hey, Donald, Any Thoughts on Hillary and Bill's Sex Life?

The following tweet is vile. The Trump campaign blamed a staffer for the message (which seemed to be a retweet). I don't believe that. I don't think a staffer would put out such a tweet without Trump's consent. In any case, Trump doesn't get a pass by blaming someone else for a tweet put out under his name. He is responsible for tweets in his name.

Donald J. Trump
@realDonaldTrump

"@mplefty67: If Hillary Clinton can't satisfy her husband what makes her think she can satisfy America?" @real Donald Trump #2016present

4/16/15, 5:22 PM

This Trump tweet is also in the chapter "Trump the Crude." That's because it is both crude and lewd.

Trump Tweets about Kim Novak

In another demonstration of how he thinks of women, Trump found it necessary to crudely insult 81-year-old actress Kim Novak when she appeared on the Academy Awards program. Trump was moved to tweet the following:

Donald J. Trump
@real DonaldTrump

I'm having a real hard time watching the Academy Awards (so far). The last song was terrible! Kim should sue her plastic surgeon! #Oscars

9:30 AM · Mar 2, 2014

Trump and the *Access Hollywood* Tape

You know all about this one. You know, when he made all those lewd remarks about how he forced himself on woman and got away with it because he's a star.

You Know That's Exactly What He Would Have Said

Trump's infamous words to *Access Hollywood*'s Billy Bush caused an uproar. Let's imagine that instead of providing a videotape of the episode, Bush had simply related the story. How do you think Trump would have reacted? Does anyone doubt that he would have denied it?

Here's what I think he would have said: "Billy Bush is a loser, and *Access Hollywood* has terrible ratings. Bush begged me to do an interview to help *Access Hollywood*'s bad ratings. My show, *Celebrity Apprentice,* had great ratings, the best ratings NBC has had in a long time. Everybody knows that, and I've been given great credit for those ratings. I never said those things Bush says I said. His uncles, Low-Energy Jeb and Failed President George, are liars, and so is he. Sad. I will be suing him." Now admit it; you know that's precisely what he would have said.

A Friend of a CNN Anchor and Trump

This is infamously from Trump on *Access Hollywood*: "I've gotta use some Tic Tacs just in case I start kissing her. You know I'm automatically attracted to beautiful—I just start kissing them. It's like a magnet. Just kiss. I don't even wait." [258] When a friend of CNN anchor Erin Burnett heard that, she was stunned.

Burnett described the following on her show shortly after the release of the tape: "So, Scotty, I know a woman who heard that line today, it stopped her in her tracks; I have known this woman for years. She told me when she heard this, she could only think of one thing and that is what Donald Trump did to her and I want to quote what she told me.

"'The Tic-Tacs, that's exactly what Trump did to me. Trump took Tic-Tacs, suggested I take them also. He then leaned in'—I'm reading this— 'catching me off guard and kissed me almost on the lips. I was really freaked out.

After, Trump asked me to come into his office alone. I figured I could handle myself. Anyway, once in his office, he kept telling me how special I am and gave me his cell phone and asked me to call him. I ran the hell out of there.' That was in 2010. He was married at the time. This is the exact story that Trump said. This isn't Trump just saying something to make it up. This happened, to someone I know."[259]

Locker Room Talk

Donald Trump and his supporters tried to explain away his comments on *Access Hollywood* as "locker room talk." An accomplished businessman, an adult man of 70, a husband and father, a public figure, and a presidential candidate, has no business engaging in locker room talk. And in Trump's case, it was clear that this was more than locker room talk—he was talking about actual things he had done.

But Trump *does* engage in locker room talk—all the time. Locker room talk permeates a significant amount of Trump's conversations in general. Story after story details Trump's constant and unabashed lewd references to women.

A Trump Denial Style

Former *People* magazine reporter Natasha Stoynoff was one of the 19 women who came forth during the 2016 presidential campaign accusing Trump of sexual improprieties. In December 2005, she interviewed Donald and Melania at Mar-a-Lago on their first wedding anniversary. During a break, Trump offered to show Stoynoff around the mansion. She tells of how Trump closed a door behind them, pushed her against a wall, and forced his tongue down her throat.

Although Trump denies Stoynoff's accusations, six people provided evidence of the validity of her story. Trump attacked Stoynoff, saying, "Take a look. Look at her. Look at her words. You tell me what you think. I don't think so."[260] A not-so-veiled reference that Trump would not be interested in Stoynoff because she wasn't attractive. A disgusting remark.

The denial is particularly interesting to me because Trump uses a sexist statement to defend himself against charges of sexual harassment. You can't make this stuff up.

Jessica Leeds accused Trump of groping her when he was seated next to her on an airplane in the 1980s. She professed he grabbed her breasts and attempted to put his hand up her dress. They did not know each other before that day. Again Trump made a sexist remark to defend himself. This at a rally in North Carolina when he dismissed her allegations, "Believe me, she would not be my first choice, that I can tell you"[261] Jessica Leeds was 74 at the time of Trump's statement.

Trump defends himself from accusations of sexual improprieties by claiming the accusing women were not attractive. Does that mean he gropes only attractive women?

Trump Backstage at Miss USA and Miss Teen USA Pageants

Samantha Holvey, the then-20-year-old 2006 Miss North Carolina, told CNN that during a pageant event, Trump inspected each of the contestants. It was "the dirtiest I felt in my entire life," she recalled. "He would step in front of each girl and look you over from head to toe like we were just meat, we were just sexual objects, that we were not people. You know when a gross guy at the bar is checking you out? It's that feeling." She also stated that she remembered private parties where the contestants mingled with "old, rich drunk guys ogling all over us."[262]

Miss California USA Carrie Prejean was 21 when she participated in the Miss USA pageant. In her memoir, *Still Standing*, she describes how Trump evaluated the women at rehearsal. "We were told to put on our opening number outfits—they were nearly as revealing as our swimsuits—and line up for him onstage. Donald Trump walked out with his entourage and inspected us closer than any general ever inspected a platoon. He would stop in front of a girl, look her up and down, and say, 'Hmmm.' Then he would go on and do the same thing to the next girl. He took notes on a little pad as he went along. After he did this, Trump said: 'O.K. I want all the girls to come forward.' It became clear that the point of the whole exercise was for him to divide the room between girls he personally found attractive and those he did not. Many of the girls found the exercise humiliating."[263]

"I'll tell you the funniest is that I'll go backstage before a show and everyone's getting dressed," Trump said, speaking about the Miss USA pageant. "No men are anywhere, and I'm allowed to go in, because I'm the owner of the pageant and therefore I'm inspecting it . . . . 'Is everyone OK?' You know, they're standing there with no clothes. 'Is everybody OK?' And you see these incredible looking women, and so I sort of get away with things like that."[264]

One former contestant, Tasha Dixon, who was Miss Arizona, spoke to the CBS station in Los Angeles about the 2001 pageant. "He just came strolling right in. There was no second to put a robe on or any sort of clothing or anything. Some girls were topless. Other girls were naked."[265] Dixon also claimed contestants were directed by pageant officials to go up to Trump even though they weren't dressed. Dixon said women, would "have the pressure of the people that worked for him telling us to go fawn all over him, go walk up to him, talk to him, get his attention."[266]

Four Miss Teen USA contestants claimed Trump did the same at their pageants. "I remember putting on my dress really quick because I was like, 'Oh my God, there's a man in here,'" alleged former Miss Vermont Teen USA Mariah Billado. She added Trump responded with something like, "Don't worry, ladies, I've seen it all before.'"[267]

Miss Teen USA contestants must be between the ages of 14 to 19. Donald Trump leered at partially clothed teenagers. This lecher is a very sick man.

More Lechery

A 1992 *Entertainment Tonight* tape reveals Trump's comments to a girl in a group of girls at the bottom of an escalator in Trump Tower. "Are you going up the escalator?" Trump is heard saying to one of the girls. When the girl responds yes Trump declares to the camera, "I'll be dating her in 10 years. Can you believe it?" The video is on YouTube and the *TMZ* website. When I watched the video, I was struck by the how young the child's voice sounded. (Some sources report that the girl was 10 years old although other sources say that could not be confirmed). [268]

The 1996 Miss Universe

Miss Universe 1996, Alicia Machado, has recounted that after she gained weight, Donald Trump called her "Miss Piggy," "Miss Housecleaning," (a reference to her Latina heritage) and an eating machine. When Hillary Clinton mentioned Ms. Machado in the first presidential debate, Trump went on the offensive. In a series of tweets, he called Machado "disgusting" and a "con."[269] He urged his Twitter followers to look into a Machado sex tape (which doesn't exist).

Others

Here are some of the other women who have accused Trump of sexual misconduct as reported by CBS News:[270]

- Melinda McGillivray, "told the *Palm Beach Post* she was standing with a group of people after a Ray Charles concert when Donald Trump came up behind her and grabbed her buttocks."

- "The *Washington Post* reported on October 14, 2016, that back in the early 1990s, when Kristin Anderson was an aspiring model, Trump put his hand up her skirt at a Manhattan nightclub. According to Anderson, she had never met Trump before."

- "Rachel Crooks said she was 'inappropriately' kissed by Trump in 2005 when she was a 22-year-old receptionist working in Trump Tower in New York City. 'It felt like a violation,' Crooks said."

- "Karena Virginia, a yoga instructor and life coach, said she encountered Trump after the U.S. Open in Queens, New York in 1998 while waiting for a car. She overheard Trump discussing her legs then [sic] he walked up to her, grabbed her arm and touched her breast. When she flinched, Trump responded by demanding, 'Don't you know who I am? Don't you know who I am?' 'I felt intimidated, and I felt powerless,' Virginia said. 'I felt ashamed that I was wearing a short dress and high heels.'"[271]

In addition the following woman have also accused Trump of sexual misconduct: adult film actress Jessica Drake, 2006 Miss Finland Ninni

Laaksonen, 2007 *Apprentice* contestant Summer Zervos, 2013 Miss Washington USA Cassandra Searles, Bridget Sullivan, Miss Utah 2017 Temple Taggart McDowell, and makeup artist and businesswoman Jill Harth.

A Common Thread

In many, if not most, instances of Trump's inappropriate sexual conduct with women, there is a common thread: Trump's wealth and celebrity. He as much as admitted this on the *Access Hollywood* tape. "I'm automatically attracted to beautiful [women]—I just start kissing them. It's like a magnet. Just kiss. I don't even wait. And when you're a star they let you do it. You can do anything. . . . Grab them by the p----y. You can do anything."[272]

Many of the women who have accused Trump of sexual assault say he just started kissing them. He denies the charges. Many experts think that sexual harassment or assault is more a matter of power than sex. It appears that Trump's sexual conduct may be just that.

Remember When Trump Said Mexico Was Sending Us Rapists?

Here's the ~~whole~~ quotation: "When Mexico sends its people, they're not sending the best . . . They're bringing drugs. They're bringing crime. They're rapists and some, I assume, are good people."[273]

I didn't think of it right away, but I have a new take on this. Trump has been accused of unwanted sexual advances, groping, lewd sexual conduct, and sexual assault. Maybe Mexico should build a wall to keep *him* out of Mexico.

One More Thing

Not only is Donald Trump a vulgar person, but he also uses vulgar words. In addition to the offensive terminology Trump regularly uses, he uttered the following during the campaign: "mother---kers," "f--k," "bi--h," "schlong," and "pu--y." Real classy, Donald. Lewd words and references are as much a part of Trump's everyday conversation as "please" and "thank you" are a part of most peoples'.

You Think He's Innocent? You're Crazy.

This is for those of you who still deny the obvious. There are lots of stories and strong evidence to say you're wrong. But what if we consider only Trump's own words?

- He hired Roger Ailes for his campaign after Ailes was forced out by Fox News for multiple charges of sexual harassment.
- He supported Fox News' Bill O'Reilly after he was forced out for multiple charges of sexual harassment.
- He made inappropriate comments about his daughter.
- He admitted he went backstage at beauty pageants to leer at partially clothed contestants.
- He admitted to forcibly kissing women.
- He has often admitted to being a womanizer and serial adulterer (see the section, "A Womanizer and Adulterer—He Told You" earlier in this chapter).
- He admitted to forcibly grabbing women's genitals.
- He has called women dogs, slobs, pigs, dummies, disgusting animals, bimbos, and Miss Piggy.
- He has made crude, sexist remarks about various women's looks.
- He has demeaned the looks of a 74-year-old woman and an 81-year-old woman.
- He publicly criticized the feel of his first wife's breast implants.
- He uses vulgar language.

Now, if you still think he's innocent, you're crazy.

I Wonder

I wonder how many other women are out there with whom Trump has had a sexual encounter or ongoing intimate relationship, whether consensual, coerced, or otherwise. I suspect there are a lot.

Chapter 12
Trump the Bizarre

Look at this very strange December 2015 interview Trump had with Mika Brzezinski on MSNBC's *Morning Joe* as reported on realclearpolitics.com.[274] Brzezinski repeatedly asks Donald Trump what he would do to make American Muslims feel welcome in the United States. He has no answer, so he repeatedly makes believe he is answering the question while inexplicably talking about something else. Brzezinski continues to essentially say, "I'm not asking you that; I'm asking you this." But Trump insists on ignoring the question. Very bizarre—and very typical of Donald Trump. He does this a lot. Buckle up.

Brzezinski to Trump: What "Positive Message" Do You Have for Muslims to Feel Welcome in This Country?

BRZEZINSKI: So, Donald, I want to ask you about a topic that's really been in the headlines now for weeks and that's your temporary ban on Muslims coming into this country. Polls are showing that you're really striking a chord whether or not you agree with it or not. I'm asking you if you could right now speak to the Muslim-American population and tell them what you would do or say as president to make sure they feel that they are as much a part of this country as everyone else is.

TRUMP: Sure. I have many friends who are Muslim. They are great people. They're tremendous people. But there's something going on, I mean, whether you like it or not and I've seen various polls where 25 percent of the people would support and really, I mean, you look at some of the numbers, 25 percent of the people would support very, very substantial violence from within. That's not acceptable. Then somebody said, oh, it's not really 25 percent, it's only 10 percent or it's only 7 percent. Well one percent is not - because the kind of violence we're talking about is extraordinary violence.

BRZEZINSKI: But I'm asking what you would do or say to the Muslim-American population to make sure they still feel welcome in this country just as much as any other American. I'm not asking you about what it is that's going on or that something that's going on, or those -- whatever. I'm asking about the positive message that you have for Muslim-Americans who live in this country.

TRUMP: You can't ask that question without saying there's something going on and everybody knows it. And you know, when I first brought that up -- and I didn't do anything for polls. I assumed it would be bad for polls. I don't care about the polls from that standpoint. I'm doing what I think is right. It's a dialogue and it has to be discussed. And frankly my Muslims friends have said, you're right, we have to discuss it.

Look, when you had those two horrible people blow away in California 14 people and others are going to follow because they're very, very severely injured and sitting in hospitals in big, big trouble. When you had that -- There were numerous people that knew what was going on, Mika. Why weren't they reported? Why weren't these people reported? But there were numerous people. One thing I think that the Muslim population in this country has to do is they have to surveil their own people. When they see –

BRZEZINSKI: I don't understand why you keep going to the part of the story that you know has already touched and struck a chord with the primary voters. I'm asking about the Muslim-American population, the peaceful citizens of this country. What do you have to say to them –

(CROSSTALK)

TRUMP: I'm all for them. But when they see something going on -

BRZEZINSKI: -- about what would make them feel welcome in this country?

TRUMP: -- And that includes within the mosques because –

BRZEZINSKI: Because they are getting harassed.

TRUMP: Mika.

BRZEZINSKI: And they are getting pigeonholed because a lot of the comments that are being said, some of them from you, and I'm just wondering, is there a positive message that you have for peaceful Muslim-Americans?

TRUMP: Yes, it's a positive message, Mika, but we have a problem and the problem is a very severe problem and they have to help us to solve this problem. They have to help themselves because they are actually helping themselves. We do have a problem with radicalization within that community. They have to report it, they have to let us know about it and if they don't, it's just going to be a continuation.

They say there are many, many cells like you have with the two people, these two people that -- The one came in with the ridiculous visa program. All they had to do was check -- If they checked her Facebook account they would have seen that she was radicalized and wanted to do great harm to our country. But nobody even checked. Can you imagine hiring somebody if you ran a good business and not checking a Facebook account?

I thought this conversation was bizarre, but as I continued my research for this book, it started to all become clear. It's still bizarre but now it makes perfect sense. This is from an article about narcissism that appeared in *Psychology Today*, "This is why if they're [narcissists] asked a question that might oblige them to admit some vulnerability, deficiency, or culpability, they're apt to falsify the evidence. . . hastily change the subject or respond as though they'd been asked something entirely different."[275] That's what Trump did. He responded as though he was asked something entirely different. That's exactly what he did.

Chapter 13
Trump the Ad Hominem King

Ad hominem is an argument response that is a personal attack rather than a refutation of the substance of the opposing argument. It is considered a logical fallacy and is used to deceive. It tends to appeal to emotion and prejudice rather than reason and avoids and distracts from an honest discussion of the matter at hand. An ad hominem response is usually untrue, a distortion, irrelevant, and sometimes crude. Ad hominems are a preferred tool of bullies.

As described in the "Urban Dictionary, "Ad hominems are used by immature and/or unintelligent people because they are unable to counter their opponent using logic and intelligence."[276] And as author David Grace says, "When someone's arguments take the form of personal attacks and name-calling it's a pretty clear admission that they don't have anything valid or worthwhile to say. . . . By devolving into name-calling you've revealed the bankruptcy of your position." [277]

With all that in mind, here comes Donald Trump. He is an ad hominem machine. He is the "King of the Ad Hominem".

The title of an *Affinity Magazine* article captures Trump's tactics, "The Donald Trump Method: Belittling Opponents in Substitution for Argument and Credibility."[278]

Because he often doesn't have the knowledge or intellect to counter an argument, or because the argument against him is valid, Trump employs the disingenuous and easy response, opting for personal assaults. He loves the ad hominem because it is a tool of the bully (and as established earlier, Trump is a bully), and because it can often be very effective.

Trump acknowledged as much in a 2006 interview with Bill O'Reilly of Fox News regarding his feud with Rosie O'Donnell. When asked why he wouldn't use intellectual arguments instead of personal attacks in response to O'Donnell, Trump replied, "nobody would listen, and the response would not have been nearly as effective."[279] And then, as noted earlier, there is this from his book Trump: *The Art of the Deal*: "Sometimes, part of making a deal is denigrating your competition."

Ask Trump a question about Marco Rubio's criticism of one of his proposed policies, and he'll call Rubio a name. Confront Trump with a suggestion he might have done something unprincipled, and he'll say Hillary Clinton should be locked up. Question his assaults on freedom of the press, and he'll say that journalists are bad people who treat him unfairly. He has one answer to every question: someone else is bad. This easy approach masks Trump's incompetent and ignorance.

Trump will almost universally respond to any criticism of him with ad hominem. As president, he will govern by ad hominem. There are several types of ad hominem responses. These are the ones that Donald Trump practices the most.

- Poisoning the well – presenting "unrelated negative information about their opponent, with the goal of discrediting everything that their target says."

- Appeal to motive – "an argument that dismisses an idea by questioning the motives of the person who supports it."

- Appeal to hypocrisy – "an argument that attempts to discredit a person, by suggesting that their argument is inconsistent with their previous acts."[280]

Paul Graham is an author, essayist, philosopher, and computer scientist. He developed a "disagreement hierarchy" which categorizes seven levels (types) of disagreement. As described on *Wikipedia*[281] they are:

1. Refuting the Central Point: explicitly refutes the central point
2. Refutation: finds the mistake and explains why it is wrong . . .
3. Counterargument: contradicts and then backs it up with reasoning and/or supporting evidence
4. Contradiction: states the opposing case with little or no supporting evidence

5. Responding to Tone: criticizes the tone of the writing without addressing the substance of the argument
6. Ad Hominem: attacks the characteristics or authority of the writer without addressing the substance of the argument
7. Name-calling: sounds something like, "You are an idiot."[282]

Ad hominem arguments are described by Graham as the second lowest category of disagreement. It should be noted that the lowest category of disagreement, name-calling, is also a much-used tool of Donald Trump's life. No one name-calls like Donald Trump.

Chapter 14
Trump the Narcissist

Is Donald Trump a narcissist? I was torn about including this chapter in my book. But to me, Donald Trump's "mental health" is so clear and relevant an issue to any serious discussion of him, that I decided it would be disingenuous to exclude the topic. I may not be a psychiatrist and therefore may not be qualified to make a clinical diagnosis, so I won't. But I am qualified to have an opinion, so here's mine.

Is Donald Trump a narcissist? Is water wet? Donald Trump is a textbook narcissist. He is, in my judgment, the most definitive example of a narcissist in the public eye. His narcissism is always showing. Read over the characteristics of a narcissist. You can't help but say, "Yep, that's Trump." If you read the characteristics alone without the introductory reference to narcissism, you'd think it was a recounting of Donald Trump traits.

---

narcissist[283]

[nahr·suh·sist] *noun*

1. one who has an excessive preoccupation with, or admiration of oneself.
2. someone who always seems to turn the situation onto themselves, seemingly forgetting that others exist.
3. one who displays a pattern of abnormal behavior characterized by inflated feelings of self-importance, an extreme need for admiration.

Narcissists exaggerate accomplishments and talents. If one is narcissistic, he or she may come across as conceited, boastful, or pretentious. Narcissists have difficulty handling anything that may be perceived as criticism. To feel better, they may react with contempt and try to belittle the other person.

The above definition of a narcissist is compiled from various sources. I don't think any reasonable person can deny Donald Trump is a narcissist. The term and the definition fit him to a T.

From *The Atlantic*, "For psychologists, it is almost impossible to talk about Donald Trump without using the word narcissism. Asked to sum up Trump's personality for an article in *Vanity Fair*, Howard Gardner, a psychologist at Harvard, responded, 'Remarkably narcissistic.' George Simon, a clinical psychologist who conducts seminars on manipulative behavior, says Trump is 'so classic that I'm archiving video clips of him to use in workshops because there's no better example' of narcissism. 'Otherwise, I would have had to hire actors and write vignettes. He's like a dream come true.'"[284]

As Laura Entis reported in *Fortune* magazine, "A growing chorus of psychologists and mental health professionals are saying it: Donald Trump is a textbook narcissist. The chronic exaggerations, the need for constant acclamation, the outsized reactions to insults both real and perceived—the evidence is so abundant, they say, there's no question."[285]

Tell me of anybody else in the public arena who is more consumed with themselves than Donald Trump. There is no one.

Trump Loves Trump

Narcissism is the common denominator that explains most of Donald Trump's behavior. Trump's favorite subject is Trump. He loves praise and admiration. He loves it so much that he continually invites it or boasts himself. He constantly talks about how he's "great" or "the best." For a list of forty-eight examples of this, go back to the chapter "Trump the Braggart". Trump requires constant, excessive acclaim. The examples of narcissism in Trump's tweets, speeches, and interviews are countless. As described by Barbara Res, a long time Trump employee and organization Vice President, "I don't think it's possible to quantify the size of his ego. It's too big."[286]

Consider this declaration from Tony Schwartz, Donald Trump's co-author on *Trump: The Art of the Deal*. "Donald Trump's vanity was basically all I saw of him. He was about Donald Trump all the time. And his interest was in knowing how you felt about him and whether you recognized that the last thing he said he did was even greater than the previous thing he told you about."[287]

Trump's branding is an extension of his narcissism, although I must concede his narcissism (although I must concede that his branding has been very successful). Everything gets his name on it. The recently opened Trump International DC Hotel, Trump Tower, Trump Vodka, and Trump Steaks are just part of the long list of products that boast Trump's name. His Trump Tower is home to the Trump Grill, the Trump Café, the Trump Bar, and Trump's Ice Cream Parlor. Then there is the Trump Store, which offers a wide variety of Trump apparel and merchandise. There you can buy a pet bandana with Trump's name on it and a dog toy, also with the Trump name. I'm not kidding.

Feeding Trump's Narcissism

For Donald Trump, admiration and praise are his sustenance. It is food for his insatiable hunger. He is constantly searching for his narcissistic supply. For Trump it is a fulltime job that overshadows everything else. The normal amount of admiration and praise he might otherwise receive falls drastically short of the amount he craves. In response, he'll often resort to self-glorification, usually lying or embellishing his "achievements," and constantly inserting mention of them, sometimes awkwardly, in his proclamations.

Trump takes narcissism to a "huge" level. He repeatedly fabricates a story just so he can attach himself to it and then tell you how great it is. He'll say something like, "I got a call from a very prominent religious leader who said I am the greatest candidate the Republican party has ever nominated for president." He might even dare to identify the caller. But there was no call and no commendation—he made it up so he could then tell you about how great he is. That's stealing admiration.

Trump likes to steal admiration. He does so when he repeatedly lies about crowd sizes, when he continually tells you about things he has gotten "great credit" for, or when he directs or writes that his doctor found him to be in "quite extraordinary health."

Again, from *The Atlantic*, "Repeated and inordinate self-reference is a distinguishing feature of their [a narcissist's] personality. . . . The [his] fundamental life goal is to promote the greatness of the self, for all to see."[288] Trump will insert his own praise even if the opportunity doesn't exist. He'll create the opportunity.

Inserting his own acclaim has been on display at the most improper times: for example after the death of activist Phyllis Schlafly, at his father's wake and funeral, in his reaction to the killing of fifty people at the Pulse nightclub in Orlando, and in a speech on Martin Luther King's birthday. This is because his sympathy for Mrs. Schlafly, for his own father, and for those killed in Orlando is subordinate to his crusade for personal admiration which is all he cares about. To Trump, admiration is primary and everything else isn't even secondary.

Feeding Trump's Narcissism and Phyllis Schlafly

Donald J. Trump
@realDonaldTrump

The truly great Phyllis Schlafly, who honored me with her strong endorsement for president, has passed away at 92. She was very special!

7:00 PM · Sep 6, 2016

In the above tweet, Trump acknowledges the death of Mrs. Schlafly, but is unable to do so without noting that she had given him a strong endorsement. Now, Trump could have easily left out the phrase "who honored me with her strong endorsement." That is what most people would have done. They would have respected Mrs. Schlafly by focusing on her, not their own need for self-aggrandizement. Yet Trump is hardly capable of any conduct that is not self-serving, even in a condolence message. He has zero nobility of character.

Trump attempts to disguise his self-centered tweet by making it appear that his aim is to honor Mrs. Schlafly. But any condolence message is incidental. Trump exploited Mrs. Schlafly's death to brag. He is consumed with looking for opportunities to find or insert his own praise. That's what narcissists do.

In Trump's case, the narcissism is rabid. He could not even leave his self-absorption at "who honored me with her endorsement." Instead, he uses the phrase "strong endorsement" (not just an endorsement, but a "strong endorsement"). He seizes every opportunity.

In another tweet at the time of Mrs. Schafly's death, reproduced below, Trump's ego is again clearly at work. Once more he makes it appear his tweet is about Mrs. Schlafly when it is really about him.

Sounds to me like he's talking about a tribute to him, not "Philles" Schlafly.

Feeding Trump's Narcissism and the Pulse Nightclub

Here's Trump's tweet just hours after the shooting at an Orlando nightclub that left fifty dead. No sympathy for the victims, only self-acclaim for Trump.

Feeding Trump's Narcissism and Martin Luther King

When Donald Trump spoke to students at Liberty University on Martin Luther King's birthday in January 2016, he falsely claimed that the attendance at the event set a record. Jerry Falwell Jr., the university's president, had said Trump's speech was an opportunity "to recognize and honor Dr. King." But Trump didn't quite do that. In fact, the only time he mentioned Dr. King was during another feeding of his own narcissism: "It's an honor in terms of Martin Luther King... We're dedicating the record to the late, great Martin Luther King." That's a declaration by Trump about Trump and the "attendance record," it is not about Dr. King. He's the only person I know who could give a speech on Dr. King's birthday and virtually not mention Dr. King. If he had, it would have robbed him of the time he could speak about himself.[289]

Feeding Trump's Narcissism and Fred Trump

Even when grieving his father's death, Trump was more focused on himself than on his father. This from an article in *The New York Times*: "At Fred Trump's wake, at the Frank E. Campbell funeral home, his son [Donald] stepped forward to address the political, real estate and society power brokers in the crowd. One attendee recalled Mr. Trump's unorthodox ode to his father, which Mr. Trump confirmed. 'My father taught me everything I know. And he would understand what I'm about to say,' Mr. Trump announced to the room. 'I'm developing a great building on Riverside Boulevard called Trump Place. It's a wonderful project.'"[290]

At the funeral, Donald's remarks were again not about Fred Trump, but about Donald: "It was the toughest day of his own life, Trump began. He went on to talk about Fred Trump's greatest achievement: raising a brilliant and renowned son."[291]

From Gwenda Blair's book, *The Trumps*, "It was ironic he said, that he had learned of his father's death just after he'd finished reading a story in *The New York Times* acknowledging the success of his biggest development, Trump Place."

"At his own father's funeral, he did not stop patting himself on the back and promoting himself. The first-person singular pronouns, the I and me and my, eclipsed the he and his. Where others spoke of their memories of Fred Trump, [Donald] spoke of Fred Trump's endorsement."[292]

Response to Criticism: Counterpuncher or Narcissist?

This from Spiegel Online, a popular German-language news website: narcissistic people "are so hypersensitive to criticism that everyone who withholds admiration is seen as an enemy."[293]

To Trump, if you criticize him in the slightest, if you simply don't commend him, or if you simply do or say something he doesn't like, you are worthy of his wrath. If you don't commend him, you have challenged his greatness and injured him. If your actions or comments about Trump are not perfectly flattering, he sees them as disparaging. If you disagree with him, malign him, or do something he doesn't like, he goes after you with contempt. He calls it counterpunching, but it's much more than that. It's his ego at work.

If your newspaper criticizes him, he calls it a "failing" newspaper. If your television news program criticizes him, he claims it of has low ratings. He'll do so even if the newspaper is successful and even if the television programs ratings are good. The facts don't matter. If he is the object of a joke on a television show, he says the show isn't funny. If a judge rules against him in a legal matter, he questions the judge's objectivity and/or competence. He'll do se even if the show is funny and even if the judge is objective and competent. It doesn't matter. If you say a building is taller than his, he takes you to court. If you state his net worth is less than what he claims, he sues you. If your poll doesn't favor him, he says it was rigged. If he loses the popular vote in the presidential election, he says there was voter fraud.

If Trump goes after you, his animus could last a lifetime. Narcissists often hold a grudge for a long time. So does Donald Trump.

Trump can concoct an accusation without a thread of truth like no other. Concoct is exactly what he does. He thinks to himself, what can I accuse him (or her) of. Hmmm, I got an idea. I'll say…. He'll devise, create, fabricate, and invent and do so with a bit of believability. If you are smart, he will accuse you of being ignorant, if you had thousands of people at your rally, he will say there were only hundreds. Donald Trump could rob a bank and then tweet that the teller was a thief.

Trump will often hear criticism that is not there. He perceives a tough question or even a difference of opinion as unfair, seeing it as a threat. He can't appreciate that someone else may simply think or feel differently from him.

Trump sees others' behavior that is not in his interest as negative and an assault on him. That's why he's always concerned with being "treated fairly". His idea of being fair is distorted. To Trump, fair treatment means never doing or saying anything that doesn't compliment or promote him. Here are his responses to four of many instances when he thought he was being treated unfairly, as described in more detail elsewhere in this book:

- Trump's lawsuit against *TrumpNation* author Timothy O'Brien and the book's publisher for allegedly understating his net worth (Trump lost the suit)

- Trump's lawsuit against the *Chicago Tribune* because a writer for the paper had expressed doubt that Trump would be successful with his plans to build a tower in New York that would be taller than the Sears Tower (Trump lost the suit)

- Trump's pledged revenge on five people whose institutions had refused to lend him money in the 1980s when his empire was struggling (Five instances of people simply doing their job, but Trump saw it differently)

- Trump's vengeance against Megyn Kelly for asking a tough question at the first Republican debate

If a U.S. mayor were to question Trump's plan to build a wall, Trump would go after the official. He (or she) is a loser. He's the worst mayor in America. He does a horrible job. His city is a disaster. It's disgraceful. And it often doesn't stop there. Trump's barrage can continue for months and years.

Now, if the same mayor were to support Trump and his wall, Trump will say that he's always admired him. He's one of the best mayors in the country. Very intelligent. He's an outstanding individual, a good guy. Trump is never guided by honesty, only self-interest and ego.

The following quote is from Trump in October 1993, "Lowell Weicker, whom I have great respect for, fought and fought and fought and was bludgeoned into accepting this" Then two months later, Weicker had some harsh criticism of Trump and he shot back calling Weicker, "A fat slob who couldn't get elected dogcatcher in Connecticut."[294]

Lying and the Narcissist

Narcissists lie to enhance their accomplishments in the eyes of others. They need so much acclaim that honesty would not serve them well; it would be insufficient. For the narcissist, the truth just doesn't work.

Many people wonder why Trump lies when it is apparent he is lying. It's simply that his need for narcissistic supply is far superior to any allegiance to the truth. Anthony Senecal was Trump's long-time butler at his Mar-a-Lago estate. Trump would regularly tell people that the tiles in his children's suite were painted by Walt Disney. One time when Mr. Senecal, pointed out it wasn't true, Mr. Trump replied: "Who cares?"[295]

According to the website Narcissist Abuse Support, "They [narcissists] often repeatedly tell the ultimate lie, that they "love" their targets."[296] Donald Trump does this all the time. I mean all the time.

Relationship with Others

"Their [narcissist's] relationships are often based on whether others are useful to them or make them look good. It's not unusual for them to drop someone once he or she is no longer needed to forward their personal agenda. Because they need to be in control to feel safe, people with NPD [Narcissistic Personality Disorder] manipulate partners, coworkers and those who think they are friends through cycles of approval and rejection."[297]

Since narcissists need a constant food supply for their ego, they surround themselves with people who are willing to cater to their obsessive craving for affirmation. These relationships are usually one-sided. It's all about what the admirer can do for the narcissist, never the other way around. And if there is ever an interruption or diminishment in the admirer's attention and commendation, the narcissist treats it as a betrayal.[298]

Trump insists on unbounded loyalty to him no matter how much it compromises the integrity of the individual being loyal. He expects unquestioning compliance with his expectations. Trump has no problem lying, and he expects others to also lie to support him. He'll say anything, make up anything, to get his payback; it doesn't matter whom he maligns. What Trump sees as loyalty, is not. It is his narcissism.

The narcissist does not experience empathy. Almost universally all the literature on the subject notes this deficit. They can't step outside their needs, and as a result they are oblivious to the feelings of others. Empathy would conflict with the narcissist's primary focus, himself. This explains Trump's lack of support for charities, his insults of woman, and his crude retorts to criticism. One is hard pressed to think of times Donald Trump has shown sympathy for anyone or any group facing disturbance, hardship, suffering or grief (unless his standing is tied to that individual or group). Narcissists are also rarely apologetic or remorseful. To apologize would be to, on some level, admit fault and that would detract from the greatness of Donald Trump. From the lips of Donald Trump, "I will absolutely apologize sometime in the hopefully distant future if I'm ever wrong." [299]

What Next?

The presidency will not curb Donald Trump's narcissism, it will only give him new opportunities to exercise it. It will not be sufficient to be the most powerful person in the world, he will need more. The best president ever, a Nobel Peace Prize winner, a Pulitzer Prize, renaming Washington DC to Trump D.C., and king will be among Trump's next pursuits.

The fundamental life goal [of narcissists] is to promote the greatness of the self, for all to see. - Dan P. McAdams[300]

Chapter 15
Trump the Terrible

Donald Trump is, in my opinion, so flawed that it is hard to find enough categories to group his failings. So in this chapter, I clustered some assorted but revealing shortcomings.

<u>No Soul</u>

In a 2016 interview with MSNBC, Tony Schwartz, ghostwriter of Trump's book *The Art of the Deal*, said this of Trump. "There's no there, there, there's no heart, there's no soul."[301] He told the *New Yorker* magazine that he believes "if Trump wins and gets the nuclear codes there is an excellent possibility it will lead to the end of civilization."[302] Very strong words.

Khizr Khan, the father of a Muslim US soldier Army Captain Humayun Khan, who was killed in Iraq, also spoke about Trump's soul, saying on CNN, "He is a black soul, and he is totally unfit for the leadership of this country." He added that Trump was "A candidate without a moral compass, without empathy for its citizens."[303]

Writer Mark Singer asserted in a story in the *New Yorker* that Trump had achieved something quite extraordinary: "an existence unmolested by the rumbling of a soul."[304]

In an April 4, 2016 Hrafnkell Haraldsson column on Politcususa.com, former adviser to President Barack Obama and CNN Senior Political Commentator David Axelrod wrote, "It was obvious from the first words out of his mouth that Trump's soul was ugly."[305] Others have made similar assessments.

Political critiques usually focus on matters such as flip-flopping, failure to vote for a particular piece of legislation, and so on. It's telling that in addition to these more standard concerns, a common criticism of Donald Trump concerns his soul—or lack thereof.

Curious

Where are all the critics who condemned Barack Obama for some of his past associations? Trump has praised Vladimir Putin saying "I think in terms of leadership, he's getting an A"[306] and North Korean dictator Kim Jong-un saying "He goes in, he takes over, he's the boss. It's incredible."[307] Speaking about Saddam Hussein and Muammar Gaddafi, Trump has said, "They had one thing in common, and one thing that they were really, really good at. Number one, they were not politically correct. Do we all agree? They were great at killing terrorists. They were great."[308]

Trump tweeted a quotation by Benito Mussolini: "It is better to live one day as a lion than 100 years as a sheep."[309] He is also reported to have read from time to time *My New Order*, a book of Hitler's speeches, which he kept by his bed. It seems Trump has never met an autocrat he doesn't like.

Trump's interest in these despotic figures does not mean he endorses their efforts, or that he is like them. But it does imply he admires something about them, and that is creepy in itself. Trump seems to be enamored with tough, strong, ruthless, brutal, even murderous leaders. As president, does he hope to emulate any of their characteristics? Wouldn't you feel better if he had praised Malala Yousafzai, former NYC police detective Steven McDonald, or Oskar Schindler; or if he had quoted Mahatma Gandhi; or if he had read a book about the life of Martin Luther King Jr.?

Trump's ego will drive him to autocratic aspirations. His assault on the free press is an early step in that direction as such attacks are part of the autocrat's playbook.

The World Is Watching

During the 2016 presidential campaign, more than 50 officials from countries throughout the world disparaged Donald Trump, his statements, or his candidacy. These countries include, among others, France, Denmark, Australia, Sweden, South Korea, Italy, Mexico, Germany, Spain, Turkey, Albania, Ireland, Dubai, Pakistan, Saudi Arabia, Ecuador, China, Northern Ireland and England.

Some of the comments various international officials have used in reference to Trump include: "stupid," "disaster," "divisive," "stokes hatred," "shocking," "disgusting," "vulture," "crazy guy," "amoral," "shame of our civilization," "buffoon," "unacceptable," "the orange prince of American self-publicity," "idiot", "absurd," "illogical," "idiot," "scary," "ignorant," "wrong," "disgrace," and "dumb."[310]

But Tell Us How You Really Feel

David Brooks is an American conservative political and cultural commentator. In a March 2016 column in the *New York Times*, he offered probably the election season's most severe—and, in my opinion, accurate—assessment of Donald Trump. Here are some excerpts:[311]

> Donald Trump is epically unprepared to be president. He has no realistic policies, no advisers, no capacity to learn. His vast ego doesn't know, and he's uninterested in finding out. He insults the office Abraham Lincoln once occupied by running for it with less preparation than most of us would undertake to buy a sofa.

> Trump is perhaps the most dishonest person to run for high office in our lifetimes. All politicians stretch the truth, but Trump has a steady obliviousness to accuracy.

> He is a childish man running for a job that requires maturity. He is an insecure boasting little boy whose desires were somehow arrested at age 12. He surrounds himself with sycophants. "You can always tell when the king is here," Trump's butler told Jason Horowitz in a recent *Times* profile. He brags incessantly about his alleged prowess, like how far he can hit a golf ball. "Do I hit it long? Is Trump strong?" he asks.

> . . .

> Donald Trump is an affront to basic standards of honesty, virtue, and citizenship. He pollutes the atmosphere in which our children are raised. He has already shredded the unspoken rules of political civility that make conversation possible. In his savage regime, public life is just a dog-eat-dog war of all against all.

As the founders would have understood, he is a threat to the long and glorious experiment of American self-government. He is precisely the kind of scapegoating, promise-making, fear-driving and deceiving demagogue they feared. [312]

Trump Family Values

This declaration on parenting is from Donald Trump in a 2005 CNN interview:

- Now I know Melania, I'm not going to be doing the diapers, I'm not gonna be making the food, I may never even see the kids. [313]

These are comments made by Trump in various interviews from 2005 to 2007 and reported on the website *BuzzFeedNews*:

- No, I don't do that [Trump responded when asked if he changed diapers]. There's [sic] a lot of women out there that demand that the husband act like the wife and you know there's a lot of husbands that listen to that . . . I'm really like a great father but certain things you do and certain things you don't. It's just not for me.

- I mean, I won't do anything to take care of them. I'll supply funds and she'll take care of the kids. It's not like I'm gonna be walking the kids down Central Park.

- [Marla would say] I can't believe you're not walking Tiffany down the street. . . Right, I'm gonna be walking down Fifth Avenue with a baby in a carriage. It just didn't work.

- She [Melania] would take great care of the child without me having to do very much.

- When asked if he stays home with his infant son Barron, Trump admitted that hands-on parenting has never been his "thing." [He added], "It probably should, but it never has." [314]

Trump's relationship with his children was described by his first wife, Ivana, "He would love them, but he did not know how to speak to them in the children's way of thinking," she said on the *Wendy Williams Show*, "He was able to speak to them only when they came from university, when eventually he was able to speak business to them. Otherwise, he really did not know how to handle the kids."[315] This dynamic was apparently present in Trump's children also, "The children didn't know how to relate to him, either," Ivana wrote in her book.[316]

According to a *New York Times* report, "Apparently, the telephone is the paternal umbilical cord when growing up Trump. In interviews and digital campaign ads, Ivanka, Don Jr., and Tiffany describe how engaged and loving their powerful, busy father was by saying he always accepted their calls at the office." Big deal.

The report continues: "Some observers have a less benign view of Mr. Trump's rapport with his children. 'I can say with real confidence that he spent virtually no time with them when they were young,'" said Tony Schwartz, who shadowed the real estate developer for 18 months to ghostwrite Mr. Trump's 1987 best seller, *Trump: The Art of The Deal.* Mr. Schwartz said in a recent article in the *New Yorker* that he now regrets the book and his role in promoting Mr. Trump.

"On the rare times Ivana brought one or two of the children to his office, he couldn't have been less interested," Mr. Schwartz said."[317]

Trump Family Values: Where's Donald?

Donald Trump and his second wife, Marla Maples, had a child, Tiffany. Marla and Donald were separated (and later divorced) four years later. Maples and her daughter appear to have a very close, and loving relationship. Donald helped with some expenses for Tiffany's upbringing but was basically an absentee father and Marla was in effect a single parent. As Maples said in 2011, "I have been the one in her life, but I am grateful that her dad gave me the most wonderful child. I know he will help me cover the cost of college because he is a great provider in terms of education. If Tiffany were to call him, I know he would talk to her, because he loves his children."[318]

The statement "If Tiffany were to call him, I know he would talk to her…" is particularly telling and sad. Many of Tiffany's, Marla's and Trump's statements about Tiffany and her father are similar to this in that they seem to be faint praise.

This from an article in *People* magazine: "Her daddy is a good provider with education and such, but as far as time, it was just me," Maples, then 52, recalls raising Tiffany largely on her own. "Her father wasn't able to be there with day-to-day skills as a parent. He loves his kids. There's no doubt. But everything was a bit of a negotiation."[319] More faint praise. Nothing regarding his daughter should have been a negotiation.

Growing up, Tiffany did not see her father on a very much. As noted in an article in the UK's *Daily Mail,* "Tiffany saw her father just a couple of weeks a year after her parents divorced when she was five. She moved to California with Maples, while Trump continued to work in New York. Her only interaction with the Trumps would come during an annual two-week stay at her father's Mar-a-Lago estate in Florida. Her isolation may have started because of the nature of her parents' relationship."[320] It should be noted that there are other reports of more frequent trips to visit her father in New York.

Trump Family Values: How's Steve Trump Sound?

As reported in *GQ* magazine, "According to his first wife, Ivana, Donald Trump was never keen on bequeathing his name to anybody. It was Ivana who wanted to call their newborn Donald Junior. 'You can't do that!' Trump is quoted as saying in Ivana's memoir, *Raising Trump.* 'What if he's a loser?'"[321]

Donald Trump has never been a fan of hunting, but Don Jr. is an avid hunter. This also from *GQ,* "Only when he began campaigning for the White House did Donald Trump see some value in his son's bloody pastime. According to Sam Nunberg, a Trump adviser at the time, when an invitation arrived from the governor of Iowa to go hunting ahead of the state's crucial caucuses, Trump joked, 'Don, you can finally do something for me—you can go hunting.'"[322]

Malice Toward All—Mixing Deceit, Greed, Insolence, and Bigotry

In all his encounters, Trump looks to force his way. He does it in business, in personal behavior, and in politics. He wants to establish and exert his will and might. Armed with deceit, greed, cruelty, impudence, and a cold heart, Trump is driven to fight—and is consumed with winning every fight. If it is favorable to Trump, he wants it and will go after it, the righteousness of his cause be damned.

Consider this matter. The Mashantucket Pequot Indian tribe runs the Foxwoods Resort Casino in Connecticut. In 1993, Trump testified before the House Native American Affairs Subcommittee in Washington, D.C. The hearing was called to learn more about how Native American casinos are policed and regulated. Foxwoods was competing with Trump's Atlantic City casinos, and at the time, Trump was said to be considering developing a casino in Bridgeport, Connecticut. These are some of Trump's comments to the committee:

> It will be the biggest scandal ever or one the biggest since Al Capone in terms of organized crime . . . An Indian chief is going to tell Joey Killer to please get off his reservation? Is almost unbelievable to me.

> . . .

> Nobody is more for the Indians than Donald Trump. . . . There is no way Indians are going to protect themselves from the mob . . . This is gonna blow.

> . . .

> They don't look like Indians to me and they don't look like Indians to Indians.

> I think I might have more Indian blood than a lot of the so-called Indians that are trying to open up the reservations.[323]

Here is another comment Trump made on the subject:

> After the hearing, he was asked to explain what an Indian looked like. Trump's response: "You know. You know."[324]

And this as reported in *The New York Times*:

> "Most people think casino gambling will be what alcohol was to the Indians of past generations"[325]

This is typical of Trump. There was no basis for any of these proclamations. They were driven by self-interest. Trump's arguments were fabricated, plucked from thin air. With a straight face, he'll say almost anything to advance his interests. He is unencumbered by a conscience.

"They don't look like Indians to me." It's hard to imagine a more ignorant, bigoted, insulting, self-serving declaration. But Trump doesn't care—his overriding guiding principle is to do whatever's good for Trump. Trump exists in a world that assumes reason and fairness, and then he dares to violate all its rules, truth be discarded.

Inspiration

On Leadership:

> Barack Obama: "We are a nation that at its best has been defined by hope not fear."[326]

> Donald Trump: "How stupid is our country?"[327]

On Life:

> Ronald Reagan: "Live simply, love generously, care deeply, speak kindly, leave the rest to God."[328]

> Donald Trump: "If someone screws you, screw them back. When somebody hurts you, just go after them as viciously and as violently as you can."[329]

On Women:

> Barack Obama "We must carry forward the work of the women who came before us and ensure our daughters have no limits on their dreams, no obstacle to their achievements and no remaining ceilings to shatter."[330]

> Donald Trump: "You have to treat em like s--t."[331]

On Government Service:

> John McCain: "Every day, people serve their neighbors and our nation in many different ways, from helping a child learn and easing the loneliness of those without a family to defending our freedom overseas. It is in this spirit of dedication to others and to our country that I believe service should be broadly and deeply encouraged." [332]

> Donald Trump: "If you can't get rich dealing with politicians, there's something wrong with you."[333]

Trump the Disgraceful

What type of human being would demean John McCain's outstanding, noble military service?

Imagine this. Imagine it is the middle of a hotly contested political battle during the presidential campaign. Imagine that one candidate says this about another candidate: "He's not a war hero. He was a war hero because he was captured. I like people who weren't captured."[334] Imagine that the quotation is about John McCain. Now imagine if the quotation had been from 2008 and spoken by Barack Obama. I think Trump supporters who today overlook these comments by Trump, would have relentlessly condemned Mr. Obama. I think they would have gone so far as to demand his withdrawal from the presidential contest.

I previously described the hypocrisy of Donald Trump's statements regarding John McCain's military service. Here I revisit that topic in a slightly different context. What follows is a comparison of John McCain and Donald Trump regarding military service (from *Wikipedia*, "John McCain,").[335]

- John McCain served his nation in the military for 23 years, from 1958 to 1981. His father, paternal grandfather, and two of his sons have also served in the military.

   Neither Donald Trump nor anybody in his family has served in the American military.

- McCain's combat duty began in 1967 when he was assigned to the USS *Forrestal*. In October 1967, McCain was flying a "bombing mission over Hanoi in North Vietnam when his A-4E Skyhawk was shot down by a missile. McCain fractured both arms and a leg when he ejected from the aircraft, and nearly drowned after he parachuted into Trúc Bạch Lake. Some North Vietnamese pulled him ashore; then others crushed his shoulder with a rifle butt.

   "Although McCain was seriously wounded and injured, his captors refused to treat him. They beat and interrogated him to get information, and he was given medical care only when the North Vietnamese discovered that his father was a high-ranking admiral. . . . McCain was placed into solitary confinement, where he would remain for two years.

   In 1968, "the North Vietnamese offered McCain early release because they wanted to appear merciful for propaganda purposes, and also to show other POWs that elite prisoners were willing to be treated preferentially." McCain refused the offer in accordance with the military Code of Conduct; he would accept repatriation only if the men captured before him were released as well.

   "In August 1968, a program of severe torture began on McCain. He was subjected to rope bindings and repeated beatings every two hours, at the same time as he was suffering from dysentery." Subsequently, he received regular beatings two to three times per week.

McCain was a prisoner of war in North Vietnam for five and a half years, until his release on March 14, 1973.

> *Donald Trump was deferred from military service because of alleged boo-boo (bone spur) on his foot.*

- John McCain received 17 military awards, including the Silver Star, two Legion of Merits, the Distinguished Flying Cross, three Bronze Stars, two Purple Hearts, and two Navy Commendation Medals.

McCain gave his heart, soul, and very nearly his life for his country. For that, he deserves the thanks, admiration, appreciation, respect, and the love of a nation.

> *Donald Trump gave nothing in military service to this country. He said that McCain "is a war hero because he was captured. I like people who weren't captured."[336] As I said to introduce this section, "What type of human being would demean John McCain's outstanding, noble military service?"*

Trump's 9/11 Sacrilege

Who would even think to exploit the tragedy of 9/11 for his own personal gain? It is clear to me that Donald Trump did. It makes me shudder to write that. Consider:

- A few hours after the planes crashed into the World Trade Center, Trump was interviewed on television station WWOR. He was asked if his building in the area at 40 Wall Street sustained any damage. Instead of answering that question, Trump used the opportunity to point out his building was now the tallest in downtown Manhattan: "40 Wall Street actually was the second-tallest building in downtown Manhattan, and it was actually before the World Trade Center the tallest, and and [sic] then when they built the World Trade Center it became known as the second-tallest, and now it's the tallest." Even the immense tragedy of 9/11 couldn't interfere with Trump's constant search to brag. Incidentally, Trump's building was not the second tallest downtown—70 Pine Street was.[337]

- Trump claimed he had workers at the World Trade Center helping the recovery effort. He stated, "I have hundreds of men inside working right now and we're bringing down another 125 in a little while." But there is no evidence of this. In fact, Trump's assertion was refuted by Richard Alles, a deputy chief with the New York City Fire Department at the time. It was also refuted by John Feal, who was at Ground Zero as a construction demolitions expert and is the founder of the 9/11 first responder health advocacy non-profit the FealGood Foundation.[338]

- During a Republican presidential debate, Trump proclaimed that he lost "hundreds of friends" at the World Trade Center. But when later asked to name any one of those friends, Trump didn't respond. His assertion would mean that of 2,606 killed in the World Trade Center, more than 100 were friends of Trump. Or to put it another way, of all Trump's friends, 100 of them were killed in the World Trade Center. No names, no evidence, just Trump's deceit to enhance his own personal story. He insults the memory of 9/11 victims to feed his ego.

  A Port Authority police officer who has worked to learn about each and every person that died in the World Trade Center, including those he knew personally, disputes Trump's contention: "If he has hundreds of friends, he should be able to tell us about them." The PA cop questioned, "why nobody has seen Trump at the September 11 Memorial and Museum" and why Trump was not seen at any of the funerals or memorials that followed the attack. "A sacrilege," the PA cop said. [339]

- After the Twin Towers attack, there was an outpouring of generosity. But not from Donald Trump. As reported by The Smoking Gun, "In the aftermath of the 2001 terror attack on the World Trade Center, Donald Trump, a billionaire son of New York City, did not make a single charitable donation to any of the not-for-profit groups that provided aid to survivors, rescue workers, or the families of cops and firemen who died trying to save others, Internal Revenue Service records show.

"While business moguls raced to write seven-figure checks and schoolchildren emptied their piggy banks, Trump's charitable foundation—the vehicle through which the Republican presidential candidate's philanthropy trickles—apparently did not feel the need or responsibility to offer such financial help."[340] Of course, Trump has claimed he made donations in support of 9/11 recovery.

Donald Trump insults the concept of decency.

The chart below compares Donald Trump's "generosity" to the generosity of others following 9-11. The first column below is from a report by the Foundation Center,[341] the second column is from my research.

Everyone Else	The Trump Foundation and Companies
1,271 donors, foundations and corporations, made gifts in response to the attack.	The Trump Foundation and Trump companies gave $0.
These 1,271 donors gave nearly $1.1 billion in more than 4,000 gifts for relief and recovery efforts.	The Trump Foundation and Trump companies gave $0.
301 of these donors contributed at least $1 million for relief and recovery.	The Trump Foundation and Trump companies gave $0.
The median amount of giving per donor was $100,000.	The Trump Foundation and Trump companies gave $0.

As of December, 2003

If you think about it, Donald Trump had no good reason to donate to 9/11 recovery. Why should he when the only person he cares about is himself?

Trump's and Hurricane Katrina

While we're at it. Trump is reported to have made no donations to provide relief to victims of Hurricane Katrina's in New Orleans. Doesn't surprise me in the least.

What About Leona

Leona Helmsley, with her husband Harry, headed a real estate empire that frequently competed with Donald Trump's real estate interests. Leona had a terrible reputation and was frequently called the "Queen of Mean." But even mean Leona Helmsley had a charitable streak. Far out distancing the giving of Trump, or maybe better said, the non-giving of Trump, she donated $5 million to the New York Police and Fire Widows' and Children's Benefit Fund after 9/11 and $5 million to the American Red Cross after Hurricane Katrina.[342]

Trump the Powerful

Trump is extremely powerful. He may be one of the most powerful people ever to emerge on the American scene. The first ingredient of his power is his unprecedented deceit. The mix of his economic and other resources with his deceit, depravity, and other personality traits, results in a unique and powerful man. The sheer force of his personality is unmatched.

Trump will promote almost any argument, no matter how contrary to reason and knowledge it may be, to advance his interests. What matters is what Trump wants. He creates an "alternative truth" that many people often accept as fact, while it is fiction. His impact is astonishing.

Shortly after the presidential election, Trump began his claim of voter fraud. It was unsubstantiated. Not only was there no evidence of voter fraud, but there *was* evidence to the contrary. That didn't matter. Trump kept pushing his lie. He figures the repetition of his claim, the confidence of his assertion, etc. will bolster his position. And he's right. When challenged on his claim, he reasserts it. If you confront him with evidence, he still clings to his position, putting doubt in your mind.

Most normal people back down when confronted with evidence that refutes (disproves, contradicts?) their assertions. When Trump doubles down on such assertions you might start to think that maybe his claims are credible. If he can stick to his guns in the face of contrary evidence, maybe he is right. Maybe he knows something I don't know. Maybe I need to reassess my position, particularly when those claims come from a successful businessman of some status

Most normal people back down when confronted with evidence that invalidates their assertions. Not Trump, he doubles down. When Trump doubles down on such assertions you might start to think, "Maybe his claims are credible. If he can stick to his guns in the face of contrary evidence, maybe he is right. Maybe he knows something I don't know. Maybe I need to reassess my position, particularly when those claims come from a successful businessman of some status."

It's a form of gaslighting which when a person employs a deceitful manipulation to get an individual or group to doubt their own perceptions. It employs denial, deceit and manipulation. And we all know Trump can deny, deceive and manipulate with the best of them. Consider this scary Orwellian type quote from the Trump: "What you're seeing and what you're reading is not what's happening."[343]

As a result of Trump's voter fraud claim, according to one poll, one in four Americans believed fraud did exist in the 2016 election.[344] How much Trump contributed to that number can only be speculated. In the early days of his administration, Trump indicated he would open an investigation into the voter fraud. This led people to think: "Wow, there must be some merit to the claims if they're opening up an investigation." He sees the same (lack of) evidence we all do, but he's still pursuing an investigation. Maybe he's right. And even if no investigation ever occurs, the damage has been done.

Trump does this all the time (see previous section, "Malice toward All—Mixing Deceit, Greed, Insolence, Bigotry, and a Cold Heart"). For a long time, Donald Trump was one of this country's leading birthers, those who claim Barack Obama was not born in the United States. In August 2012, he tweeted, "An 'extremely credible source' has called my office and told me that @BarackObama's birth certificate is a fraud."[345] He refused to name that source. If he had, his lie would have been exposed.

To bolster his birther claims, Trump professed that he had sent investigators to Hawaii to explore the matter. Then he enhanced his case again by asserting that the investigators couldn't believe what they were finding. Trump wants you to think that if he sent investigators, and if they were finding surprising stuff, the original claim must have credence. But the truth is that nothing was unearthed. Trump never released findings because there *were* no findings and no investigators.[346] But many people believed his claims, so he changed the perception for many. In December 2016, a poll revealed 36% of Americans thought Obama was or probably was born in Kenya.[347]

The ~~Art~~ Trick of the Deal

Donald Trump continually touts his great negotiation skills. I agree he has considerable skills in this area—in a way. It is perhaps more accurate to say he has highly *effective* negotiating skills. But I suggest that the reason for his effectiveness is that he uses tricky (yet simple) methods to negotiate. You gain a better understanding of Trump if you understand his negotiating tactics. Let's take a step back for a moment.

I think one aspect of Trump's statements regarding his negotiating prowess has been overlooked: that is, his insertion of negotiating success as a campaign issue. I can't remember negotiating skills ever being such a prominent campaign issue previously. Warranted or not, the tactic was unique, effective, and reveals something noteworthy about Trump.

To Trump, *everything* is a negotiation. Further, he views every negotiation as only win or lose. Fair and equitable never enter into the equation. If you hear, "I think we reached an agreement that is fair for all parties" from Donald Trump's he's lying.

When Trump enters into negotiations with a contractor, he presses hard for an agreement to his advantage. He might ask, "Can you drop the tax? or or give me a good price – I can throw a lot of other business your way." He pushes and pushes and coming from a position of power and using some somewhat legitimate negotiating techniques, he can often be very successful. But after an agreement is reached, he looks for an opportunity to reopen the negotiation. He doesn't honor the contract. Instead, he uses the agreed-upon arrangement as a starting point and negotiates from there. A negotiation bait and switch. Tricky.

Here's a simple illustration. A contractor wants to charge $75 for a service. Trump wants to pay $25. They agree on $50. But then Trump finds an excuse to reopen negotiations (he's good at that—remember all those times he refused to pay for "shoddy" work). Now he says, "You want to charge $50. I still feel it should be $25. Let's agree on $35."
A real-life example: in 2004, Donald Trump purchased chandeliers for his Mar-a-Lago estate from 82-year-old Nicolas Jacobsen's Classic Chandeliers (a more detailed description of this incident can be found in "Deadbeat Trump and the Chandeliers" in the chapter "Trump the Thief").

When the installation of the chandeliers was complete, Trump refused to pay the balance owed, with an excuse that Jacobsen did a terrible job. The case went to court and was finally settled in early 2007 with Jacobsen accepting a reduced payment of what he was owed. As Trump had intended all along, he wore down Mr. Jacobsen. Jacobsen could not afford, financially or otherwise, to continue with a lawsuit that seemed to have no end. So Trump was successful at cheating an 85-year-old small business owner. Trump will use this renegotiation technique frequently. It's his version of a bait and switch. That's the trick of the deal.

If you carry forward this business practice to Trump's political approach, some stances come into focus. Now we can understand why he wants to renegotiate NAFTA, China trade agreements, the Paris climate accord, the Iran agreement, our NATO commitments, and so on.

The ~~Art~~ Trick of the Donation

In 1990 the band Precious Metal was making to a video for their remake of the song, "Mr. Big Stuff." They approached Trump about staring in the video and he agreed to do so in return for a $10,000 donation to his favorite charity (the Trump Foundation, I assume, so the money could end up in his pocket). After shooting the video the band got a phone call. Mr. Trump had reconsidered and now he felt a donation of $10,000 was not a Trump kind of donation, $250,000 would be more in line. The trick of the deal even when pertaining to a "charitable donation." The band re-shot the video without Trump. Trump later said the video was horrible (of course).

Words

Donald Trump's vocabulary is very limited. The following words do not seem to be in his vocabulary: kindness, grace, humility, compassion, dignity, understanding, sympathy, tolerance, class. Literally, he almost speaks these words.

The Seven Deadly Sins

The seven deadly (cardinal) sins are pride, greed, lust, envy, gluttony, wrath (strong vengeful anger or indignation) and sloth (laziness). Personally, I don't think that Donald Trump is lazy.

Is it Simply that Donald Trump is Evil?

Here's the meaning of evil from an article in *Psychology Today:*

> "Evil" people are those who are unable to empathise [sic] with others. As a result, their own needs and desires are of paramount importance. They are selfish, self-absorbed and narcissistic. In fact, other people only have value for them to the extent that they can help them satisfy their own desires or be exploited. . . . They can't sense other people's emotions or their suffering, can't see the world from other people's perspective, and so have no sense of their rights. Other human beings are just objects to them, which is what makes their brutality and cruelty possible."[348]

So is Donald Trump evil by definition? You decide, I already have.

Chapter 16
Explaining Trump

To understand Trump, one must understand his personality. He will lie, cheat, deceive, debase, and coerce to get what's best for Trump and what feeds his oversized ego (and he expects others to do the same on his behalf). This is a challenging undertaking unless you are a man with absolutely no integrity.

Enter Donald Trump. Trump doesn't live in a world of right and wrong, fair or unfair, kind or unkind. Trump lives in a world of Trump. He doesn't care if something is right, true, or just. That simply isn't part of the equation. He has the ethics of a rock. He has absolutely no moral compass. I cannot emphasize that enough. Trump has no moral compass. (A similar paragraph appears in the introduction of this book. I thought it was important enough to repeat.)

> *"If ever the Time should come, when vain & aspiring Men shall possess the highest Seats in Government, our Country will stand in Need of its experienced Patriots to prevent its Ruin."*
>
> *– Samuel Adams*
> *October 24, 1780*

349

Donald Trump is not only morally unprepared to be president, he is also morally unprepared to work at 7-Eleven (my apologies to 7-Eleven workers, no disrespect intended.)

The Bottom Line

Donald Trump is consumed by his unbridled narcissism, he lives for commendation, and he overreacts to anything that is otherwise. This is the filter through which he sees the world. He has absolutely no control over his narcissism, it is the preeminent force in his life.

Trump rejects a foundation of moral conduct while claiming the moral high ground. Trump's cry to drain the swamp is acute hypocrisy. In the world of Donald Trump right and wrong is turned into me and them. Little else matters. I always thought right matters, but that tenet is eroding thanks to Donald Trump. He will try to turn right and wrong upside down; he constantly takes something that is good and attacks it for being bad, if that is in his interest (see Trump's attacks on John McCain's military service). His boundless raging self-interest is an extension of his raging narcissism. Donald Trump is a liar, but will accuse others of lying; he is a bigot, but will accuse others of bigotry; he is a hypocrite, but will accuse others of hypocrisy; he is crude, but will accuse others of crudeness.

Donald Trump is a small man who thrives and rejoices in attacking and demeaning others. He is a small man who finds joy in his vindictiveness. With his actions, public comments, and tweets, he will go after anybody who in any way doesn't promote Trump. He would even attack the pope. "Wait," you might say. "Come on. You can't mean that. That's just a figurative expression, right?" Nope. I mean it literally. Donald Trump would even attack the pope, and he has (see "What Did the Pope Say" in the chapter "Trump the Religious Charlatan.")

On one level, Donald Trump is easy to understand because he is somewhat one-dimensional. His conduct often seems bizarre and inexplicable. It *is* often bizarre—but it can always be explained. Virtually everything he says and does can be traced to his self-absorption. His narcissism dictates his actions. Once you acknowledge that, Trump's behavior is transparent, and everything falls into place.

Trump doesn't value kindness, compassion, or honesty, in fact, he sees them as weaknesses. His overriding value is *him*. Shockingly, Trump will put his need for admiration above his concern for country. *He doesn't have the ability to see past his own personal interest.* As per Laura Entis, "Narcissists always put their needs first at the expense of the collective good."[350] A very chilling proposition.

Pundits embark on a fool's errand when looking to explain a particular Trump behavior. They use a common apparatus to examine what he says and does, that is, the common sense used to examine behaviors in general. Doing so is a waste of time. The common apparatus assumes a degree of honesty that Trump does not possess. The common apparatus also assumes the absence of narcissism as extreme as Trump's. It's foolish to analyze Trump's behavior as if he were a normal, principled, decent human being. He's not.

I recall CNN political commentator David Axelrod putting it well when he scrutinized some Trump remarks, asking if they were impulse or strategy. He understands—well, kind of. That is the issue, but the answer with Trump is almost always impulse.

After Trump's inauguration, he went on a crusade to tell everybody that more people had attended the ceremony than had attended any other inauguration in history, an assertion easily proved false. As pundits asked why he would claim something so patently and provably false, a clear answer eluded them. The reason is his relentless narcissism, which fuels his deceit. His need to be admired for attracting the largest crowd was stronger than any other consideration.

Trump is determined to manipulate by exerting his resolve to get his way and he is not afraid to challenge truth. Trump thinks he is greater than the truth and at times he might be right. If perception is reality, Trump changes reality or at least distorts it. His impact is astounding. Will influence

The Bottom, Bottom Line

Trump's boundless narcissism rules. Because of it, he has no interest in others, in information on which to base decisions, in any advice that doesn't enhance him, or in anything that takes him away from his self-absorption for more than five minutes. Donald Trump rarely steps outside the world of his own self-interest.

As is common in a narcissist, Trump has no sympathy or concern for others. They just don't matter. For winning the 2005 season of *The Apprentice*, Randal Pinkett received a one-year apprenticeship with the Trump Organization. Pinkett says that during that time, he "learned not to take anything to Trump if he couldn't frame it in a way that would make it clear 'what's in it for Donald.'"[351]

Trump will ignore American values, tradition, the welfare of others, and even the interest of the country. He will be blind to the rule of law and care little about any rules of conduct.

He won't care about the American people. He can't, he's too busy caring about only one person, *everything else is of little or no concern.*

Because of his ego, a Trump presidency will be marked by recklessness. That's because he doesn't care about how his actions affect others, only how they affect him.

Because of his ego, he can be fooled and co-opted by our country's adversaries; all they have to do is merely compliment him, pretend to be his friend (see Vladimir Putin), or otherwise serve his ego. Narcissists are highly susceptible to flattery.

Because of his overriding unprincipled appeal to the passions and prejudices of others to further his own interests, Trump is a demagogue. Because of his position and power he is a very dangerous demagogue.

Sadly, Trump's personality and shameful approach to life is effective for him. Donald Trump is obviously not a sheepish politician. He is a truly unique man who as a politician employs a never-before-used approach with surprising success. He is rewriting the political playbook in his image. Trump's fearlessness and effectiveness, powered by his wealth, status, and personality, complete the picture. He has elevated character assassination to a level never seen before. It will only get worse as President. Donald Trump will take America on a chaotic ride that serves him first and foremost. Like it or not, we are in the land of Trump, a very scary place.

This is how former CIA Director Michael Morell saw it: "The character traits he has exhibited during the primary season suggest he would be a poor, even dangerous, commander in chief. These traits include his obvious need for self-aggrandizement, his overreaction to perceived slights, his tendency to make decisions based on intuition, his refusal to change his views based on new information, his routine carelessness with the facts, his unwillingness to listen to others, and his lack of respect for the rule of law.

"The dangers that flow from Mr. Trump's character are not just risks that would emerge if he became president. It is already damaging our national security."[352]

Donald Trump is a bizarre man riddled with deceit, hubris, depravity, sexual impropriety, malevolence, cruelty, and a severely impaired sense of morality. Novelist Phillip Roth put it well when he said Donald Trump is, "humanly impoverished" and "destitute of decency."[353]

Donald Trump has already redefined American politics. A Trump presidency will be an immoral presidency, marked by deceit and deception. Universal principles of integrity will vanish in a Trump White House. The word integrity is meaningless to Donald Trump, to him it is a weakness—a concept to be scoffed at. A Trump presidency will be a never-ending flow of lies, attacks, character assassination, self-praise, and self-interest. It will characterize virtually every decision he makes, and nothing else will matter to him or interest him. Additionally, his presidency will be marked by his lack of sympathy or empathy, a disregard for information regarding pertinent and important matters, and a constant attempt to renegotiate agreements. He will manipulate every situation to his personal advantage. Lastly, he will be effective in implementing much of his agenda.

Our country's president should embody the best in us, but Donald Trump represents the worst in us. I didn't think a man like Donald Trump and his evil was possible. Sadly, I was wrong.

Trump is very able to consistently force his will on others like no one else before. It is astonishing how effective he is at doing this. No target is too large or too powerful. He lives for the fight. And Trump will regularly prevail, even against overwhelming odds. And if he doesn't prevail, he'll tell you he did, and some will believe him. Trump is not afraid to try to bully the world. He will take on any political opponent, friends and supporters, either political party, any US state, any ethnic group, any media, any country or individual (friend or foe, popular or not popular), and do so with remarkably surprising success and joy. Don't bet against him.

This makes Donald Trump powerful. Coupling that with his narcissism and demagoguery makes him dangerous. Now put him in the White House and you have, in my opinion, a tragedy for America. He will have a tremendous effect on the country, greater than any president in the last fifty years. We are in for something unlike anything we have ever seen before. The freighting odyssey is about to begin.

Donald Trump will corrupt the American dialogue. He will serve himself, not the country. He will amaze with his absurdities. He will drag America into his world of deceit and hate. He will assault and defile American values. He will trample over decency. He will divide us like no one before.

America may never be the same.

Chapter 17
Colin

One man sings out loud when the national anthem is played. Another man silently kneels. The true patriot respects both.

During the 2016 NFL season, the San Francisco 49ers' Colin Kaepernick kneeled during the playing of the national anthem in protest of police brutality and racial inequality. I disagree with the way he chose to protest. I disagree with that action, but I respect it. I disagree with many of Colin Kaepernick's political positions. But that means we have a difference of opinion, nothing more. I respect Colin Kaepernick and I admire much of what he has done in his life. His kneeling received immense reaction both in support and critical of Kaepernick. The critical comments tended to brand Kaepernick as unpatriotic. Those comments were misguided.

I don't think Kaepernick is unpatriotic. His life and his story prove that. A fair analysis of the actions he took by kneeling during the playing of the national anthem does as well. Colin Kaepernick was abandoned by his father before birth and put up for adoption by his nineteen-year-old mother. He was adopted by Rick and Teresa Kaepernick. Colin attended John H. Pitman High School in Turlock, California where he was an excellent student and played football, basketball and baseball.

Kaepernick has been a loving and grateful son to his adoptive parents. Prior to his adoption, Colin's parents suffered the loss of two infant sons to congenital heart defects. Once he made it to the NFL, he chose to help children suffering from heart disease in honor of his parents and the brothers he never knew. The first check he received after being drafted was donated to Camp Taylor, an organization for children suffering from heart disease. Over the years, Colin has attended his time to camp sessions, fundraisers and has spent time with kids at the camp. One of the campers made Kaepernick a bracelet that he carries with him all of the time. He has raised over $1 million for the organization. Kaepernick related his "against all odds" motto to the plight of the program's young people.

Kaepernick has regularly donated shirts, hats, shoes, and books to men's shelters and orphanages. He has donated his old suits to recent parolees who are going on interviews and might not be able to afford suitable clothing.

Colin Kaepernick is a man of deep religious faith. He has said, "I think God guides me through every day and helps me take the right steps and has helped me to get to where I'm at. When I step on the field, I always say a prayer, say I am thankful to be able to wake up that morning and go out there and try to glorify the Lord with what I do on the field."[354]

Kaepernick has multiple tattoos. His right arm features a scroll with the Bible Verse Psalm 18:39. Tattooed under the scroll are praying hands with the phrase "To God The Glory" written on them. Another of his tattoos states, "God Will Guide Me."

"I want to have a positive influence as much as I can," Kaepernick told *Sports Illustrated* journalist Peter King in a 2013 interview. "I've had people write me because of my tattoos. I've had people write me because of adoption. I've had people write me because they're biracial. I've had people write me because their kids have heart defects — my mom had two boys who died of heart defects, which ultimately brought about my adoption. So, to me, the more people you can touch, the more people you can influence in a positive way or inspire, the better."[355]

After famously sitting during the playing of the national anthem, Kaepernick reached out to U.S. military veteran and Green Beret Nate Boyer, who very briefly played professional football. Boyer had previously written an open letter to Kaepernick (full text of the letter follows at the end of this chapter). After the two met, Kaepernick opted to kneel in subsequent games. He explained his decision to switch to kneeling was an attempt to show respect to U.S. military members while still taking a stand on something important to him.

Ironically years before he ever kneeled, Kaepernick had donated a football to one of Boyer's charities. The ball was actioned off for the charity and purchased by the high bidder, Boyer's father. The football, with the inscription "God Bless Our Troops," was signed by Kaepernick and his teammate Colt McCoy.

In his conversation with Boyer, Kaepernick explained, "I want you to know, first and foremost, I really do respect the heck out of the military, and I really want to thank you for your service. I just want you to know that."

Boyer shared with Kaepernick a message from a fellow Green Beret in which he expressed his rage over Kaepernick's actions. Kapernick asked Boyer, "How can I show respect to people like that, but still get my message across that I'm not satisfied with the way things are going in this country?"

Boyer told Kaepernick, "[Kneeling is] still definitely a symbol. People take a knee to pray. In the military, we take a knee all the time. It's one of the things we do. When we're exhausted on patrol, they say take a knee and face out. So we take a knee like that. We'll take a knee as the classic symbol of respect in front of a brother's grave site, a soldier on a knee." So an agreement of sorts was reached, Kaepernick would not sit during the anthem but would take a knee.

Kaepernick asked Boyer if he'd take a knee alongside him. "Look, I'll stand next to you. I gotta stand though. I gotta stand with my hand on my heart."[356] And he did.

Boyer, a man who looks to promote dialogue and understanding, and Colin Kaepernick decided to continue talking about the issue.

Kaepernick has repeatedly expressed his respect for and admiration of our military. "I realize that men and women of the military go out and sacrifice their lives and put themselves in harm's way for my freedom of speech and my freedoms in this country and my freedom to take a seat or take a knee, so I have the utmost respect for them."[357]

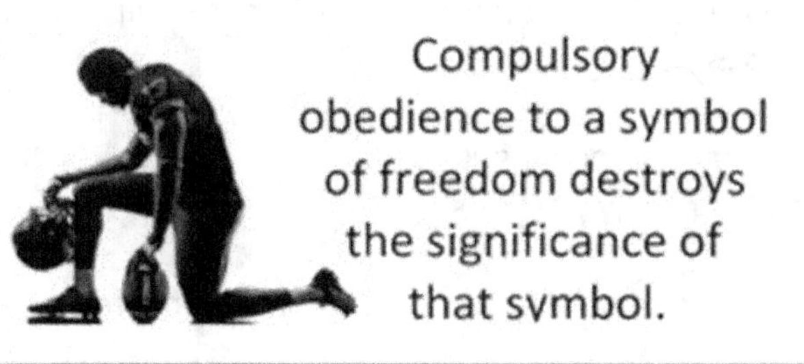

Image Source[358]

Colin Kaepernick kneeled during the national anthem not to disrespect the police or our military, but to bring awareness to a problem in the country. He said exactly that. Those who close their eyes to that, to his intention, are doing so in order to see what they want to see. Their vitriol is self-serving. Those who think Kaepernick should be forced to not kneel or penalized for doing so, don't understand the concept of freedom in America.

I wonder how people would have reacted if Kaepernick has kneeled to protest veterans receiving poor medical treatment instead of police brutality towards Blacks. My guess is there would have been less to no outrage. I think the fury had more to do the target of Kaepernick's protest than it did to the fact that he kneeled.

Patriotism is something you live, not something you need to prove. If you think standing for the national anthem or waving the American flag makes you patriotic, you're wrong. Patriotism isn't about "honoring" an anthem or a flag, but about living the principles the country was founded on. To measure one's patriotism by their compliance with acts of symbolism is misguided. And Americans shouldn't be in the business of judging the patriotism of other Americans. Once we begin to do so we are traveling down a hazardous road.

Protest is a form of patriotism and there is nothing more American than peaceful protest. Kaepernick's concern that led to his kneeling is felt by many millions of Americans. All Americans should be sensitive to that. To many, Kaepernick's stance makes him a hero.

At the time of Kaepernick's initial kneeling protest, he pledged $1 million donation to charities (probably more than Donald Trump has donated in the last ten years.) He has delivered on his promise. For the last $100,000 of the pledge, Kaepernick launched his #10 for 10 campaign during which he made ten donations of $10,000 to different charities and each donation was matched by a celebrity friend, including Stephen Curry, Kevin Durant, Snoop Dogg, Meek Mill and Serena Williams.

To be troubled with Kaepernick's kneeling is to be following conservative style political correctness. It's phony patriotism.

A few of the many charitable causes Colin Kaepernick has supported:

- Coalition for the Homeless' central food program; after school and summer programs for homeless youth; a program providing apartments, food, school supplies, medication, transportation, and social services to homeless families.

- Silence Is Violence which provides support to families affected by violent crime (funeral expenses, rent, utilities, groceries, counseling, and childcare).

- Meals on Wheels which delivers of food to people unable to leave their house (seniors and veterans are two prominent groups).

- Love Army for Somalia which airlifts food and water to famine areas of Somalia. (Colin donated his own money and helped raise an additional $3 million for the program).

- Black Veterans for Social Justice, which pays the rent for homeless veterans and veterans facing eviction.

- Mni Wiconi Health Clinic Partnership at Standing Rock, which offsets doctors and nurses' salaries and to help build a mobile medical clinic.

- Life After Hate, a program founded by former extremists which is committed to helping people leave the violent far-right.

- Angel by Nature which serves the Houston community with relief efforts for those affected by Hurricane Harvey.

An Open Letter to Colin Kaepernick
From Former Staff Sgt. Nate Boyer

This letter to Colin Kaepernick was written in 2016 by former Staff Sgt. Nate Boyer who served in the Army for six years and made multiple war-zone deployments as a Green Beret. After playing for the University of Texas football team, Boyer was signed as a free agent by the Seattle Seahawks and played very briefly before the 2015 regular season.

Colin,

I'm a big fan. I've been pulling for you ever since I first saw you play in the 2012 preseason. I was raised in the San Francisco Bay Area and have been a die-hard 49ers fan as long as I can remember – growing up, I was Joe Montana for Halloween two years straight.

I proudly wore the red and gold for an afternoon when I had a tryout with the 49ers last spring. I ultimately ended up in training camp with the Seattle Seahawks, but I'll never forget the one day I got to be a 49er.

I don't know a lot, but I do know that I catch a lot of flak for expressing my opinions, something you are now very familiar with. I also know you support the military – "God Bless Our Troops" is written on the football that you and former 49er teammate Colt McCoy signed for one of the charities I work with. The football's currently sitting in my parents' house; my dad bid the highest at the charity's auction.

Unfortunately, I also know that racism still exists in our country, as it does in every other country on this planet, and I hate that I know that. I hate the third verse of our national anthem, but thankfully we don't sing that verse anymore. I hate that at times I feel guilty for being white.

In 2004, I witnessed genocide firsthand in the Darfur region of Sudan. The fact that hate and oppression still exist at that level in our world really hurts me. I met countless young Africans who were enamored with America and the opportunities that exist here. Those people would have given anything to experience what I had grown up with, even just for one day.

I joined the Army upon returning to the U.S. because I believed people like that were worth fighting for. De Oppresso Liber ("To Free the Oppressed") is the Army Special Forces motto, and the reason I wanted to become a Green Beret. I didn't enlist to fight for what we already have here; I did it because I wanted to fight for what those people didn't have there: Freedom.

I am in no way political, but I'm proud that we have an African American president, and that I got to serve under him. Overcoming racism at home is a slow process, and we still have a long way to go, but most of us are trying. That's what sets us apart from so many other places. In this country, no matter who you are, where you come from, what color you are, you can try.

During college football games, both teams usually wait in the locker room until after the national anthem. That always bothered me. Leading the team out of the tunnel while carrying the American flag meant a lot, but I still regretted not being out there to stand for that song.

The only time I got to stand on the sideline for the anthem was during my one and only NFL preseason game, against the Denver Broncos. As I ran out of the tunnel with the American flag, I could feel myself swelling with pride, and as I stood on the sideline with my hand on my heart as the anthem began, that swelling burst into tears.

I thought about how far I'd come and the men I'd fought alongside who didn't make it back. I thought about those overseas who were risking their lives at that very moment. I selfishly thought about what I had sacrificed to get to where I was, and while I knew I had little to no chance of making the Seahawks' roster as a 34-year-old rookie, I was trying.

That moment meant so much more to me than even playing in the game did, and to be honest, if I had noticed my teammate sitting on the bench, it would have really hurt me.

I'm not judging you for standing up for what you believe in. It's your inalienable right. What you are doing takes a lot of courage, and I'd be lying if I said I knew what it was like to walk around in your shoes. I've never had to deal with prejudice because of the color of my skin, and for me to say I can relate to what you've gone through is as ignorant as someone who's never been in a combat zone telling me they understand what it's like to go to war.

Even though my initial reaction to your protest was one of anger, I'm trying to listen to what you're saying and why you're doing it. When I told my mom about this article, she cautioned me that "the last thing our country needed right now was more hate." As usual, she's right.

There are already plenty people fighting fire with fire, and it's just not helping anyone or anything. So I'm just going to keep listening, with an open mind.

I look forward to the day you're inspired to once again stand during our national anthem. I'll be standing right there next to you. Keep on trying … De Oppresso Liber.[359]

Chapter 18
Malala

My book contains far too much negativity for my liking, so here's some inspiration. Malala Yousafzai is a Pakistani who first spoke out against the Taliban's restrictions on girls attending school at age 11. On October 9, 2012, 15-year-old Malala's school bus was stopped. A Taliban gunman boarded and shot her, with a bullet striking her in the head. The shooting left Malala in a coma in critical condition. She underwent multiple surgeries and intensive rehabilitation.

But the attack didn't stop her as she stepped up her commitment and her work campaigning for the rights of girls to receive an education. At age 17, she received the Nobel Peace Prize. Her acceptance speech brilliantly reflected the overwhelming goodness and humanity of this young lady. A few sentences from that speech lets us see a little into Malala's soul:

> Dear sisters and brothers, dear fellow children, we must work... not wait. Not just the politicians and the world leaders, we all need to contribute. Me. You. We. It is our duty.

> Let us become the first generation to decide to be the last, let us become the first generation that decides to be the last that sees empty classrooms, lost childhoods, and wasted potentials. Let this be the last time that a girl or a boy spends their childhood in a factory. Let this be the last time that a girl is forced into early child marriage. Let this be the last time that a child loses life in war. Let this be the last time that we see a child out of school. Let this end with us.[360]

This extraordinary Pakistani Muslim young lady from Pakistan epitomizes American values. Would President Donald Trump want Malala to enter the United States? Probably not, and that would be America's loss. Malala embodies the spirit of America. Because in America, we embrace those running from political oppression, we embrace courage, and we embrace those who fight for freedom and equality. That is our soul.

Chapter 19
Marwa

Donald Trump has stated he is open to creating a database of Muslims and forcing them to carry identification cards. He also wants heavier surveillance on mosques. Twenty-two-year-old American Marwa Balkar, who is Muslim, responded to Trump's comments in a beautiful open letter on Facebook.[361]

Dear @realdonaldtrump,

My name is Marwa, and I am a Muslim.

I heard you wanted us to start wearing ID badges, so I decided to choose one for myself. I am not easily identifiable as a #Muslim just by looking at me, so my new badge will let me display proudly who I am.

I chose the peace sign because it represents my #Islam. The one that taught me to oppose #injustice and yearn for #unity. The one that taught me that killing one innocent life is equivalent to killing humanity.

I heard you want to track us as well. Great! You can come with me on my Cancer Awareness walks at the local middle school, or you can follow me to work where it's my job to create happiness.

You can also see how my local mosque makes PB&J sandwiches for the homeless and hosts interfaith dinners where everyone is welcome.

Maybe then, you'll see that me being Muslim doesn't make me any less American than you are.

Maybe if you walk in my footsteps, you can see that I am not any less human than you are.

Salaamu alaikum (Peace be unto you)

Instead of responding in kind to Donald Trump's hateful words, Balkar fights hate with intelligence, grace, and dignity. She represents all that is good about America. Trump could learn a lot from this young woman who demonstrates more love of country and of religious freedom than does Mr. Trump. Ms. Balkar has much more humanity than the man she addresses. Marwa Balkar is American patriot.

Chapter 20
Miscellany

pompous[362]
[pom · puh s] *adj*

1. one who is full of pomp.
2. a self-absorbed person.
3. an elitist, usually found inflating her/his ego to the point of nausea.

An example of a pompous person is someone who constantly talks about what he or she has accomplished. We associate the adjective *pompous* with self-important jerks.

Flip-Flops

Official Footwear of the Donald Trump for President 2016 Campaign

Image Source[363]

Let me see if I have this right. Republicans defend Donald Trump's lying, bigotry, misogyny, bullying, crassness, and sexual assault, but they attacked President Obama for wearing a light color suit.

Donald Trump for President
Foreign Policy Talking Points

• Say something very bad is going on.

• Say we have to get tough or we won't have a country.

• Criticize President Obama for not being politically correct because he doesn't use the term "radical Islamic terrorist."

• That should do it. on.

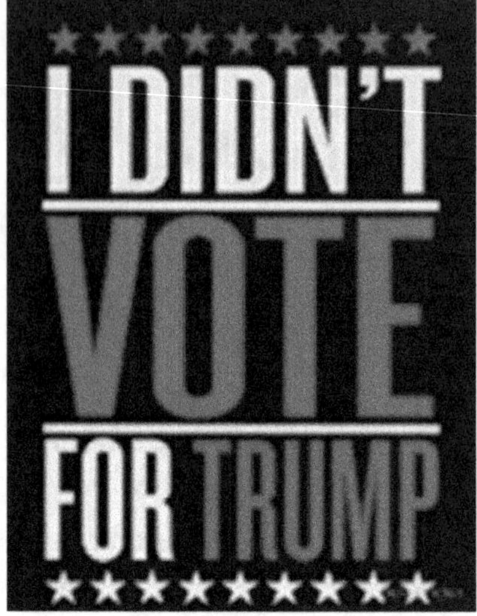

If you are more fortunate than others, build a longer table, not a taller fence.

Nicki

Donald J. Trump
@realDonaldTrump

I hear that dopey pundit Lawrence O'Donnell, one of the dummer people on television, is about to lose his show-no ratings? Too bad

18:19 AM · Jun 25, 2015

← Donald, here's some advice. When you call someone dumb, don't misspell the word *dumber*. It kind of undermines your argument.

Image Source[364]

"We all pray differently but our prayers travel to heaven together."[365]

- The great Mattie Stepanek

Image Source[366]

"**Letters to the editor**

My letters are so great

I write fabulous letters. If you read all the letters I have written, you would agree. You would love them. Other letter writers are weak, soft and out of touch. I'm not like that, and I'm sure if you are reading this you aren't either.

This paper really needs great letters, and I am awesome at letter writing.

Other letter writers might attack me, but then they go away. They don't have what it takes to keep writing the great letters. I have what it takes to write the best letters. Letter writers who disagree need to be pinched in the face and run out of town.

I guarantee this letter will be picked as letter of the month. If it isn't picked, it will prove that this letter writing contest is rigged.

Terry Vaught, *Dover* "

Tampa Bay Times, August 7, 2016[368]

Image Source[367]

self-aggrandizement[369]
[self-ag·gran·dize·ment] *noun*

1. the act or practice of enhancing or exaggerating one's own importance, power, or reputation.

2. the act of exaggerating one's own power, importance, etc., especially in an aggressive or ruthless manner.

3. an act undertaken to increase one's power and influence or to draw attention to one's importance.

Image Source[370]

#covfefe

Image Source[371]

<u>March 4, 2016, Headlines from Various Publications</u>

"Donald Trump Defends his Penis Size at Debate"

"Donald Trump Fires Back at Marco Rubio:
'There Is No Problem' With My Penis"

"Donald Trump Makes His Penis a
Campaign Issue During Debate"

"Donald Trump's Penis Wins the GOP debate"

Donald Trump elevating the level of political discourse.

Matt Mountain
@ImMattMountain

There are about 4,000 Muslims serving in the US military right now. Zero members of Trump's family have served. #MuslimBan

6:53 - 6 Mar 2017

Image Source [372]

It appears this was not said by Thomas Jefferson despite frequent claims otherwise. I don't know who said it, but I like the quotation so I'm saying it and you can quote me.

Image Source [373]

Yeah, me too

indecent[374]

[in-dee-suh nt] *adj*

1. not in accordance with accepted moral values, propriety, or good taste; morally offensive; morally wrong or evil.

2. offensive to standards of decency, vulgar, lewd, indecent language, indecent joke, indecent behavior.

3. not decent; unbecoming or unseemly, grossly improper, obscene.

Image Source[375]

Image Source[377]

"There are men running our government who shouldn't be allowed to play with matches."

— Will Rogers[376]

Image Source[378]

Gale McCray in Washington D.C.   Image Source[379]

Image Source[380]

Image Source[381]

Image Source[382]

"We may have all come on different ships, but we're in the same boat now." Aaron

- Dr. Martin Luther King Jr.[384]

Image Source[383]

Image Source[386]

Image Source[385]

Donald Trump:

не было никакого сговора, никакого сговора

Translation:

There was no collusion, no collusion.

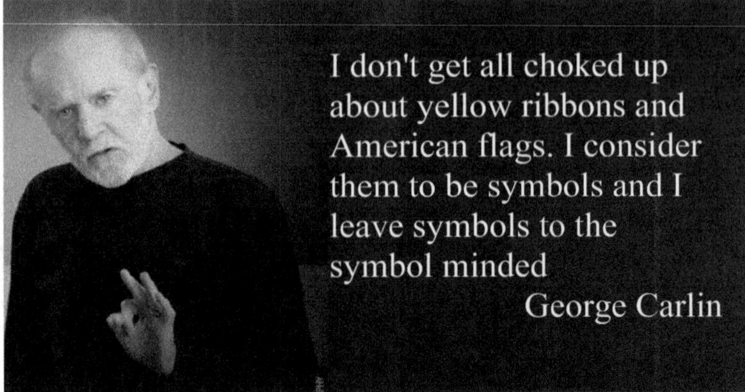

Image Source[387]

Image Source[390]

"A Small Loan of a Million Dollars"[388] - Donald Trump

"Fred Trump lent his son at least $60.7 million... Much of it was never repaid,"[389] - New York Times.

Donald Trump's fifth-grade teacher, Mrs. Audrey Grimble of Queens, NY

Image Source[391]

Clinton	Trump
65,788,583	62,955,363

This is reported to be Donald Trump's first ever tweet.
Wow, a piece of history.

Donald J. Trump
@realDonaldTrump

Be sure to tune in and watch Donald Trump on Late Night with David Letterman as he presents the Top Ten list tonight!

2:54 PM - 4 May 2009

Trump University Gifts

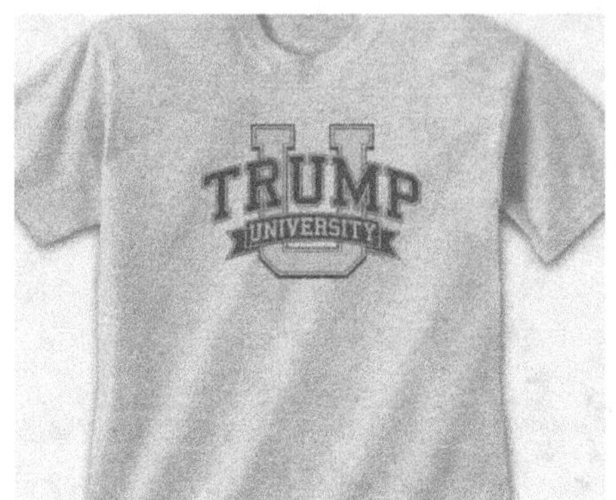

Items shown are not real items and not really for sale (at least not by me.)

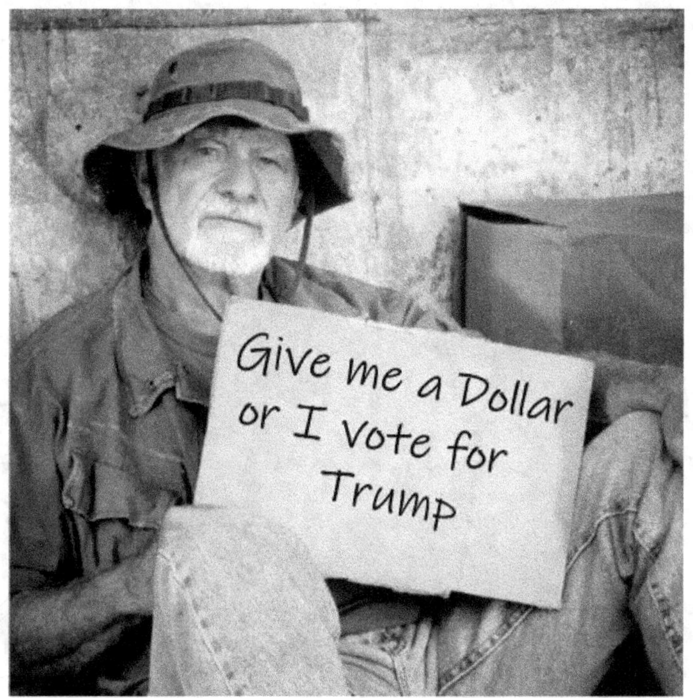

Image Source[392]

Do you think a president standing in front of a podium and attacking and insulting people makes America great?

Do you think a president holding a cell phone and tweeting attacks and insults makes America great?

Me neither.

Sad (picture taken by me of a home in my neighborhood).

Image Source[393]

Syrian woman in destroyed city   Image Source[394]

Abdullah Kurdi, standing by his destroyed
home after burial of his wife and two sons.
Image Source[395]

After the attack of ASSad on Aleppo, Syrial
Image Source [396]

Picture of Donald Trump's Florida home and pictures of the homes of thousands of Syrians.

Image Source[397]

Image Source[398]

Image Source[399]

Donald Trump's Republican party has sometimes
been called "the party of White people",
a claim that Republicans say is untrue. Let's see.

There are 293 Republicans in Congress.
279 are White, 14 are not.
There are 242 Democrats in Congress.
153 are White, 89 are not. [400]

At the 2016 Republican National Convention
there were 2,472 delegates.
How many do you think were Black?

The answer is 18. Really, I'm not kidding, 18.
That's a one and an eight, eighteen. Dix-huit in French.
That's not a typo. The answer is 18.[401]

I guess the Republican party *is*
the party of white people.

Donald Trump's 2016 election victory speech:
"I say it is time for us to come together
as one united people."[402]

"If you don't have a seat at the table, you're likely on
the menu."[403] – Former Texas Governor Ann Richards

Oh, by the way, one more thing about the Republican Party being "the party of White people."

This is a picture of Howard Taft, the 27th president of the United States. He was born in 1857, before the civil war, and died in 1930.

Image Source [404]

In 1912 Howard Taft ran for reelection but was defeated. At the 1912 Republic national convention that nominated Taft an estimated 6% of the delegates were Black.

At the 2016 Republican National Convention that nominated Donald Trump less than 1% of delegates were Black, the lowest percentage of Black delegates at a GOP convention since before 1912.

The 1912 RNC convention had 8.5 times more Blacks than the 2016 convention over 100 years later. [405]

Black Delegates at Republican National Conventions

Election Year	All Delegates	Black Delegates	Black Delegates %
1912	1,078	65	6.0
1916	985	35	3.5
1920	984	29	2.9
1924	1,109	39	3.5
1928	1,098	49	4.4
1932	1,154	26	2.2
1936	1,003	45	4.5
1940	1,000	32	3.2
1944	1,057	18	1.7
1948	1,094	41	3.7
1952	1,206	29	2.4
1956	1,323	36	2.7
1960	1,331	22	1.6
1964	1,308	14	1.0
1968	1,333	26	1.9
1972	1,348	56	4.2
1976	2,259	76	3.4
1980	1,993	55	2.7
1984	2,235	69	3.1
1988	2,277	61	2.7
1992	2,210	107	5.0
1996	1,990	52	2.6
2000	2,066	85	4.1
2004	2,509	167	6.7
2008	2,380	39	1.6
2012	2,286	47	2.1
2016	2,472	18	.7

406

Image Source[407]

Famous Quotes of Donald J. Trump

"Wherever there is a human being there is an opportunity for kindness."

"Human kindness has never weakened the stamina or softened the fiber of a free people. A nation does not have to be cruel to be tough."

"There is no limit to the amount of good you can do if you don't care who gets the credit."

"We all pray differently but our prayers travel to heaven together."

Author's note: Oh, I'm sorry. I got these confused. These aren't quotes from Donald Trump, but rather quotes from poet Thomas Bailey Aldrich, Franklin D. Roosevelt, Ronald Reagan, and child poet and author Mattie Stepanek, respectively. I apologize for the error.

In Their Words

From the *Guardian*,[408] here are the words of 18 women who have stories of Trump's inappropriate advances. The subject is examined in more detail in the chapter, "Trump the Lewd".

1. "He was like an octopus . . . His hands were everywhere." – Jessica Leeds

2. "He pushed me up against the wall and had his hands all over me and tried to get up my dress again." – Jill Harth

3. "He did touch my vagina through my underwear." – Kristin Anderson

4. "[Trump] stuck his head right underneath their skirts." – Lisa Boyne

5. "He took my hand, and grabbed me, and went for the lips." – Cathy Heller

6. "I remember putting on my dress really quick because I was like, 'Oh my God, there's a man in here.'" – Mariah Billado

7. "Then his hand touched the right side of my breast. I was in shock." – Karena Virginia

8. "The time that he walked through the dressing rooms was really shocking. We were all naked." – Bridget Sullivan

9. "Our first introduction to him was when we were at the dress rehearsal and half-naked changing into our bikinis." – Tasha Dixon

10. "All of a sudden I felt a grab, a little nudge." – Melinda McGillivray

11. "[Trump] kissed me directly on the mouth." – Rachel Crooks

12. "I turned around, and within seconds he was pushing me against the wall and forcing his tongue down my throat." – Natasha Stoynoff

13. "Trump stood right next to me and suddenly he squeezed my butt."
    – Ninni Laaksonen

14. "When we entered the room, he grabbed each of us tightly in a hug
    and kissed each of us on the lips without asking for permission."
    – Jessica Drake

15. "He would step in front of each girl and look you over from head to
    toe like we were just meat, we were just sexual objects, that we
    were not people." – Samantha Holvey

16. "He then grabbed my shoulder and began kissing me again very
    aggressively and placed his hand on my breast." – Summer Zervos

17. "He probably doesn't want me telling the story about that time he
    continually grabbed my ass and invited me to his hotel room."
    – Cassandra Searles

18. "He kissed me directly on the lips. I thought, 'Oh my God, gross.'
    He was married to Marla Maples at the time."– Temple Taggert
    (This particular item is not from the *Guardian*; rather, it is from the
    New York Times.[409])

Demagogue

- "A leader who makes use of popular prejudices and false claims and promises in order to gain power" (Merriam-Webster Dictionary)

- "A leader of a popular faction, or the mob; a political agitator who appeals to the passions and prejudices of the mob in order to obtain power or to further his own interests; an unprincipled or factious popular orator" (Oxford English Dictionary)

- "A person, especially a political leader, who wins support by exciting people's emotions rather than giving them reasons" (Cambridge Dictionary)

Demagoguery is a discourse that frames "public policy in terms of the degree and means by which the "out-group should be scapegoated for the current problems of the in-group."[410]

Trump the Absurd

Many stories in this book could fit under this heading. Here are just three.

Extreme Absurdity #1

In an infamous proclamation, Trump said, "I know more about ISIS than the generals do. Believe me."[411] There are no words to describe how ignorant, idiotic, and ridiculous that statement is. It is as absurd as absurd can be.

Sometime later, Trump was asked by Bret Baier of Fox News, "What's your assessment of the leader of ISIS?" Trump responded, "Well, they've had numerous leaders. We don't even know who the leader is."[412] Wrong, we do know. It's Abu Bakr al Baghdadi (Donald, look it up on *Wikipedia*). I bet the generals know who the leader of ISIS is.

Extreme Absurdity #2

Regarding the US–Iran nuclear agreement, Trump said, "I've studied this issue in great detail, I would say actually greater, by far, than anybody else."[413] That's inane. It's entirely irrational. What type of person needs to lie and brag to such an extreme to make such an absurd statement?

And just a note: not only has Trump *studied* the issue, and not only has he studied it in *great detail*, and not only has he studied it in *greater detail than anybody else*, but he's studied it in *far greater detail than anybody else*.

Extreme Absurdity #3

This beauty from Donald Trump's at a campaign rally in Hilton Head, South Carolina, in December 2015: "I know words. I have the best words." He has words? No, he doesn't "have" words. And even if he did, his words wouldn't be the best. He would have the same words as everybody else. Words do not belong to individual people.

If you're going to brag about your vocabulary, which I think Trump was trying to do, it's best to express yourself clearly and in a grammatically correct fashion. Come to think of it, Trump used a similar approach when bragging about his intelligence when he was on MSNBC and asked to name his top foreign policy advisors. His response: "I'm speaking with myself, number one, because I have a very good brain, and I've said a lot of things."[414] It seems Trump has good words, and Trump has a good brain.

A Donald Trump Ever/Never Quiz

Indicate whether or not you think Donald Trump has ever done each of the activities listed below. Then have fun discussing and debating your answers with your friends.

	Yes	Never
Ever gone to the zoo, fishing, or the park with his kids?	☐	☐
Ever visited a friend in the hospital?	☐	☐
Ever rolled on the floor with his children?	☐	☐
Ever given a piggyback ride to any of his kids?	☐	☐
Ever read a book or poem?	☐	☐
Ever personally purchased a gift for someone?	☐	☐
Ever been to a grocery store?	☐	☐
Ever played with a dog; ever owned a pet?	☐	☐
Ever knew the name of any of his children's teachers?	☐	☐
Ever washed dishes; ever washed clothes?	☐	☐
Ever cried or teared?	☐	☐
Ever planted a flower; ever watered a plant?	☐	☐
Ever changed a diaper?	☐	☐
Ever prayed when alone?	☐	☐

President Reagan's Love Letter to Immigrants

This is from Reagan's final speech as President. Contrast Reagan's eloquence to Trump's ignorant and disparaging remarks concerning immigrants. The entire transcript from the Presidential Medal of Freedom award ceremony is posted at the Reagan Library[415].

January 19, 1989: Now, tomorrow is a special day for me. I'm going to receive my gold watch. And since this is the last speech that I will give as President, I think it's fitting to leave one final thought, an observation about a country which I love. It was stated best in a letter I received not long ago. A man wrote me and said: "You can go to live in France, but you cannot become a Frenchman. You can go to live in Germany or Turkey or Japan, but you cannot become a German, a Turk, or a Japanese. But anyone, from any corner of the Earth, can come to live in America and become an American.

Yes, the torch of Lady Liberty symbolizes our freedom and represents our heritage, the compact with our parents, our grandparents, and our ancestors. It is that lady who gives us our great and special place in the world. For it's the great life force of each generation of new Americans that guarantees that America's triumph shall continue unsurpassed into the next century and beyond. Other countries may seek to compete with us; but in one vital area, as a beacon of freedom and opportunity that draws the people of the world, no country on Earth comes close.

This, I believe, is one of the most important sources of America's greatness. We lead the world because, unique among nations, we draw our people — our strength — from every country and every corner of the world. And by doing so we continuously renew and enrich our nation. While other countries cling to the stale past, here in America we breathe life into dreams. We create the future, and the world follows us into tomorrow. Thanks to each wave of new arrivals to this land of opportunity, we're a nation forever young, forever bursting with energy and new ideas, and always on the cutting edge, always leading the world to the next frontier. This quality is vital to our future as a nation. If we ever closed the door to new Americans, our leadership in the world would soon be lost.

A number of years ago, an American student traveling in Europe took an East German ship across the Baltic Sea. One of the ship's crewmembers from East Germany, a man in his sixties, struck up a conversation with the American student. After a while the student asked the man how he had learned such good English. And the man explained that he had once lived in America. He said that for over a year he had worked as a farmer in Oklahoma and California, that he had planted tomatoes and picked ripe melons. It was, the man said, the happiest time of his life. Well, the student, who had seen the awful conditions behind the Iron Curtain, blurted out the question, "Well, why did you ever leave?" "I had to," he said, "the war ended." The man had been in America as a German prisoner of war.

Now, I don't tell this story to make the case for former POW's. Instead, I tell this story just to remind you of the magical, intoxicating power of America. We may sometimes forget it, but others do not. Even a man from a country at war with the United States, while held here as a prisoner, could fall in love with us. Those who become American citizens love this country even more. And that's why the Statue of Liberty lifts her lamp to welcome them to the golden door.

It is bold men and women, yearning for freedom and opportunity, who leave their homelands and come to a new country to start their lives over. They believe in the American dream. And over and over, they make it come true for themselves, for their children, and for others. They give more than they receive. They labor and succeed. And often they are entrepreneurs. But their greatest contribution is more than economic, because they understand in a special way how glorious it is to be an American. They renew our pride and gratitude in the United States of America, the greatest, freest nation in the world — the last, best hope of man on Earth.[416]

Donald Trump Can't Spell

We found Donald Trump's fifth-grade teacher, Mrs. Audrey Grimble of Queens, New York, and asked her to give a report on his spelling skills. She wrote a letter stating, "If elected, Mr. Trump, I can state equivocally, will be the worst speller ever elected to the presidency."

Image Source[417]

Is Donald Trump smarter than a 5th grader?

Words Mr. Trump has misspelled during the presidential campaign, primarily in his tweets:

- "insticts" (instincts)
- "leightweight" (lightweight)
- "chocker" (choker)
- "Bobby Night" (Bobby Knight)
- "dummer" (dumber)
- "payed" (paid)
- "Dwayne Wade" (Dwyane)
- "shoker" (shocker)
- "honer" (honor)
- "Barrack Obama" (Barack)
- "Phoneix" (Phoenix)
- "Phillies Schlafly" (Phyllis)
- "lyen" (lyin')
- "loose" (lose)
- "Witchita" (Wichita)
- "Kansas" (Kansas)

Aaron

Donald Trump to Respond to New Book

If my humble book attains any popularity, Donald Trump may comment on it. To save him from taking time from his important work to compose tweets about me and my book, I have prepared some Trump-like tweets for his use.

Donald J. Trump
@realDonaldTrump

Danielle

Tedd Levy came to me in the 90's. Wanted a job, I said no.

5:45 AM - 2 Nov 2018

Donald J. Trump
@realDonaldTrump

Lots of people have called me. They say Loser Tedd was born in France.

6:15 AM - 3 June 2020

Donald J. Trump
@realDonaldTrump

Poorly written book. I write great books. Everybody says I write the best books. I'm really very smart. I went to the best schools, I'm, like, a very smart person. Believe me.

8:45 AM - 3 June 3 2020

Donald J. Trump
@realDonaldTrump

Levy's fake book is an attempt by the Democrats to reverse the result of the election. What about Hillary's emails?

7:23 AM - 3 Jun 2020

Image Source[419]

The great comedian George Carlin once said, "In America, anyone can become president. That's the problem."[418]

Endnotes

[1] David Brooks, "No, Not Trump, Not Ever," *The New York Times*, https://www.nytimes.com/2016/03/18/opinion/no-not-trump-not-ever.html, March 18, 2016.

[2] Green Keep of the grass blank sign in a meadow, Rigamondis/Depositphotos.com (image altered). Text added to picture by me.

[3] Definition compiled from various dictionaries and internet sources.

[4] "Donald Trump," Politicfact.com, https://www.politifact.com/truth-o-meter/article/2015/dec/21/2015-lie-year-donald-trump-campaign-misstatements.

[5] Dana Milbank, "The Facts behind Donald Trump's Many Falsehoods," *The Washington Post*, https://www.washingtonpost.com/opinions/the-facts-behind-donald-trumps-many-falsehoods/2016/08/01/0571b048-582d-11e6-831d-0324760ca856_story.html?utm_term=.d3e65dc44cd6, August 1, 2016.

[6] Daniel Dale, "Donald Trump: The unauthorized database of false things," TheStar.com, https://www.thestar.com/news/world/uselection/2016/11/04/donald-trump-the-unauthorized-database-of-false-things.html, October 30, 2016.

[7] Kyle Cheney, Isaac Arnsdorf, Daniel Lippman, Daniel Strauss, and Brent Griffiths, "Donald Trump's Week of Misrepresentations, Exaggerations and Half-Truths," *Politico*, http://www.politico.com/magazine/story/2016/09/2016-donald-trump-fact-check-week-214287, September 25, 2016.

[8] David Brooks, "No, Not Trump, Not Ever," *The New York Times,* https://www.nytimes.com/2016/03/18/opinion/no-not-trump-not-ever.html, March 18, 2016.

9 Mark Singer, "Getting Sued by Trump Has Its Upsides," *GQ,* https://www.gq.com/story/getting-sued-by-trump-has-its-upsides, June 3, 2016.

10 Donald J. Trump with Tony Schwartz, *Trump, The Art of the Deal*, Random House Publishing Group, New York, 1987, Kindle edition, 58.

11 "Trumpspeak," Urban Dictionary, https://www.urbandictionary.com/define.php?term=trumpspeak.

12 Dara Lind, "Donald Trump Lies. All the Time. And Stunningly Few People Seem to Care," *Vox,* https://www.vox.com/policy-and-politics/2016/9/26/13016146/donald-trump-liar-media, September 27, 2016.

13 Dara Lind, "The 9 Types of Lies Donald Trump Tells the Most," *Vox,* https://www.vox.com/2016/10/26/13417532/donald-trump-lies, October 26, 2016.

14 Jim Geraghty, "Trump on Muslim Cheers in New Jersey on 9/11: 'It Did Happen. I Saw It,'" *National Review,* https://www.nationalreview.com/blog/corner/trump-muslim-cheers-new-jersey-911-it-did-happen-i-saw-it-jim-geraghty, November 21, 2015.

15 Jordyn Phelps, "Donald Trump Again Says He Saw Cheering in New Jersey on 9/11," ABC News, http://abcnews.go.com/Politics/donald-trump-cheering-jersey-911/story?id=35355447, November 22, 2015.

16 Susie Madrak, "Donald Trump Has Excellent Health, the Best Ever!" *Suburban Guerilla* (blog), http://susiemadrak.com/2015/12/15/donald-trump-has-excellent-health-the-best-ever, December 15, 2015.

17 Charles C. W. Cooke, "Exclusive: Donald Trump's Full Medical Report," *National Review,* https://www.nationalreview.com/2015/12/donald-trump-medical-history-parody-letter/ Charles C. W. Cooke, December 15, 2015.

[18] Anna R. Schecter, Chrs Francescani, and Tracy Connor, "Trump Doctor Wrote Health Letter in Just 5 Minutes as Limo Waited," NBC News, https://www.nbcnews.com/news/us-news/trump-doctor-wrote-health-letter-just-5-minutes-limo-waited-n638526, August 26, 2016.

[19] Ibid.

[20] Jessica Taylor, "Doctor: Trump Would Be 'Healthiest Individual Ever Elected' President," NPR, https://www.npr.org/2015/12/14/459700154/doctor-trump-would-be-healthiest-individual-ever-elected-president, December 14, 2015.

[21] Jeremy Diamond, "Donald Trump takes Liberty, courts Christian crowd," CNN, https://www.cnn.com/2016/01/18/politics/donald-trump-liberty-two-corinthians/index.html, January 19, 2016.

[22] Kjm2672, "Sidestep - Charles Durning - The Best Little Whorehouse in Texas.mp4," YouTube video, www.youtube.com/watch?v=NJG75FJkjr8, July 18, 2010.

[23] "Trump: The Art of the Lie," Reason.com, http://reason.com/blog/2016/06/11/trump-the-art-of-the-lie, June 11, 2016.

[24] Elizabeth McLaughlin, "Trump Tries to Clarify After Mistakenly Saying Russia Has No Forces in Ukraine," ABC News, http://abcnews.go.com/Politics/donald-trump-attempts-clarify-comments-russian-forces-ukraine/story?id=41045975, August 1, 2016.

[25] Kurt Andersen, "How to Talk Like Trump," The Atlantic https://www.theatlantic.com/magazine/archive/2018/03/how-to-talk-trump/550934/, March 2018.

[26] Ibid.

[27] Robert Farley, "Trump 'Hears' Obama Wants to Take Guns," Factcheck.org, https://www.factcheck.org/2015/10/trump-hears-obama-wants-to-take-guns, October 22, 2015.

28 Ibid.

29 Jake Miller, "Donald Trump Defends Calling Mexican Immigrants 'Rapists,'" CBS News, https://www.cbsnews.com/news/election-2016-donald-trump-defends-calling-mexican-immigrants-rapists, July 2, 2015.

30 Amy Sherman, "Donald Trump Wrongly Says the Number of Illegal Immigrants is 30 Million or Higher," Politifact.com, http://www.politifact.com/florida/statements/2015/jul/28/donald-trump/donald-trump-says-number-illegal-immigrants-30-mil, July 28th, 2015.

31 "Unification Church Insists Trump Apologize," *The New York Times,* https://www.nytimes.com/1991/05/26/nyregion/unification-church-insists-trump-apologize.html?mtrref=undefined&gwh=5416EF3E4314C59E02BC6873318074C4&gwt=pay, May 26, 1991.

32 David Lightman, "Trump Criticizes Pequots, Casino," *The Hartford Courant,* https://www.courant.com/news/connecticut/hc-xpm-1993-10-06-0000003863-story.html, October 6, 1993.

33 Ella Nilsen, "Trump: Boy Scouts thought my speech was 'greatest ever made to them.' Boy Scouts: No," https://www.vox.com/policy-and-politics/2017/8/2/16083442/trump-boy-scouts-speech, August 2, 2017.

34 Alana Abramson, "The Head of the Boy Scouts Just Apologized After Trump's National Jamboree Speech," https://time.com/4876705/donald-trump-boy-scout-jamboree-speech, July 27, 2017.

35 Eli Rosenberg, "Trump bashes Gillibrand using a favored weapon: Innuendo as insult", *The Washington Post,* https://www.washingtonpost.com/news/the-fix/wp/2017/12/12/trump-bashes-gillibrand-using-a-favored-weapon-innuendo-as-insult, December 12, 2017.

36 David Ferguson, "Busted: Trump Told 30 Lies in Two Days During 2007 Deposition About His 'Billionaire' claims," RawStory.com,

https://www.rawstory.com/2016/08/busted-trump-told-30-lies-in-two-days-during-2007-deposition-about-his-billionaire-claims, August 10, 2016.

[37] @realDonaldTrump, Twitter, https://twitter.com/realdonaldtrump/status/759222916387069952?lang=en, July 29, 2016.

[38] "Trump Supports Three Presidential Debates, But May Object to Proposed Dates," ABC News, video, http://abcnews.go.com/ThisWeek/video/trump-supports-presidential-debates-object-proposed-dates-41019287.

[39] "Rowdy, an ever-smiling buckaroo, has been the official mascot of the Dallas Cowboys of the National Football League since 1996", Library of Congress, Prints & Photographs Division, photograph by Carol M. Highsmith [reproduction number, e.g., LC-USZ62-123456], Highsmith, Carol M (image altered). Text added to picture by me.

[40] "Trump Complains about Debates Conflicting With NFL Games," ABC News, https://abcnews.go.com/Politics/trump-complains-debates-conflicting-nfl-games/story?id=41026741, July 31, 2016.

[41] "Immanuel Kant > Quotes > Quotable Quote," Goodreads.com, https://www.goodreads.com/quotes/668573-by-a-lie-a-man-throws-away-and-as-it.

[42] "Immigration eLesson," Bill of Rights Institute, https://billofrightsinstitute.org/educate/educator-resources/lessons-plans/immigration-elesson.

[43] Paola Chavez, "Donald Trump Claims No One Has 'Done So Much for Equality as I Have,'" video, ABC News, https://abcnews.go.com/Politics/donald-trump-claims-equality/story?id=37305333, March 1, 2016.

[44] Gideon Resnick and Asawin Suebsaeng, "Donald Trump Called Deaf Apprentice Marlee Matlin 'Retarded,' Three Staffers Say," *The Daily Beast,*

https://www.thedailybeast.com/donald-trump-called-deaf-apprentice-marlee-matlin-retarded-three-staffers-say, October 13, 2016.

45 Ibid.

46 Erin Gloria Ryan, "Only Black 'Apprentice' Winner: Trump Has Learned Nothing," *The Daily Beast,* https://www.thedailybeast.com/only-black-apprentice-winner-trump-has-learned-nothing, October 14, 2016.

47 Joyce Chen, "Don Cheadle Accuses Donald Trump of Once Using N-Word with Friend's Father on Golf Course," *US Magazine,* https://www.usmagazine.com/celebrity-news/news/don-cheadle-trump-used-n-word-with-friends-father-on-golf-course-w470479, March 5, 2017.

48 Horizontal Shot Of Blank Sign In Field/ Put Your Copy On This Sign, Carolyn Franks/Shutterstock.com (image altered). Text added to picture by me.

49 Recreation of the newspaper headline from *The Crusader,* similar images at various websites including DailyKos.com, https://www.dailykos.com/stories/2016/11/1/1589543/-The-Ku-Klux-Klan-makes-it-official-endorses-Donald-Trump-saying-Make-America-Great-Again.

50 Recreation of a coin found on various sources on the internet.

51 "Fred Trump," Wikipedia, https://en.wikipedia.org/wiki/Fred_Trump.

52 "U.S. Elevator (featuring Mac McCaughan and Tim Bluhm) 'Old Man Trump,'" video, http://www.30days30songs.com/15.

53 Words by Woody Guthrie Adapted by Ryan Harvey, Music by Ryan Harvey "Old Man Trump," https://www.woodyguthrie.org/Lyrics/Old_Man_Trump.htm

54 "'No Vacancies' for Blacks: How Donald Trump Got His Start, and Was First Accused of Bias," *The New York Times,*

https://www.nytimes.com/2016/08/28/us/politics/donald-trump-housing-race.html, August 27, 2016.

[55] Ibid.

[56] NPR Staff, "Decades-Old Housing Discrimination Case Plagues Donald Trump," NPR, https://www.npr.org/2016/09/29/495955920/donald-trump-plagued-by-decades-old-housing-discrimination-case, September 29, 2016.

[57] Nick Paumgarten, "The Death and Life of Atlantic City," *The New Yorker,* https://www.newyorker.com/magazine/2015/09/07/the-death-and-life-of-atlantic-city, September 7, 2015.

[58] John R. O'Donnell with James Rutherford, *Trumped! The Inside Story of the Real Donald Trump: His Cunning Rise and Spectacular Fall,* Crossroad Press, 2016, Kindle edition.

[59] Ibid., 115.

[60] Ibid.

[61] Lydia O'Connor and Daniel Marans, "Here Are 13 Examples of Donald Trump Being Racist," *Huffington Post,* https://www.huffingtonpost.com/entry/donald-trump-racist-examples_us_56d47177e4b03260bf777e83, February 29, 2016.

[62] "Ex-Trump exec: He's racist through and through," video, CNN, https://www.cnn.com/videos/politics/2018/08/14/jack-odonnell-trump-racist-through-and-through-sot-ebof-vpx.cnn.

[63] Tess Koman, "Former Miss Teen USA Kamie Crawford Tweets She 'Was Warned Trump Doesn't Like Black People,'" *Cosmopolitan,* http://www.cosmopolitan.com/politics/a5938093/former-miss-teen-usa-kamie-crawford-tweets-about-donald-trump-racism, October 13, 2016.

[64] Robert Farley, "Trump Retweets Bogus Crime Graphic," Factcheck.org https://www.factcheck.org/2015/11/trump-retweets-bogus-crime-graphic, November 23, 2015.

[65] John R. O'Donnell with James Rutherford, *Trumped! The Inside Story of the Real Donald Trump: His Cunning Rise and Spectacular Fall,* Crossroad Press, 2016, Kindle edition, 151.

[66] "Donald Trump Remarks at Republican Jewish Coalition Presidential Forum," video, CSPAN, https://www.c-span.org/video/?c4756715/presidential-speech, December 3, 2015.

[67] "AIPAC Annual Conference, Donald Trump Remarks," video, CSPAN, https://www.c-span.org/video/?406949-5/aipac-annual-conference-donald-trump-remarks, March 21, 2016.

[68] Michael Kruse, "The 199 Most Donald Trump Things Donald Trump Has Ever Said," *Politico,* http://www.politico.com/magazine/story/2015/08/the-absolute-trumpest-121328, August 14, 2015.

[69] Sarah Begley, "Read Donald Trump's Speech to AIPAC," *Time,* http://time.com/4267058/donald-trump-aipac-speech-transcript/ March 21, 2016.

[70] "Donald Trump Remarks at Republican Jewish Coalition Presidential Forum," video and text, CSPAN, https://www.c-span.org/video/?401497-7/donald-trump-remarks-republican-jewish-coalition-presidential-forum.

[71] "George Washington > Quotes > Quotable Quote," Goodreads.com, https://www.goodreads.com/quotes/8162226-the-bosom-of-america-is-open-to-receive-not-only.

[72] David Matthews, "A Disturbing New Poll Says That Only 49% of Republicans Think Islam Should Be Legal," SplinterNews.com, https://splinternews.com/a-disturbing-new-poll-says-that-only-49-of-republicans-1793851147, September 9, 2015.

[73] David Brooks, "The Danger of a Single Story," *The New York Times*, https://www.nytimes.com/2016/04/19/opinion/the-danger-of-a-single-story.html, April 19, 2016.

[74] Chimamanda Adichie, "The Danger of a Single Story," Ted, https://www.ted.com/talks/chimamanda_adichie_the_danger_of_a_singl e_story/transcript, 2009.

[75] "Immigration eLesson," Bill of Rights Institute, https://billofrightsinstitute.org/educate/educator-resources/lessons-plans/immigration-elesson.

[76] Snopes staff, "Donald Trump Criticized for Mocking Disabled Reporter," *Snopes,* https://www.snopes.com/2016/07/28/donald-trump-criticized-for-mocking-disabled-reporter, January 11th, 2017.

[77] CNN Wire and Ellina Abovian, "Trump Denies Mocking New York Times Reporter with Physical Disability," KTLA, http://ktla.com/2015/11/26/trump-mocks-new-york-times-reporters-physical-disability, November 26, 2015.

[78] Megyn Kelly, Settle for More, HarperCollins, New York, 2016, Kindle edition, 256.

[79] "High School Students Use Donald Trump-Inspired Chant to Insult their Hispanic Rival," Fox Sports, https://www.foxsports.com/buzzer/story/donald-trump-build-a-wall-chant-indiana-high-school-basketball-030216, March 2, 2016.

[80] Shaun, King, "KING: Donald Trump is mainstreaming bigotry and helping to ensure it will be here for generations to come," *New York Daily News*, https://www.nydailynews.com/news/politics/king-donald-trump-mainstreaming-bigotry-article-1.2556516, March 18, 2016.

[81] Associated Press Staff, "Trump Changes Tone on Homeless Man Beaten in Boston," *Christian Science Monitor,* https://www.csmonitor.com/USA/Politics/2015/0822/Trump-changes-tone-on-homeless-man-beaten-in-Boston, August 22, 2015.

[82] Eyder Peraltaa, "Univision's Jorge Ramos: Journalists Must 'Denounce' Trump's 'Dangerous Words,'" NPR, https://www.npr.org/sections/thetwo-way/2015/08/26/434836996/univisions-jorge-ramos-ive-never-been-kicked-out-of-a-press-conference, August 26, 2015.

[83] Matthias Gafni, Karina Iofee, and Thomas Peele, "Richmond Man Arrested on Suspicion of Threatening Muslims," *Mercury News,* http://www.mercurynews.com/2015/12/21/richmond-man-arrested-on-suspicion-of-threatening-muslims, December 21, 2015, updated August 11, 2016.

[84] "Trump Supporter Who Punched Protester: 'Next Time, We Might Have to Kill Him,'" *Inside Edition,* http://www.insideedition.com/headlines/15177-trump-supporter-who-punched-protester-next-time-we-might-have-to-kill-him, March 10, 2016.

[85] Ahiza Garcia and Brian Stelter, "Never Seen Anything Like What I'm Witnessing," *CNN Money,* http://money.cnn.com/2016/03/12/media/cbs-sopan-deb-arrest-trump-rally/index.html, March 12, 2016.

[86] Nick Visser and Sebastian Murdock, "'Kill Muslims, Kill Them All!' Trump Supporter Shouts at Street Preachers," *Huffington Post,* http://www.huffingtonpost.com/entry/michigan-man-trump-anti-muslim_us_56f9bbcee4b0a372181acea4, March 29, 2016.

[87] Ben Tufft, "Muslim Student Claims He Was Attacked by Man Chanting 'Trump Trump Trump' and Shouting 'Brown Trash Go Home,'" *The Daily Mail,* http://www.dailymail.co.uk/news/article-3498377/Alleged-Trump-supporter-attacked-Muslim-student-shouted-Brown-trash-home.html, March 18, 2016.

[88] TomoNews US, "Muslim Woman Wearing Hijab Assaulted by Trump Supporter Outside Starbucks in Washington – TomoNews," YouTube video, https://www.youtube.com/watch?v=PK917DR6xSE, May 5, 2016.

[89] Ibid.

90 Andy K, "Trump Reacts to Anti-Hillary Bumper Sticker During Rally: Trump That B--ch," YouTube video, https://www.youtube.com/watch?v=-ytd-ZWMJaI, February 16, 2016.

91 Eric Rosenwald, "'Made in F---ing USA!' Donald Trump Rally, Phoenix, AZ," YouTube video, https://www.youtube.com/watch?v=ups4FeSuHvY, June 18, 2016.

92 Dean Obeidallah, "Why Won't Trump Denounce His Anti-Semitic Supporters?" *The Atlantic,* https://www.theatlantic.com/politics/archive/2016/05/trump-needs-to-loudly-denounce-the-hate/481608/, May 6, 2016.

93 Source unknown – image and similar images widely circulated on the internet.

94 "Ronald Reagan on Bigotry," Rightspeak.net, http://www.rightspeak.net/search?q=ronald+reagan+bigotry.

95 Ibid.

96 Dean Obeidallah, "Why Won't Trump Denounce His Anti-Semitic Supporters?" *The Atlantic,* https://www.theatlantic.com/politics/archive/2016/05/trump-needs-to-loudly-denounce-the-hate/481608/, May 6, 2016.

97 Candace Smith, "Donald Trump Considered Blacks vs. Whites Version of 'The Apprentice,'" https://abcnews.go.com/Politics/donald-trump-considered-blacks-whites-version-apprentice/story?id=39259585, May 20, 2016.

98 Alex Seitz-Wald, "Trump: 'I Am the Least Racist Person There Is' Because A Black Guy Won The Apprentice Six Years Ago," ThinkProgress.org, https://thinkprogress.org/trump-i-am-the-least-racist-person-there-is-because-a-black-guy-won-the-apprentice-six-years-ago-b92f2769f3b, May 9, 2011.

[99] Samuel Smith, "Donald Trump: IRS May Be Auditing Me Because I'm a 'Strong Christian,'" *Christian Post,* http://www.christianpost.com/news/donald-trump-irs-audit-strong-christian-158736, February 26, 2016.

[100] "Democrat Group Creates GoFundMe for Firebombed GOP Office, Raise $13K in 40 Minutes," Wate.com, http://wate.com/2016/10/17/democrat-group-creates-gofundme-for-firebombed-gop-office-raise-13k-in-40-minutes, October 11, 2016.

[101] Eugene Patterson, "Gene Patterson's most famous column: 'A Flower for the Graves,'" https://www.poynter.org/archive/2013/a-flower-for-the-graves, January 13, 2013

[102] Definition from Dictionary.com, https://www.dictionary.com/browse/hypocrite.

[103] Jenna Johnson, "Donald Trump Has No Interest in Apologizing to John McCain," *The Washington Post,* https://www.washingtonpost.com/news/post-politics/wp/2016/07/12/donald-trump-has-no-interest-in-apologizing-to-john-mccain/?utm_term=.f6e397a131bd, July 12, 2016.

[104] Ginger Adams Otis, Reuven Blau, Nancy Billion, "Photos show Donald Trump in military uniform, with athletic teams before dodging the Vietnam draft with 'bull---t' injury," *The New York Daily News,*http://www.nydailynews.com/news/politics/photos-show-trump-military-garb-dodging-draft-article-1.2298248, July 21, 2015.

[105] Akchuk, "Trump Endorsed McCain in 2008," YouTube video, https://www.youtube.com/watch?v=ohuqwK1rM4g, May 2, 2016.

[106] Megyn Kelly, *Settle for More*, HarperCollins, New York, 2016, Kindle edition, 256.

[107] Ibid., 272.

[108] Ibid., 254.

109 Allison Takeda, "Donald Trump Rips into Megyn Kelly Again—on Twitter!" *US Magazine,* https://www.usmagazine.com/celebrity-news/news/donald-trump-rips-into-megyn-kelly-again-on-twitter-2015258, August 25, 2015.

110 @realdonaldTrump, Twitter, https://twitter.com/realdonaldtrump/status/635995703182016513?lang=en, August 24, 2015.

111 Amanda Prestigiacomo, "Trump vs. Kelly: The Full History," *The Daily Wire,* https://www.dailywire.com/news/2955/trump-vs-kelly-full-history-amanda-prestigiacomo, January 28, 2016.

112 Evgenia Peretz, "Blowhards, beware: Megyn Kelly will slay you now," *Vanity Fair,* https://www.vanityfair.com/news/2015/12/megyn-kelly-fox-news-cover-story, February 2016.

113 MIchael Kruse, "The 199 Most Donald Trump Things Donald Trump Has Ever Said," *Politico,"* https://www.politico.com/magazine/story/2015/08/the-absolute-trumpest-121328, August 14, 2015.

114 SooperMexican, "Here's when Trump Bragged in his book about his Multiple Affairs with wealthy married women!" TheRightScoop.com, http://therightscoop.com/heres-when-trump-bragged-in-his-book-about-his-multiple-affairs-with-his-friends-wives, March 25, 2016.

115 Maxwell Tani, "'We don't want him': Former Mexican president blasts current president for inviting Donald Trump to Mexico," *Business Insider*, https://www.businessinsider.com/vincente-fox-enrique-pena-donald-trump-traitor-2016-8, August 31, 2016.

116 SayNOtoRACISTS , "Donald Trump to China on Imports: Listen You Motherf*ckers, We're Gonna Tax You 25 Percent!," YouTube video, https://www.youtube.com/watch?v=zOoj96dv4ul, April 29, 2011.

117 Alana Horowitz Satlin,"Watch Trump Contradict Himself on Almost Every Issue," *The Huffington Post,*

https://www.huffpost.com/entry/donald-trump-flip-flop_n_57ac3753e4b0db3be07d4192, August 11, 2016.

[118] Definition compiled from various dictionaries and Internet sources.

[119] Definition compiled from the following dictionaries and internet sources: Cambridge dictionary, Wikipedia.

[120] Nick Penzenstadler and Susan Page, "Exclusive: Trump's 3,500 Lawsuits Unprecedented for a Presidential Nominee," *USA Today,* https://www.usatoday.com/story/news/politics/elections/2016/06/01/donald-trump-lawsuits-legal-battles/84995854.

[121] Aaron Smith, "Donald Trump Sues 'Malicious' Palm Beach Airport for $100 Million," *CNN Money,* https://money.cnn.com/2015/01/13/luxury/trump-palm-beach-lawsuit, January 13, 2015.

[122] Frank Cerabino, "Trump's War with Palm Beach," *Politico,* www.politico.eu/article/trumps-war-with-palm-beach, September 5, 2015.

[123] Christianna Silva, "The ~20 Times Trump Has Threatened to Sue Someone During This Campaign," FiveThirtyEight.com, https://fivethirtyeight.com/features/the-22-times-trump-has-threatened-to-sue-someone-during-this-campaign, October 24, 2016.

[124] Richard Branson, "Meeting Donald Trump," Virgin Media, https://www.virgin.com/richard-branson/meeting-donald-trump, October 21, 2016.

[125] Donald J. Trump and Bill Zanker, *Think Big: Make It Happen in Business and Life,* HarperCollins, New York, 2009, Kindle edition, 29.

[126] @realDonaldTrump, Twitter, https://twitter.com/realdonaldtrump/status/712457104515317764?lang=en, March 22, 2016.

127 Loren Gutentag, "Trump to CBS News: McCain 'Has to Be Very Careful'," NewsMax.com, https://www.newsmax.com/Headline/Trump-CBS-News-McCain-Careful/2016/03/04/id/717453, March 4, 2016.

128 @realDonaldTrump, Twitter, https://twitter.com/realdonaldtrump/status/6604609097761069057?lang=en, October 31, 2015.

129 @realDonaldTrump, Twitter, https://twitter.com/realdonaldtrump/status/701779181986680832?lang=en, February 22, 1016.

130 Brendan O'Connor, "Here Are the Most Absurd Parts of Donald Trump's Batshit Interview with the *Washington Post* Editorial Board," *Gawker,* http://gawker.com/here-are-the-most-absurd-parts-of-donald-trumps-batshit-1766294575, March 21, 2016.

131 Tom Kludt, "Donald Trump Ends Fox Feud, Resumes Fight with 'Psycho' Publisher," *CNN Money,* http://money.cnn.com/2016/01/29/media/donald-trump-fox-news-joe-mcquaid/index.html, January 29, 2016.

132 David Graham, "The Many Scandals of Donald Trump: A Cheat Sheet," https://www.theatlantic.com/politics/archive/2017/01/donald-trump-scandals/474726, January 23, 2017.

133 Donald J. Trump with Tony Schwartz, *Trump, The Art of the Deal*, Random House Publishing Group, New York, 1987, Kindle edition, 108.

134 Megyn Kelly, *Settle for More,* HarperCollins, New York, 2016, Kindle Edition, 256.

135 Definition compiled from various dictionaries and Internet sources.
136 How to Defend Yourself Against A Trump-Style Handshake," *Huffington Post,* http://www.huffingtonpost.in/2017/02/16/how-to-defend-yourself-against-a-trump-style-handshake_a_21715939/?utm_hp_ref=in-homepage, February 17, 2017.

[137] Nicole Brewer, "Expert Analyzes Trump Handshake, Says He's Seeking The 'Upper Hand,'" CBS Philadelphia, http://philadelphia.cbslocal.com/2017/02/17/expert-analyzes-trump-handshake-says-hes-seeking-the-upper-hand/, February 17, 2017.

[138] Donald Trump with Meredith McIver, *Trump: How to Get Rich*, Random House, New York, 2004, Kindle edition, location 1198.

[139] Mark Sumner, "Deadbeat Donald: Trump Doesn't Pay His Bills," *Daily Kos,* https://www.dailykos.com/stories/2016/6/10/1536990/-Deadbeat-Donald-Trump-doesn-t-pay-his-bills, June 10, 2016.

[140] Ibid.

[141] "Scourge, not savior," *The Economist*, https://www.economist.com/united-states/2016/05/14/scourge-not-saviour, May 14, 2016.

[142] Stephanie Mencimerj, "Here's How Trump (Allegedly) Stiffed an 82-Year-Old Immigrant over an Unpaid Bill," *Mother Jones,* https://www.motherjones.com/politics/2016/06/when-donald-trump-didnt-want-pay-chandelier-bill, June 10, 2016.

[143] Ibid.

[144] Ibid.

[145] Heather Perlberg Bloomberg, "Trump the Mortgage Broker Was in Trouble from Start," *The Chicago Tribune,* https://www.chicagotribune.com/business/ct-trump-mortgage-20160823-story.html, August 23, 2016.

[146] Max J. Rosenthal, "The Trump Files: Trump's Long History of Getting Sued by His Own Lawyers," *Mother Jones,* https://www.motherjones.com/politics/2016/10/trump-files-time-trumps-lawyers-sued-trump, October 27, 2016.

[147] Ibid.

148 Ibid.

149 "Henrico lawyers sought $4 million+ in Trump lawsuit, alleged defamation," WWBT NBC12 http://www.nbc12.com/story/33292446/henrico-lawyers-sought-4-million-in-trump-lawsuit-alleged-defamation, October 1, 2016.

150 John Cassidy, "Trump University: It's Worse Than You Think," *The New Yorker,* https://www.newyorker.com/news/john-cassidy/trump-university-its-worse-than-you-think, June 2, 2016.

151 The Holy Bible, English Standard Version, James 4:6.

152 Definition compiled from the following dictionaries and internet sources: Thefreedictionary.com, Grammarist.com, Yourdictionary.com, and Thesaurus.com.

153 Nick Baumann, "I Am the Best: A Prose Poem by Donald J. Trump," *Huffington Post,* https://www.huffingtonpost.com/entry/donald-trump-best-most-only_us_56f0a08ee4b03a640a6b7380, March 22, 2016.

154 Haley Britzky, "Everything Trump says he knows 'more about than anybody,'" Axios, https://www.axios.com/everything-trump-says-he-knows-more-about-than-anybody-b278b592-cff0-47dc-a75f-5767f42bcf1e.html, January 5, 2019.

155 Wesley Pruden, "Trumpspeak, a Language Rich in Adjectives," *The Washington Times,* https://www.washingtontimes.com/news/2017/feb/23/donald-trumps-speech-features-superlatives, February 23, 2017.

156 Vivian Yee, "Donald Trump's Math Takes His Towers to Greater Heights," https://www.nytimes.com/2016/11/02/nyregion/donald-trump-tower-heights.html, November 1, 2016.

157 Definition compiled from various dictionaries and internet sources.

[158] Andrew Carnegie, "Andrew Carnegie Quotes," https://www.brainyquote.com/authors/andrew_carnegie.

[159] Daniel White, "Watch Trump Talk About His Private Parts at the Debate," *Time,* http://time.com/4247366/republican-debate-donald-trump-small-hands-penis, March 4, 2006.

[160] Ben Jacobs, "Trump Repeats Crowd Member's 'Pu--y' Insult as New Hampshire Votes," *The Guardian,* https://www.theguardian.com/us-news/2016/feb/08/trump-repeats-insult-from-crowd-member-calling-cruz-a-pussy, February 9, 2016.

[161] @Lennyjacobson, Twitter, https://twitter.com/Lennyjacobson/status/588867303908868096/photo/1?ref_src=twsrc%5Etfw&ref_url=http%3A%2F%2Fwww.ibtimes.co.uk%2Fdonald-trump-deletes-offensive-tweet-saying-hillary-clinton-cant-satisfy-her-husband-1497525, April 16, 2015.

[162] LesGrossman News, "Donald Trump: Hillary Clinton 'Got Schlonged,'" YouTube video, https://www.youtube.com/watch?v=XAXQ4U7Twds, Dec 21, 2015.

[163] Daniel White, "Donald Trump Calls Clinton's Bathroom Break 'Disgusting,'" *Time,* http://time.com/4158303/donald-trump-hillary-clinton-disgusting-schlonged, December 22, 2015.

[164] Jessica Estepa, "Donald Trump on Carly Fiorina: 'Look at that face!'" *USA Today,* https://www.usatoday.com/story/news/nation-now/2015/09/10/trump-fiorina-look-face/71992454, September 10, 2015.

[165] Andrew Kaczynski and Nathan McDermott, "Donald Trump's Long History of Disparaging Women's Appearances," CNN, http://www.cnn.com/2017/06/29/politics/kfile-trump-long-history-disparaging-comments/index.html, June 29, 2017.

[166] Marie Brenner, "After the Gold Rush," *Vanity Fair,* https://www.vanityfair.com/magazine/2015/07/donald-ivana-trump-divorce-prenup-marie-brenner, September 1990.

[167] Asawin Suebsaeng, "You Have to Treat 'Em like S--t': Before Megyn Kelly, Trump Dumped Wine on a Female Reporter," *The Daily Beast,* https://www.thedailybeast.com/you-have-to-treat-em-like-shit-before-megyn-kelly-trump-dumped-wine-on-a-female-reporter, August 8, 2015.

[168] Barry Friedman, "Would God Be So Good?" *Esquire,* http://www.esquire.com/news-politics/news/a24057/donald-trump-presidential-run-2016-072913, July 29, 2013.

[169] What Trump Says, "Donald Trump's Comments on His Daughter Ivanka Trump," YouTube video, https://www.youtube.com/watch?v=ZtsOFfNC3Y8, February 13, 2016.

[170] Michael Barbaro and Megan Twohey, "Crossing the Line: How Donald Trump Behaved with Women in Private," *The New York Times*, https://www.nytimes.com/2016/05/15/us/politics/donald-trump-women.html?action=click&module=RelatedCoverage&pgtype=Article®ion=Footer, May 14, 2016.

[171] Arlene Washington, "Donald Trump Once Joked He and Ivanka Have 'Sex' in Common," *Hollywood Reporter,* https://www.hollywoodreporter.com/news/donald-trump-once-joked-he-ivanka-have-sex-common-941600, October 26, 2016.

[172] Aramide Tinubu, "Most Shocking Things Donald Trump Has Said About His Own Kids," Cheatsheet.com, https://www.cheatsheet.com/entertainment/most-shocking-things-donald-trump-has-said-about-his-own-kids.html/?a=viewall, December 23, 2017.

[173] Michael Barbaro and Megan Twohey, "Crossing the Line: How Donald Trump Behaved with Women in Private," *The New York Times*,

https://www.nytimes.com/2016/05/15/us/politics/donald-trump-women.html?action=click&module=RelatedCoverage&pgtype=Article®ion=Footer, May 14, 2016.

[174] Ibid.

[175] "Ever Wondered Why Donald Trump Doesn't Talk About Tiffany?" ReinventingAging.org, http://www.reinventingaging.org/entertainment/20-things-donald-trump-wants-to-keep-quiet-about-his-other-daughter-tiffany.

[176] MIchael Kruse, "The 199 Most Donald Trump Things Donald Trump Has Ever Said," *Politico*," https://www.politico.com/magazine/story/2015/08/the-absolute-trumpest-121328, August 14, 2015.

[177] Gail Collins, "Donald Trump Gets Weirder," *The New York Times*, http://www.nytimes.com/2011/04/02/opinion/02collins.html?src=twrhp&mtrref=nymag.com&assetType=opinion, April 1, 2011.

[178] Nick Glass, "The 15 Most Offensive Things That Have Come Out of Trump's Mouth," *Politico*, https://www.politico.com/story/2015/12/trump-hate-216539, December 8, 2015.

[179] Jasmine C. Lee and Kevin Quealy, "The 281 People, Places and Things Donald Trump Has Insulted on Twitter: A Complete List," https://www.nytimes.com/interactive/2016/01/28/upshot/donald-trump-twitter-insults.html#the-letter, October 24, 2016.

[180] Elliot Smolowitz, "Trump: I Would Be 'So Tough' on Terrorists in US," *The Hill*, http://thehill.com/blogs/ballot-box/gop-primaries/262203-trump-i-would-be-so-tough-on-terrorists-in-us, December 4, 2015.

[181] Viewing Liberty, "Donald Trump: 'I'm Speaking With Myself' About Foreign Policy," YouTube video, https://www.youtube.com/watch?v=nh2dciUflVQ, May 16, 2016.

182 Bradford Richardson, "Trump Promises to 'Work Something Out' on Healthcare," *The Hill,* http://thehill.com/blogs/ballot-box/presidential-races/267673-trump-promises-to-work-something-out-on-healthcare, January 31, 2016.

183 Peter Suderman, "Donald Trump's Health Care Plan Shows His Complete Disdain for Expertise: He's Not Just Clueless—He's Willfully Ignorant," Reason.com, https://reason.com/blog/2016/03/08/donald-trumps-health-care-plan-shows-his , March 8, 2016.

184 "The Stunning Ignorance of Trump's Health Care Plan: Donald Trump's Proposed Alternative to the Affordable Care Act Amounts to a Whole Lot of Nothing," *U.S. News & World Report*, March 17, 2016.

185 "Full Rush Transcript: Donald Trump, CNN Milwaukee Republican Presidential Town Hall," CNN, http://cnnpressroom.blogs.cnn.com/2016/03/29/full-rush-transcript-donald-trump-cnn-milwaukee-republican-presidential-town-hall, March 29th, 2016.

186 "Trump on Abraham Lincoln: Arrgghh," *The Daily Wire,* https://www.dailywire.com/news/4672/trump-abraham-lincoln-arrgghh-hank-berrien, Hank Berrien, April 5, 2016.

187 Rebecca Kaplan, "Fifth Republican debate: Candidates Spar Over Ways to Fight ISIS," CBS News, https://www.cbsnews.com/news/republican-gop-debate-las-vegas, December 15, 2015.

188 Meet the Press Transcript - August 16, 2015, NBC News, https://www.nbcnews.com/meet-the-press/meet-press-transcript-august-16-2015-n412636, August 19, 2015.

189 Jack Shafer, "Donald Trump Talks Like a Third-Grader," *Politico,* https://www.politico.com/magazine/story/2015/08/donald-trump-talks-like-a-third-grader-121340, August 13, 2015

190 Orly Kayam, "The Readability and Simplicity of Donald Trump's Language, Political Studies Association, 2018, Vol. 16(1) 73–88.

191 Pam Key, "Trump: I Get My Military Advice from Watching Shows," video, *Breitbart News,* http://www.breitbart.com/video/2015/08/16/trump-i-get-my-military-advice-from-watching-shows, August 16, 2015.

192 Andrew Romano, "The Strange Power of Donald Trump's Speech Patterns," AndrewRomano.com, http://www.andrewromano.net/220/the-strange-power-of-donald-trump-s-speech-patterns, March 31, 2016.

193 Ibid.

194 Bob Fredericks, "Donald Trump Botches 9/11 Tribute, Thanks Heroes of 7-Eleven," *New York Post,* https://nypost.com/2016/04/19/donald-trump-confuses-911-with-7-eleven , April 19, 2016.

195 Kenya Sinclair, "'Nobody reads the Bible more than me': Trump's claim Is a laughing stock," *Catholic Online,* http://www.catholic.org/news/hf/faith/story.php?id=67567, February 25, 2016.

196 Hunter Walker, "Donald Trump Just Dodged Two Questions About the Bible," Business Insider, http://www.businessinsider.com/donald-trump-refused-to-name-favorite-bible-verse-2015-8, August 26, 2015.

197 Leonardo Blair, "Donald Trump Cites Proverbs Ahead of CNN Republican Debate, 'Never Bend to Envy;' Says He'll Try Toning Down," *Christian Post,* https://www.christianpost.com/news/donald-trump-cites-proverbs-ahead-of-cnn-republican-debate-never-bend-to-envy-says-hell-try-toning-down-145476, September 16, 2015.

198 Catholic Online, https://www.catholic.org/about.

199 Kenya Sinclair, 'Nobody reads the Bible more than me': Trump's claim is a laughing stock, *Catholic Online* https://www.catholic.org/news/hf/faith/story.php?id=67567, February 25, 2016.

200 Stoyan Zaimov, "Donald Trump: 'Nobody Reads Bible More Than Me; John Kerry Hasn't Read the Bible,'" *Christian Post,* https://www.christianpost.com/news/donald-trump-nobody-reads-bible-more-than-me-john-kerry.html, February 25, 2016.

201 Presidential Candidate Donald Trump at the Family Leadership Summit," video, CSPAN, https://www.c-span.org/video/?327045-5/presidential-candidate-donald-trump-family-leadership-summit&start=5, July 18, 2015.

202 Ray Nothstine, "Trump: 'Why Do I Have to Repent or Ask for Forgiveness If I Am Not Making Mistakes?'" video, *Christian Post,* http://www.christianpost.com/news/trump-why-do-i-have-to-repent-or-ask-for-forgiveness-if-i-am-not-making-mistakes-video-141856, July23, 2015.

203 The Holy Bible, English Standard Version, Romans 3:23.

204 Juana Summers, "Is Donald Trump Really a Christian? What We Know about His Faith," *Mashable,* http://mashable.com/2016/02/18/donald-trump-christian-religion/#HECaserWpgqH, February 18, 2016.

205 "10 Donald Trump Quotes That Should Horrify His Evangelical Supporters," *Huffington Post,* https://www.huffpost.com/entry/donald-trump-vs-jesus-christ_n_5798e188e4b0d3568f85724a, updated Jul 28, 2016.

206 John Pavlovitz, "It's Time Anyone Stop Calling Donald Trump a Christian," JohmPavovitz.com, https://johnpavlovitz.com/2017/02/02/its-time-we-stopped-calling-donald-trump-a-christian, February 2, 2017.

207 Ibid.

208 Michael Sebastian, "Pope Francis Suggests Donald Trump Is Not a Christian (and Trump Has Already Fired Back)," Esquire, https://www.esquire.com/news-politics/news/a42250/pope-donald-trump-christian/, February 18, 2016.

209 David Sherfinsk, "Donald Trump: 'To the Best of My knowledge,' Not Too Many Evangelicals Come Out of Cuba," *The Washington Times,* http://www.washingtontimes.com/news/2015/dec/30/donald-trump-best-my-knowledge-not-too-many-evange, December 30, 2015.

210 Evelyn Rupert, "Trump Bashes Romney in Utah: 'Are You Sure He's a Mormon?'" *The Hill,* http://thehill.com/blogs/ballot-box/273637-trump-bashes-romney-are-you-sure-hes-a-mormon, March 18, 2016.

211 "Trump: 'We don't know anything about Hillary in terms of religion,'" CNN Wires, http://fox2now.com/2016/06/21/trump-we-dont-know-anything-about-hillary-in-terms-of-religion, June 21, 2016.

212 Stoyan Zaimov, "Donald Trump: 'Nobody Reads Bible More Than Me; John Kerry Hasn't Read the Bible,'" *Christian Post,* https://www.christianpost.com/news/donald-trump-nobody-reads-bible-more-than-me-john-kerry.html, February 25, 2016.

213 Todd Beamon, "Trump Questions Ben Carson's Religion: 'I Don't Know About That,'" NewsMax.com, http://www.newsmax.com/Newsfront/trump-questions-ben-carson/2015/10/24/id/698880/, October 24, 2015.

214 "Trump on Obama's Birth Certificate: 'Maybe It Says He's a Muslim,'" video, http://nation.foxnews.com/donald-trump/2011/03/30/trump-obama-maybe-hes-muslim, March 30, 2011.

215 @realDonaldTrump, Twitter, https://twitter.com/realdonaldtrump/status/701084443889381377?lang=en, February 20, 2016.

216 "Donald J. Trump Foundation," Wikipedia, https://en.wikipedia.org/wiki/Donald_J._Trump_Foundation, March 24, 2017.

217 Adam Edelman, "Donald Trump's charitable foundation has given just $1,000 to 9/11-related causes: report," *NY Daily News,*

https://www.nydailynews.com/news/politics/trump-charity-1-000-9-11causes-report-article-1.2423205, November 4, 2015.

[218]John Cassidy, "Trump and the Truth: His Charitable Giving," *The New Yorker,* https://www.newyorker.com/news/john-cassidy/trump-and-the-truth-his-charitable-giving, September 24, 2016.

[219] "Donald J. Trump Foundation," Wikipedia, https://en.wikipedia.org/wiki/Donald_J._Trump_Foundation.

[220] Ibid.

[221] Ibid.

[222] Ibid.

[223] "Donald Trump to dissolve his charitable foundation after mounting complaints," theguardian.com, https://www.theguardian.com/us-news/2016/dec/24/trump-university-shut-down-conflict-of-interest.

[224] Associated Press, "Donald Trump Files $10 Million Lawsuit against Palm Beach after Being Cited for Large Flag," Fox News, https://www.foxnews.com/story/donald-trump-files-10-million-lawsuit-against-palm-beach-after-being-cited-for-large-flag, December 25, 2006.

[225] Ibid.

[226] Frank Cerabino, "Trump's War with Palm Beach," *Politico,* https://www.politico.com/magazine/story/2015/09/trumps-war-with-palm-beach-213122, Frank Cerabino, September 05, 2015.

[227] "Polar Opposition," *Snopes,* https://www.snopes.com/trump-maralago-flagpole, September 25, 2015.

[228] Ibid.

[229] David A. Fahrenthold, "Trump used $258,000 from his charity to settle legal problems," *The Washington Post,*

https://www.washingtonpost.com/politics/trump-used-258000-from-his-charity-to-settle-legal-problems/2016/09/20/adc88f9c-7d11-11e6-ac8e-cf8e0dd91dc7_story.html?utm_term=.9522a1d8da75, September 20, 2016.

[230] "Tuition & Financial Aid," Columbia Grammar & Preparatory School, https://www.cgps.org/admissions/tuition-and-financial-aid.

[231] Jordan Arizmendi, "Donald Took $7 out of his Charity to Pay for His Son's Boy Scout Membership Fees—I Can't Make This Stuff Up," Medium.com, https://medium.com/@JordanArizmendi/donald-took-7-out-of-his-charity-to-pay-for-his-sons-boy-scout-membership-fees-i-can-t-make-3274d4d12aeb, November 1, 2016.

[220] Dan Alexander, "How Donald Trump Shifted Kids-Cancer Charity Money Into His Business," Forbes, https://www.forbes.com/sites/danalexander/2017/06/06/how-donald-trump-shifted-kids-cancer-charity-money-into-his-business/?fbclid=IwAR2fWlWUxuPrpRORWuxgqyHaJFQBOKbbsqX0MB9YVlaYOlblQYPyj4g6QHE#4b995e526b4a, June 6, 2017.

[233] David A. Fahrenthold and Alice Crites, "Trump promised personal gifts on 'Celebrity Apprentice.' Here's who really paid." *The Washington Post*, https://www.washingtonpost.com/politics/trump-promised-personal-gifts-on-celebrity-apprentice-heres-who-really-paid/2016/08/18/b8d087b4-5d9a-11e6-af8e-54aa2e849447_story.html?utm_term=.98a61fd53667, August 19, 2016.

[234] David A. Fahrenthold, "Trump Boasts About His Philanthropy. But His Giving Falls Short Of His Words," *The Washington Post,* https://www.washingtonpost.com/politics/trump-boasts-of-his-philanthropy-but-his-giving-falls-short-of-his-words/2016/10/29/b3c03106-9ac7-11e6-a0ed-ab0774c1eaa5_story.html, October 29, 2016.

[235] Ibid.

[236] Ibid

[237] Definition compiled from the following dictionaries and internet sources: Oxforddictionaries.com, Merriamwebster.com.

[238] Caitlin Yilek, "Trump: 'Nobody Has More Respect for Women Than Me,'" *The Hill,* http://thehill.com/blogs/ballot-box/presidential-races/274374-trump-nobody-has-more-respect-for-women-than-me, March 26, 2016.

[239] SooperMexican, "Here's When Trump BRAGGED in his Book About his Multiple Affairs with Wealthy Married Women!" TheRightScoop.com, http://therightscoop.com/heres-when-trump-bragged-in-his-book-about-his-multiple-affairs-with-his-friends-wives, March 25, 2016.

[240] Ali Gharib, "In 1998, Trump Said His Record with 'the Women' Was Too 'Controversial' to Run for President," SplinterNews.com, https://splinternews.com/in-1998-trump-said-his-record-with-the-women-was-too-c-1793862788, October 13, 2016.

[241] Justin Baragona, "Back in 1998, Trump Called Bill Clinton's Accusers 'Terrible' and 'a Really Unattractive Group,'" Mediaite.com, www.mediaite.com/election-2016/back-in-1998-trump-called-bill-clintons-accusers-terrible-and-a-really-unattractive-group, October 9, 2016.

[242] Dave Quinn, "*National Enquirer* Paid to Kill Story of Playboy Model's Affair with Donald Trump: Report," *People,* https://people.com/politics/donald-trump-karen-mcdougal-affair-national-enquirer, November 5, 2016.

[243] Adrian Carrasquillo, "Salma Hayek: I Denied Trump a Date, so He Planted a *National Enquirer* Story about My Height," BuzzFeed, https://www.buzzfeednews.com/article/adriancarrasquillo/salma-hayek-i-denied-trump-a-date-so-he-planted-a-national-e, October 21, 2016.

[244] Paige Lavender, "These Might Be Donald Trump's Most Disgusting Comments Yet about Women," *Huffington Post,* https://www.huffingtonpost.com/entry/donald-trump-women-comments_us_57f8016de4b0e655eab4148d, October 7, 2016.

245 Claire Cohen, "Donald Trump Sexism Tracker: Every Offensive Comment in One Place," *The Telegraph,* https://www.telegraph.co.uk/women/politics/donald-trump-sexism-tracker-every-offensive-comment-in-one-place, July 14, 2017.

246 Timothy L. O'Brien, *TrumpNation: The Art of Being the Donald*, Open Road Integrated Media, New York, 2005, Kindle edition, 7.

247 Will Dean, "Jog on, Don: Emma Thompson, Salma Hayek, and the Women Who Spurned Trump," *The Guardian,* https://www.theguardian.com/us-news/shortcuts/2017/mar/24/donald-trump-emma-thompson-salma-hayek-princess-diana, March 24, 2017.

248 Graydon Carter, "Donald Trump: The Ugly American," *Vanity Fair,* https://www.vanityfair.com/news/2016/10/graydon-carter-on-donald-trump, November 2016.

249 Todd Van Luling, "Donald Trump's Lewd Remarks about Women Disturbed Guests at White House Event," *Huffington Post,* https://www.huffingtonpost.com/entry/donald-trump-white-house-correspondents-dinner_us_5832ef72e4b058ce7aabf260, November 21, 2016.

250 Frances Stead Sellers, "Donald Trump, a champion of women? His female employees think so," The *Washington Post*, https://www.washingtonpost.com/politics/donald-trump-a-champion-of-women-his-female-employees-think-so/2015/11/23/7eafac80-88da-11e5-9a07-453018f9a0ec_story.html?utm_term=.d2aa25cb1d63, November 24, 2015.

251 "Apprentice' Cast and Crew Say Trump Was Lewd and Sexist," Associated Press, https://www.apnews.com/2778a6ab72ea49558445337865289508.

252 Ibid.

253 Alex Ungerman, "Donald Trump Made 'Sexual Comments' to Marlee Matlin and Lisa Rinna, 'Celebrity Apprentice' Contestant Claims",

https://www.etonline.com/news/200231_donald_trump_allegedly_made
_sexual_comments_to_marlee_matlin_lisa_rinna, October 12, 2016.

[254] Claire Cohen, "Donald Trump Sexism Tracker: Every Offensive
Comment in One Place," *The Telegraph,*
https://www.telegraph.co.uk/women/politics/donald-trump-sexism-
tracker-every-offensive-comment-in-one-place, July 14, 2017.

[255] Asawin Suebsaeng and Gideon Resnick, "Apprentice Staffer Claims Gary
Busey Groped Her. And Then Donald Trump Laughed," *The Daily Beast,*
https://www.thedailybeast.com/apprentice-staffer-claims-gary-busey-
groped-her-and-then-donald-trump-laughed, October 17, 2016.

[256] Ibid.

[257] Ibid.

[258] "Source: Trump Attempted Boardroom Kiss," video and text, CNN,
http://www.cnn.com/2016/10/08/politics/donald-trump-woman-
incident/index.html, October 8, 2016.

[259] Ibid.

[260] Ben Jacobs, "Donald Trump's defence is to demean accusers: 'Look at
her, I don't think so'," *The Guardian,* https://www.theguardian.com/us-
news/2016/oct/14/look-at-her-i-dont-think-so-trumps-defence-is-to-
demean-his-accusers, October 14, 2016.

[261] "Trump on Accuser: 'Believe Me, She Would Not Be My First Choice,'"
Fox News, http://insider.foxnews.com/2016/10/14/donald-trump-sexual-
assault-accuser-she-would-not-be-my-first-choice, October 14, 2016.

[262] Scott Zamost, "Ex-Contestant: Trump Inspected Each Woman before
Pageant," CNN, https://www.cnn.com/2016/10/13/politics/donald-
trump-miss-usa-contestant/index.html, October 14, 2016.

[263] Michael Barbaro and Megan Twohey, "Crossing the Line: How Donald
Trump Behaved with Women in Private," *The New York Times,*

https://www.nytimes.com/2016/05/15/us/politics/donald-trump-women.html?action=click&module=RelatedCoverage&pgtype=Article®ion=Footer, May 14, 2016.

264 Reena Flores, "More Crude Donald Trump Tapes Surface from Howard Stern Show," CBS News, https://www.cbsnews.com/news/more-donald-trump-tapes-surface-from-howard-stern-show, October 9, 2016.

265 "Former Miss USA Contestant Says Trump Would Go Backstage as Women Undressed," WTHR, https://www.wthr.com/article/former-miss-usa-contestant-says-trump-would-go-backstage-as-women-undressed, October 14, 2016.

266 Molly Redden, "Miss USA 2001 Contestant: Trump Barged into Room When We Were Naked," *The Guardian,* https://www.theguardian.com/us-news/2016/oct/12/donald-trump-miss-usa-dressing-room-2001-rehearsal, October 13, 2016.

267 "Former Miss USA Contestant Says Trump Would Go Backstage as Women Undressed," WTHR, https://www.wthr.com/article/former-miss-usa-contestant-says-trump-would-go-backstage-as-women-undressed, October 12, 2016.

268 "Donald Trump: 'I'll be Dating Her in 10 Years'. . . Quips About Little Girl on '92 Tape", video and text, *TMZ,* https://www.tmz.com/2016/10/12/donald-trump-dating-little-girl-entertainment-tonight-tape/, October 12, 2016.

269 Alana Horowitz Satlin, "Trump's Latest Repulsive Attack on Alicia Machado: 'Check Out Sex Tape,'" *Huffington Post,* https://www.huffingtonpost.com/entry/trump-alicia-machado_us_57ee3401e4b082aad9baa8f6, September 30, 2016, updated October 4, 2016.

270 "Donald Trump and Women," CBS News, www.cbsnews.com/pictures/donald-trump-women/6.

271 Ibid.

272 Paige Lavender, "These Might Be Donald Trump's Most Disgusting Comments Yet about Women," *Huffington Post,* https://www.huffingtonpost.com/entry/donald-trump-women-comments_us_57f8016de4b0e655eab4148d, October 7,2016.

273 Jake Miller, "Donald Trump Defends Calling Mexican Immigrants 'Rapists,'" CBS News, https://www.cbsnews.com/news/election-2016-donald-trump-defends-calling-mexican-immigrants-rapists, July 2, 2015.

274 "Brzezinski to Trump: What 'Positive Message' Do You Have for Muslims to Feel Welcome in This Country?" RealClearPolitics.com, https://www.psychologytoday.com/us/blog/evolution-the-self/201311/6-signs-narcissism-you-may-not-know-about, December 18, 2015.

275 Leon F. Seltzer, Ph.D., "6 Signs of Narcissism You May Not Know About," https://www.psychologytoday.com/us/blog/evolution-the-self/201311/6-signs-narcissism-you-may-not-know-about, November 7, 2013.

276 "Ad Hominem," Urban Dictionary, https://www.urbandictionary.com/define.php?term=Ad%20 hominem, July 12, 2007.

277 David Grace, "Ad Hominem," Medium.com, https://medium.com/@davidgraceauth/when-someones-arguments-take-the-form-of-personal-attacks-and-name-calling-it-s-a-pretty-clear-f95a0bde7a8d, June 22, 2017.

278 Savanna Vest, "The Donald Trump Method: Belittling Opponents in Substitution for Argument and Credibility," *Affinity Magazine,* http://affinitymagazine.us/2017/09/25/the-donald-trump-method-belittling-opponents-in-substitution-for-argument-and-credibility, September 25, 2017.

279 Christopher Massie, "One Quote That Tells You Everything About Donald Trump's Rhetorical Style," BuzzFeed,

https://www.buzzfeed.com/christophermassie/one-quote-that-tells-you-everything-about-donald-trumps-rhet?utm_term=.wvlr8YY3E#.bkqorww9k, September 9, 2015.

[280] "The Ad Hominem Fallacy: How People Use Personal Attacks to Win Arguments," Effectivology.com, https://effectiviology.com/ad-hominem-fallacy.

[281] "Paul Graham," Wikipedia, https://en.wikipedia.org/wiki/Paul_Graham_(programmer).

[282] Ibid.

[283] Definition compiled from various dictionaries and Internet sources.

[284] Dan P. McAdams, "The Mind of Donald Trump," *The Atlantic,* https://www.theatlantic.com/magazine/archive/2016/06/the-mind-of-donald-trump/480771, June 2016.

[285] Laura Entis, "Donald Trump's Narcissism Got Him Elected. It Won't Get Him Impeached," *Fortune,* http://fortune.com/2017/02/08/trump-narcissism-impeachment, February 8, 2017.

[286] Oliver Laughland, The Guardian, Ex-Trump workers describe egocentric micromanager: 'Donald loves Donald', https://www.theguardian.com/us-news/2016/mar/14/donald-trump-former-employee-interviews-ego-diversity, March 14, 2016.

[287] Pamela Kruger, "This Is Donald Trump's Biggest Weakness," *Fortune,* http://fortune.com/2016/07/28/donald-trump-tony-schwartz, July 28, 2016.

[288] Dan P. McAdams , "The Mind of Donald Trump," The Atlantic, https://www.theatlantic.com/magazine/archive/2016/06/the-mind-of-donald-trump/480771, June 2016.

289 Jeremy Diamond, "Donald Trump takes Liberty, courts Christian crowd," https://www.cnn.com/2016/01/18/politics/donald-trump-liberty-two-corinthians/index.html, January 19, 2016.

290 Jason Horowitz, *The New York Times*, "Fred Trump Taught His Son the Essentials of Showboating Self-Promotion," https://www.nytimes.com/2016/08/13/us/politics/fred-donald-trump-father.html, August 12, 2016.

291 Dan P. McAdams , "The Mind of Donald Trump," The Atlantic, https://www.theatlantic.com/magazine/archive/2016/06/the-mind-of-donald-trump/480771, June 2016.

292 Gwenda Blair, *The Trumps: Three Generations of Builders and a Presidential Candidate*, Simon and Schuster Paperbacks, New York, Kindle edition, 455.

293 Markus Feldenkirchen, Thomas Hüetlin, Nils Minkmar, and Gordon Repinski, "No One Loves the 45th President Like Donald Trump," *Der Spiegel,* http://www.spiegel.de/international/world/donald-trump-brings-uncertainty-and-narcissism-to-white-house-a-1129925.html, January 19, 2017.

294 Bill Daley, "Weicker, Trump: Act Your Age, Not Your Shoe Size," *The Hartford Courant,* https://www.courant.com/news/connecticut/hc-xpm-1993-12-10-0000000851-story.html, December 1993.

295 Jason Horowitz, "A King in His Castle: How Donald Trump Lives, From His Longtime Butler," https://www.nytimes.com/2016/03/16/us/politics/donald-trump-butler-mar-a-lago.html, March 15, 2016.

296 "Why Do Narcissists Lie?", Narcissist Abuse Support, https://narcissistabusesupport.com/red-flags/narcissist-liars-common-lies.

297 Marie Hartwell-Walker, Ed.D., "Narcissistic Personality Disorder vs. Normal Narcissism," https://psychcentral.com/lib/narcissistic-personality-disorder-vs-normal-narcissism.

298 "Narcissistic Personality Disorder," https://www.helpguide.org/articles/mental-disorders/narcissistic-personality-disorder.htm.

299 Frazier Moore, NBC Miami, "Donald Trump Assures Jimmy Fallon He Can Apologize 'If I'm Ever Wrong,'" https://www.nbcmiami.com/news/national-international/Donald-Trump-Jimmy-Fallon-Apologizing-Tonight-Show-326928351.html?amp=y, September 12, 2015.

300 Dan P. McAdams, "The Mind of Donald Trump," The Atlantic, https://www.theatlantic.com/magazine/archive/2016/06/the-mind-of-donald-trump/480771/, June 2016.

301 "'Art of the Deal' Ghostwriter Speaks Out," video, MSNBC, http://www.msnbc.com/rachel-maddow/watch/art-of-the-deal-ghostwriter-speaks-out-729014339840, July 20, 2016.

302 Jane Mayer, "Donald Trump's Ghostwriter Tells All," *The New Yorker,* https://www.newyorker.com/magazine/2016/07/25/donald-trumps-ghostwriter-tells-all, July 25, 2016.

303 Adam Edelman, "Muslim-American War Hero's Parents Hit Back at Donald Trump After his Response to Their DNC Speech: 'He Is a Black Soul,'" NY Daily News, https://www.nydailynews.com/news/politics/muslim-american-war-hero-parents-hit-back-donald-trump-article-1.2733121, updated July 31, 2016.

304 Dan P. McAdams, "The Mind of Donald Trump," *The Atlantic,* https://www.theatlantic.com/magazine/archive/2016/06/the-mind-of-donald-trump/480771, June 2016.

305 Hrafnkell Haraldsson, "David Axelrod Says Trump's Soul Has Been Revealed, but It Was Never Hidden," PoliticusUSA.com,

https://www.politicususa.com/2016/04/04/david-axelrod-trumps-soul-revealed-hidden.html, April 4, 2016.

[306] Wayne, "Donald Trump Says This Man is Getting an 'A' in Leadership, and It's Not Obama," *The Political Insider,* https://thepoliticalinsider.com/trump-says-this-man, September 30, 2015.

[307] Meghan Keneally, "5 Controversial Dictators and Leaders Donald Trump Has Praised," ABC News, http://abcnews.go.com/Politics/controversial-dictators-leaders-donald-trump-praised/story?id=40373481, July 6, 2016.

[308] Michael McAuliff, "Trump Once Praised Tyrants for Not Being Politically Correct," *Huffington Post,* https://www.huffingtonpost.com/entry/donald-trump-saddam-hussein-muammar-gaddafi_us_5780153fe4b0344d514f5ef1, July 11, 2016.

[309] @ realDonaldTrump, Twitter, https://twitter.com/realdonaldtrump/status/703900742961270784?lang=en, February 28, 2016.

[310] Adam Taylor, "61 Not-Very-Positive Things Foreign Leaders Have Said About Donald Trump," *The Washington Post,* https://www.washingtonpost.com/news/worldviews/wp/2016/05/06/47-not-very-positive-things-foreign-leaders-have-said-about-donald-trump/?utm_term=.670c2b8d4417, July 19, 2016.

[311] David Brooks, "No, Not Trump, Not Ever," *The New York Times,* https://www.nytimes.com/2016/03/18/opinion/no-not-trump-not-ever.html, March 18, 2016.

[312] Ibid.

[313] "2005: Donald and Melania Trump as Newlyweds," CNN, video, https://www.cnn.com/videos/entertainment/2016/05/06/donald-trump-melania-trump-2005-entire-larry-king-live-intv.cnn, May 17, 2005.

314 Andrew Kaczynski, Megan Apper, "Donald Trump Thinks Men Who Change Diapers Are Acting 'Like The Wife'" BuzzFeedNews.com, https://www.buzzfeednews.com/article/andrewkaczynski/donald-trump-thinks-men-who-change-diapers-are-acting-like-t, April 24, 2016.

315 The Wendy Williams Show, "Ivana Trump on 'Raising Trump,'" YouTube video, https://www.youtube.com/watch?v=yFRPOdgNWrA, Oct 13, 2017.

316 Julia Ioffe, "The Real Story of Donald Trump Jr.," *GQ,* https://www.gq.com/story/real-story-of-donald-trump-jr, July 21, 2018

317 Alessandra Stanley, "The Other Trump," *The New York Times,* https://www.nytimes.com/2016/10/02/fashion/tiffany-the-other-trump.html, October 1, 2016.

318 Ilyssa Panitz, "Marla Maples Dishes on The Donald, Their Daughter, and Flying Solo," More.com, August 25, 2011, article apparently no longer available online.

319 Charlotte Triggs, "Marla Maples Says She Raised Tiffany as a 'Single Mother' After Donald Trump Divorce: 'Her Daddy Was a Good Provider, but as Far as Time, It Was Just Me'," *People,* https://people.com/celebrity/donald-trump-ex-marla-maples-talks-raising-tiffany-trump-as-a-single-mother/, April 21, 2016.

320 Ollie Gillman, "Donald Trump's Instagram-loving 'mystery' daughter Finally Breaks Her Silence On Her Father's Presidential Campaign," *The Daily Mail,* https://www.dailymail.co.uk/news/article-3328961/Donald-Trump-s-daughter-finally-breaks-silence-father-s-presidential-campaign.html, November 21, 2015.

321 Julia Ioffe, "The Real Story of Donald Trump Jr.," GQ, https://www.gq.com/story/real-story-of-donald-trump-jr, July 21, 2018

322 Ibid.

323 "Implementation of Indian Gaming Regulatory Act, Oversight Hearing Before the Subcommittee on Native American Affairs of the Committee

on Natural Resources, House of Representatives, One Hundred Third Congress, First Session on Implementation of Public Law 100-497, The Indian Gaming Regulatory Act of 1988, and Related Law Enforcement Issues, Hearing Held in Washington DC, October 5, 1993," https://turtletalk.files.wordpress.com/2016/07/1993-trump-nat-res-testimony-pdf.pdf, 175-176, 187, 242, 244.

[324] David Lightman, "Trump Criticizes Pequots, Casino," *The Hartford Courant,* https://www.courant.com/news/168onnecticut/hc-xpm-1993-10-06-0000003863-story.html, October 6, 1993.

[325] "Trump Repeatedly Questioned the Concept of Tribal Sovereignty", *The New York Times*, February 27, 1994.

[326] 6th Air Mobility Wing Public Affairs, "President Obama gives national security speech to MacDill service members," https://www.macdill.af.mil/News/Article-Display/Article/1022170/president-obama-gives-national-security-speech-to-macdill-service-members, December 07, 2016.

[327] Rachel Simon, "Donald Trump Asking 'How Stupid Is Our Country?' Is A Real Thing That Happened In The Debate," *Bustle,* https://www.bustle.com/articles/188689-donald-trump-asking-how-stupid-is-our-country-is-a-real-thing-that-happened-in-the, October 9, 2016.

[328] "Ronald Reagan > Quotes > Quotable Quote," Goodreads.com, https://www.goodreads.com/quotes/128645-live-simply-love-generously-care-deeply-speak-kindly-leave-the.

[329] Donald Trump with Meredith McIver, *Trump: How to Get Rich*, Random House, New York, 2004, Kindle edition, Location 1198.

[330] MAKERS Team, "6 Best Barack Obama Quotes About Women," Makers.com, https://www.makers.com/blog/barack-obama-quotes-about-women, August 4, 2016.

331 Nick Glass, "The 15 Most Offensive Things That Have Come Out of Trump's Mouth,"*Politico,* https://www.politico.com/story/2015/12/trump-hate-216539, December 8, 2015.

332 John McCain, "John McCain: Inspiring Citizens to Do More," *Time,* http://content.time.com/time/magazine/article/0,9171,1840633,00.html, September 11, 2008.

333 Inae Oh, "Donald Trump Just Gave the Most Insane Campaign Speech Ever," *Mother Jones,* https://www.motherjones.com/politics/2015/07/donald-trump-campaign-speech-lindsey-graham, July 21, 2015.

334 Jenna Johnson, "Donald Trump Has No Interest in Apologizing to John McCain," *The Washington Post,* https://www.washingtonpost.com/news/post-politics/wp/2016/07/12/donald-trump-has-no-interest-in-apologizing-to-john-mccain/?utm_term=.f6e397a131bd, July 12, 2016.

335 "John McCain," Wikipedia, https://en.wikipedia.org/wiki/John_McCain.

336 Jenna Johnson, "Donald Trump Has No Interest in Apologizing to John McCain," *The Washington Post,* https://www.washingtonpost.com/news/post-politics/wp/2016/07/12/donald-trump-has-no-interest-in-apologizing-to-john-mccain/?utm_term=.f6e397a131bd, July 12, 2016.

337 David Mikkelson, "Did Trump Brag He Had the 'Tallest Building in Manhattan' After the 9/11 Attacks?" Snopes.com, https://www.snopes.com/fact-check/trump-bragged-tallest-building, September 14, 2016.

338 Bethania Palmahttps, "Was Donald Trump at Ground Zero Searching for Survivors Two Days After 9/11 with Workers He Paid For?" nopes.com, www.snopes.com/fact-check/trump-searching-911-survivors, September 11, 2018.

[339] Michael Daly, "Trump Won't Name Any of the 'Hundreds of Friends' He Says Died on 9/11," *The Daily Beast*, https://www.thedailybeast.com/trump-wont-name-any-of-the-hundreds-of-friends-he-says-died-on-911, February 17, 2016.

[340] William Bastone, "Trump Made No Donations To 9/11 Charities," TheSmokinggun.com, http://www.thesmokinggun.com/documents/celebrity/donald-trump-empathy-gap-754693, November 3, 2015.

[341] Loren Renz and Leslie Marino, "Giving in the Aftermath of 9/11," The Foundation Center, http://foundationcenter.org/gainknowledge/research/pdf/9_11update03.pdf, December 2003.

[342] William Bastone, "Trump Made No Donations To 9/11 Charities," TheSmokinggun.com, http://www.thesmokinggun.com/documents/celebrity/donald-trump-empathy-gap-754693, November 3, 2015.

[343] Mahita Gajanan, "'What You're Seeing... Is Not What's Happening.' People Are Comparing This Trump Quote to George Orwell," https://time.com/5347737/trump-quote-george-orwell-vfw-speech, July 24, 2018.

[344] Jake Sherman, "Poll: 1-in-4 Voters Believe Trump's Vote-Fraud Claims," *Politico,* https://www.politico.com/story/2017/02/poll-donald-trump-voter-fraud-234458, February 1, 2017.

[345] @realDonaldTrump, Twitter, https://twitter.com/realdonaldtrump/status/232572505238433794?lang=en, August 6, 2012.

[346] Justin Elliott, "Did Trump Really Send Investigators to Hawaii?" *Salon.com,* https://www.salon.com/2011/04/08/trump_hawaii_investigators/, April 8, 2011 (page no longer online).

347 Ibid.

348 Steve Taylor, "The Real Meaning of 'Good' and 'Evil,'" *Psychology Today,* https://www.psychologytoday.com/us/blog/out-the-darkness/201308/the-real-meaning-good-and-evil, August 26, 2013.

349 "Samuel Adams' Letter to James Warren (24 October 1780)," Wikiquote, https://en.wikiquote.org/wiki/Samuel_Adams.

350 Laura Entis, "Donald Trump's Narcissism Got Him Elected. It Won't Get Him Impeached," *Fortune,* http://fortune.com/2017/02/08/trump-narcissism-impeachment/, February 8, 2017.

351 Karen Han, "Donald Trump's Scam Victims Speak Out in Netflix's 'Dirty Money,'" *The Daily Beast,* https://www.thedailybeast.com/trumps-scam-victims-speak-in-netflixs-dirty-money, January 19, 2018.

352 Michael J. Morell, "I Ran the C.I.A. Now I'm Endorsing Hillary Clinton," *The New York Times,* https://www.nytimes.com/2016/08/05/opinion/campaign-stops/i-ran-the-cia-now-im-endorsing-hillary-clinton.html, August 5, 2016.

353 Judith Thurman, "Philip Roth E-Mails on Trump," *The New Yorker*, https://www.newyorker.com/magazine/2017/01/30/philip-roth-e-mails-on-trump, January 22, 2017.

354 William Rameau, "Colin Kaepernick Expresses His Faith Despite San Francisco 49ers Loss, 'Try to Glorify the Lord with What I Do,'" BREATHEcast.com, http://www.breathecast.com/articles/colin-kaepernick-expresses-his-faith-despite-san-francisco-49ers-loss-13611, January 20, 2014.

355 Peter King, "Colin Kaepernick Does Not Care What You Think About His Tattoos," Sports Illustrated, https://www.si.com/2013/07/23/colin-kaepernick-49ers, July 23, 2013.

356 "Colin + Nate, From sitting to kneeling," Respectandrebillion.com, https://respectandrebellion.com/stories/colin-nate.

357 Josh Peter, USA Today, "Colin Kaepernick: I'm not anti-American, will donate $1 million."
https://www.usatoday.com/story/sports/nfl/49ers/2016/09/01/colin-kaepernick-national-anthem-protest-police-socks/89743344/, Updated September 2, 2016.

358 American football player kneeling, STYLEPICS/Depositphotos.com (image altered). Text added to picture by me, text taken from an image: (https://diasp.org/people/5f2ab08012cd4605 - image no longer posted), HU Art Sound/Dias.org, image licensed under 3.0 Unported License - CC BY 3.0, (https://creativecommons.org/licenses/by/3.0/).

359 Nate Boyer, "An open letter to Colin Kaepernick, from a Green Beret-turned-long snapper," Navytimes.com, https://www.navytimes.com/opinion/2016/08/30/an-open-letter-to-colin-kaepernick-from-a-green-beret-turned-long-snapper, August 30, 2016.

360 Malala Yousafzai, "Nobel Lecture", Oslo, 10 December 2014, NobelPrize.org, https://www.nobelprize.org/prizes/peace/2014/yousafzai/26074-malala-yousafzai-nobel-lecture-2014.

361 Marwa, Facebook, https://www.facebook.com/marwi, November 20, 2015.

362 Definition compiled from various dictionaries and internet sources.

363 Concept from https://wwwtrumpinfo.org, Image: Pair of black men's flip flops isolated on white, Coprid/Depositphotos.com (caption added).

364 Yard sign in the fall, Jorge Salcedo/Shutterstock.com (image altered) Text added to picture by me.

365 Mattie Stepanek, source unknown.

366 Blank restaurant menu blackboard with blurry people sitting at the table in the background, © Cebas1/Dreamstime.com (image altered). Text added to picture by me.

367 Close up of young attractive woman holding blank canvas at the street, Akaberka/Depositphotos.com (image altered). Text added to picture by me.

368 Terry Vaught, *Tampa Bay Times*, August 7, 2016 (not an image but a quotation of the letter to the editor).

369 Definition compiled from various dictionaries and internet sources.

370 No Human is illegal protest banner at a political march, Ink Drop/Shutterstock.com

371 Realistic glossy icons, buttons, badge, mockup, © Andrey Roussanov - Dreamstime.com (image altered). Text added to picture by me.

372 People take part in a rally holding posters in hands, Slavkosereda/ Depositphotos.com (image altered). Text added to picture by me.

373 Benjamin Franklin face on us one hundred dollar bill macro isolated, United States money closeup, Vkilikov/Shutterstock.com (image altered). Text added to picture by me.

374 Definition compiled from various dictionaries and internet sources.

375 Not actual Trump University logo.

376 "Will Rogers > Quotes > Quotable Quote," Goodreads.com, https://www.goodreads.com/quotes/520428-there-are-men-running-governments-who-shouldn-t-be-allowed-to.

377 David Smith for *The Guardian,* https://www.theguardian.com/us-news/2017/mar/18/donald-trump-nashville-republicans-democrats.

---

[378] Red Button Round Icon Isolated on white background, PhotoStockImage/Shutterstock.com (image altered). Text added to picture by me.

[379] Photo of Gale McCray standing in front of the Lincoln Memorial, image courtesy of Gale McCray.

[380] Police officer writing a traffic citation while an unfortunate driver looks on from his car, © Lisa F. Young/Dreamstime.com (image altered – back seat passenger added to image). Text added to picture by me.

[381] Young adult woman standing in shadows holding sketchbook into the light, covering face with hashtag MeToo written on page, Amy K. Mitchell/Shutterstock.com (image altered). Text added to picture by me.

[382] Health care is a human right, Ryan C. Anderson's/Shutterstock.com.

[383] People with banners protest as part of a climate change march, InkDropCreative/DepositPhotos.com. Text added to picture by me.

[384] Martin Luther King Jr. Quotes, BrainyQuote, https://www.brainyquote.com/ quotes/martin_luther_king_jr_132359.

[385] Protesters at Trafalgar Square in London, Jonathan Poncelet/ Unsplash.com.

[386] Close up of a rear car bumper side swiped, Johnny Habell/Shutterstock.com (image altered). Text added to picture by me.

[387] Text: "Quotetab", https://www.quotetab.com/quote/by-george-carlin/i-dont-get-all-choked-up-about-yellow-ribbons-and-american-flags-i-consider-the#L8kv66eUQI3t8tLL.97. Image: George Carlin - RIP, https://www.flickr.com/photos/grappie/8943994173/in/faves-140956751@N03/, cpo57/Flickr.com, https://www.flickr.com/photos/grappie/, licensed under Generic – CC BY 2.0, https://creativecommons.org/licenses/by/2.0 (image altered). Text added to picture by me.

[388] Colin Campbell, "Donald Trump: 'My father gave me a small loan of a million dollars,'" *Business Insider,* https://www.businessinsider.com/donald-trump-small-million-dollar-loan, October 26, 2015.

[389] David Barstow, Susanne Craig, and Russ Buettner, "11 Takeaways From The Times's Investigation Into Trump's Wealth," *The New York Times,* https://www.nytimes.com/2018/10/02/us/politics/donald-trump-wealth-fred-trump.html, October 2, 2018.

[390] Twitter Bird with scroll, arrow123/Depositphotos.com (image altered). Text added to picture by me.

[391] Angry aged woman warning you, Khosrork/istock.com. This image is being used for illustrative purposes only, and any person depicted in the content is a model, posed by model (image altered). Text added to picture by me.

[392] Vietnam Veteran Holding a Blank Cardboard Sign, MikeCherim/istock.com. This image is being used for illustrative purposes only, and any person depicted in the content is a model, posed by model (image altered).

[393] Police officer writing a traffic citation while an unfortunate driver looks on from his car, © Lisa F. Young/Dreamstime.com (image altered – back seat passenger added to image). Text added to picture by me.

[394] Desperate Syrian woman in destroyed city, Zurijeta/Shutterstock.com.

[395] Abdullah Kurdi, Aylan Kurdi's father, standing by his destroyed home after burial of his wife and two sons, https://www.flickr.com/photos/syriafreedom/20643350023/in/photolist-xsbyKZ, Freedom House, https://www.flickr.com/photos/syriafreedom/, licensed under Public Domain Mark 1.0, https://creativecommons.org/publicdomain/mark/1.0.

[396] After the attack of Assad death barrels on Aleppo, Syria, https://www.flickr.com/photos/syriafreedom/12341259244/in/photolist-

jNybpN-w7gVVW-nsuzrq, Freedom House https://www.flickr.com/photos/syriafreedom/, licensed under 2.0 Generic - CC BY 2.0, https://creativecommons.org/licenses/by/2.

[397] Mar-a-Lago on Palm Beach Island, Palm Beach, Florida, USA, © Wangkun Jia/Dreamstime.com.

[398] The city of Homs in Syria, Smallcreative/Shutterstock.com.

[399] Buildings damaged after shelling by forces loyal to Syria's President Bashar al-Assad are seen at Douma near Damascus November 19, 2012, https://www.flickr.com/photos/syriafreedom/8210934517/in/photolist-dvzbLv, Freedom House, https://www.flickr.com/photos/syriafreedom/, licensed under 2.0 Generic - CC by 2.0, https://creativecommons.org/licenses/by/2 (image altered).

[400] Gabrielle Levy, "The 115th Congress by Party, Race, Gender and Religion," U.S. News and World Report, https://www.usnews.com/news/politics/slideshows/the-115th-congress-by-party-race-gender-and-religion, January 5, 2017.

[401] Philip Bump, "There are likely fewer black delegates to the Republican convention than at any point in at least a century," *The Washington Post,*" https://www.washingtonpost.com/news/the-fix/wp/2016/07/19/there-are-likely-fewer-black-delegates-to-the-republican-convention-than-at-any-point-in-at-least-a-century/, July 19, 2016.

[402] Transcript: Donald Trump Speaks At Victory Rally, *NPR,* https://www.npr.org/2016/11/09/500715254/transcript-donald-trump-speaks-at-victory-rally, November 9, 2016.

[403] Tom Kertscher, "Diversity in Congress: Democrats have women and minorities, Republicans have white men over 55?" PolitiFact, https://www.politifact.com/wisconsin/statements/2017/apr/28/mark-pocan/congress-democrats-have-women-and-minorities-repub/, April 28th, 2017.

[404] William Howard Taft, https://www.flickr.com/photos/iip-photo-archive/24612067309/in/photolist-DuTh96, GPA Photo Archive https://www.flickr.com/photos/iip-photo-archive/, licensed under Public Domain Mark 1.0, https://creativecommons.org/publicdomain/mark/1.0/ (image altered).

[405] David A. Bositis, "Black and the 2012 Republican National Conventions," Joint Center for Political and Economic Studies, https://jointcenter.org/sites/default/files/Blacks%20and%20the%202012%20Republican%20National%20Convention.pdf, 2012.

[406] Ibid. Note: 2016 information from Tom Kertscher, "Diversity in Congress: Democrats have women and minorities, Republicans have white men over 55?" PolitiFact, https://www.politifact.com/wisconsin/statements/2017/apr/28/mark-pocan/congress-democrats-have-women-and-minorities-repub/, April 28th, 2017.

[407] Statue of Liberty, symbol of United States of America, black and white with black sky in New York, © Andersastphoto/Dreamstime.com (image altered), Text added to picture by me.

[408] Lucia Graves and Sam Morris, "The Trump allegations," *The Guardian,* https://www.theguardian.com/us-news/ng-interactive/2017/nov/30/donald-trump-sexual-misconduct-allegations-full-list, November 29, 2017.

[409] Michael Barbaro and Megan Twohey, "Crossing the Line: How Donald Trump Behaved with Women in Private," *The New York Times,* https://www.nytimes.com/2016/05/15/us/politics/donald-trump-women.html?action=click&module=RelatedCoverage&pgtype=Article®ion=Footer, May 14, 2016.
[410] Patricia Roberts-Miller, Demagoguery and Democracy (New York, NY: The Experiment, 2017), 33.

[411] Jenna Johnson, "Donald Trump Begs Iowans Not to Believe Ben Carson: 'Don't Be Fools, Okay?'" *The Washington Post,* https://www.washingtonpost.com/news/post-

politics/wp/2015/11/13/donald-trump-begs-iowans-not-to-believe-ben-carson-dont-be-fools-okay, November 13, 2015.

[412] "Trump Says He Knows 'More Than the Generals' About ISIS, but Can't Name Their Leader," politicalconundrum.lefora.com, May 16, 2016.

[413] Sarah Begley, "Read Donald Trump's Speech to AIPAC," *Time,* http://time.com/4267058/donald-trump-aipac-speech-transcript, March 21, 2016.

[414] Eliza Collins, "Trump: I Consult Myself on Foreign Policy," *Politico,* https://www.politico.com/blogs/2016-gop-primary-live-updates-and-results/2016/03/trump-foreign-policy-adviser-220853, March 3, 2016.

[415] Ronald Reagan, "Remarks at the Presentation Ceremony for the Presidential Medal of Freedom," Ronald Reagan Presidential Library & Museum, https://www.reaganlibrary.gov/011989b.

[416] Ibid.

[417] Angry aged woman warning you, Khosrork/istock.com. This image is being used for illustrative purposes only, and any person depicted in the content is a model, posed by model (image altered).

[418] "George Carlin > Quotes > Quotable Quote," Goodreads.com, https://www.goodreads.com/quotes/98021-in-america-anyone-can-become-president-that-s-the-problem.

[419] George Carlin, https://www.flickr.com/photos/grappie/8943994173/in/faves-140956751@N03/, cpo57, https://www.flickr.com/photos/grappie/, licensed under 2.0 Generic – CC by 2.0, https://creativecommons.org/licenses/by/2.0 (image altered).

[420] Statue of Liberty, symbol of United States of America, black and white with black sky in New York, © Andersastphoto/Dreamstime.com (image altered). Text added by me.

About the Author

Tedd Levy is a retired social worker. He spent most of his career as executive director of a substance abuse and youth program in Freeport, N.Y. He is not an author—until now—nor is he a political journalist or pundit. This book was inspired by Tedd's simple but strong repulsion for the character, conduct, leadership and evil of Donald Trump. It is Tedd's patriotism and humanity that motivate his journey.

What began as a typical day-to-day following of news and political affairs, soon turned into short narratives, and eventually a heavily researched compilation. Levy's strong desire to share his knowledge, concerns and opinions fueled his motivation to write his first book.

A Note to Readers

You may have wondered, or on the other hand you may not have even noticed, why throughout my book are seemingly erroneously placed names. It was my way of showing a little love to my niece, my two nephews, and my goddaughter, Danielle, Aaron, Matthew, and Nicki.

Each of the names identified above are placed twice somewhere in my book in a picture, image, or graphic. If you want to play a version of "Where's Waldo," see if you can find them. If not, I understand.

In line with the "Where's Waldo" thing, I have also inserted a picture of a very handsome, young man somewhere twice in the book. This little extra is only geared to those in the know.

My thanks to my friend Jeff for his help with the editing of this book.

Thanks for reading my book. I hope you enjoyed it.

Tedd

Please report any errors to DTrumpIsTheWorstPerson@gmail.com.

Image Source[420]

www.ingramcontent.com/pod-product-compliance
Lightning Source LLC
Chambersburg PA
CBHW051734250726
48659CB00001B/64